FROM
BALTI PIES
TO THE
BIGGEST
PRIZE

FROM
BALTI PIES
TO THE
BIGGEST
PRIZE

THE TRANSFORMATION OF
MANCHESTER CITY

STEVE MINGLE

The
History
Press

First published 2013

The History Press
The Mill, Brimscombe Port
Stroud, Gloucestershire, GL5 2QG
www.thehistorypress.co.uk

British Library Cataloguing in Publication Data.
A catalogue record for this book is available from the British Library.

ISBN 978 0 7524 9320 6

Typesetting and origination by The History Press
Printed in Great Britain

CONTENTS

THE STORY SO FAR ...

Thirty-seven years of City. It all started so well. League title. FA Cup. League Cup. Cup-Winners' Cup. When you're 12, you think the days of glory will never end, that it's the way things are ordained. By the time you're approaching 50, you can't remember what it felt like to see your team win anything.

City have spent most of the last twenty-five years as football's premier cock-up merchants, both on and off the pitch. Occasional glimmers of hope have been smothered by long spells of disappointment, depression and disaster – Big Mal's second coming, thirteen years without a derby win, Alan Ball, third tier football. And, of course, no trophies whatsoever. Periodic glimpses of the light at the end of the tunnel have invariably turned out to be an oncoming train.

Arriving in 2001, Kevin Keegan has threatened as much as anyone to change things. Promotion back to the Premiership was achieved with a rare swagger, holding packed Maine Road crowds in thrall week after week. Some of it carried over to the top flight, with Maine Road's final season embellished by a magnificent win in the derby and the chance to watch players of genuine class.

2003's move to a shiny new home at Eastlands brought much anticipation, but the first season there ended up with yet another relegation flirtation. The trophyless year ticker climbed up to twenty-eight and there seemed no realistic prospect of it ever being reset.

Unless…

2004/05

HIS EVER CHANGING MOODS

Dedicated Follower Of Fashion

16 OCTOBER 2004, PREMIER LEAGUE: CITY 1 CHELSEA 0

City's brush with relegation didn't bode well for the new season, and the summer signings weren't exactly the stuff of dreams, nor what we would have expected from Keegan – Danny Mills and Ben Thatcher. As brutal a combination of full-backs as even Sam Allardyce could have wished for, at least those in the front row seats could look forward to welcoming a few blood-splattered wingers.

A noticeably trimmer Robbie Fowler scored a beauty to put us ahead in our opening game against Fulham, only for us to concede a sloppy equaliser and finish with just a point. It took another three games to add to that tally, but we did so in some style with a 4-0 hammering of Charlton. The goals truly spanned the sublime to the ridiculous, with two superb Nicolas Anelka strikes supplemented by a comic cuts goal from Trevor Sinclair, as

Dean Kiely witlessly hoofed a clearance against his backside right in the centre of the goalmouth. The star of the show, however, was Shaun Wright-Phillips, who produced some glorious wing play, a magnificent run and through ball to set Anelka up for his second and, to top it all, an effortless twenty-five-yarder which arrowed into Kiely's top corner. Shaun was getting better and better, and the media clamour for an England call-up intensified.

A dreary home defeat to Everton was followed by a trip to the godforsaken Selhurst Park, and press speculation on Keegan's future was mounting. He was notoriously capable of reaching breaking point on a whim, and the consequences of defeat to a Crystal Palace side odds-on for the drop could be very significant. Instead, City produced an accomplished display, fully deserving our first away win of the season, and Keegan was adamant that he wouldn't be walking away under any circumstances, nor indeed that he ever had. Not quite how most of us remembered things, but maybe we shouldn't believe everything we read ...

By mid-October, we'd mustered just two wins from eight, all set for another season of mediocrity at best. The next game brought unbeaten Chelsea to Eastlands, and no one cared much for our chances. Always a highly anticipated fixture, if seldom one to bring us any joy, there was significant extra spice brought about by the prospect of our first sighting of the new superstar of British football.

José Mourinho had arrived in England to an unprecedented fanfare of publicity and hype, mostly of his own making. Proclaiming himself as 'The Special One', you wouldn't put modesty at the top of his list of attributes, although at least initially it seemed that much of his bluster was delivered tongue in cheek and with a glint in the eye. There was almost universal agreement that this guy was a breath of fresh air, and in particular someone who wouldn't be cowed when it came to taking on Ferguson. Indeed, he'd already seen United off when at Porto, his inflammatory celebration along the Old Trafford touchline instantly endearing him to right-minded football lovers everywhere.

On a drizzly Saturday teatime, City set about trying to become the first team to inflict defeat on Mourinho, indeed the first home team to score a goal against them. We got the chance to achieve the latter when Anelka was dragged down by Ferreira's clumsy challenge for an obvious penalty, even if Howard Webb's failure to bring out the red card was a big disappointment. Anelka stayed calm to bury the spot kick and instil a cup-tie atmosphere around the ground.

Despite the loss of Sun Jihai with a season-ending injury, City defended manfully in the face of increasing pressure, and restricted Chelsea to long range efforts from Frank Lampard. He was denied by David James and the woodwork, as an increasingly animated Mourinho, all brooding looks, stylish coat, designer stubble and chewing gum, watched on from the touchline. Rousing renditions of 'that coat's from Matalan' echoed around the ground, although if truth be told I suspect it probably wasn't.

Dunne and Distin both performed heroically to subdue Kezman and Gudjohnsen, illustrating that when the chips were down and they were both fully focussed, they were a central defensive pairing to match any in the division. The big problem for both of them was concentration; so often, a momentary lapse in an otherwise accomplished display would result in a fatal concession, and more points down the drain.

No chance of that today, though. City held out for a famous victory, the first English team to bloody Mourinho's nose, and the on-pitch celebrations reflected how scarce these occasions appeared likely to be. The bounce in Keegan's step had returned as he skipped gleefully into the tunnel, doubtless sensing that a corner had been turned. Surely he'd been at City long enough to know better?

Talk Of The Town

4 JANUARY 2005, PREMIER LEAGUE: ARSENAL 1 CITY 1

Shaun Wright-Phillips had made an inspired start to the season, and was rapidly reaching the status of a player you'd pay to go to see on his own. Against Barnsley in the Carling Cup, he'd produced an extraordinary performance, providing no fewer than four assists together with a wonderful dinked finish for a goal of his own. He'd won his first England cap, coming on as sub against Ukraine at St James's Park, and marked the occasion with a trademark goal, drilled low across the keeper from just inside the box. A couple of weeks later he was back there as City faced a Newcastle team seemingly in disarray, the primary movers in the latest dust-up being Craig Bellamy and manager Graeme Souness. Why any club would want to entertain Bellamy heaven only knows, the epitome of a man who'd start an argument with himself in an empty room.

Shaun again excelled, and his two superb goals looked likely to bring us a point, with the score at 3-3 with just a few minutes to go. In contrast, Bellamy had made little impact on the match, until he prodded a late chance goalwards with little force or conviction. James dived to his left for a routine save, but the ball somehow passed between his hands to nestle agonisingly in the back of the net. Calamity James was back in town, and Bellamy's redemption with the home faithful was instant. Football fans will forgive most things in return for a win. Even Alice bands.

Undeterred, Shaun continued in a rich vein of form, giving Portsmouth the complete runaround on their own turf, then clinching the points against Villa with a twenty-yard left-footer that went in like a shell. But although he was now clearly the main man, we still had plenty of other players capable of providing memorable moments, even if not always in the conventional sense.

Our Boxing Day trip to Goodison ultimately proved fruitless, but produced another classic goal celebration from Robbie Fowler. Taunted as ever by Evertonians about alleged substance abuse, he powered in a great header then ran away from the scene repeatedly patting the top of his head. Those who'd spent the previous evening honing their skills at Charades would instantly have bellowed 'smackhead!' If not quite as spectacular as his inspired touchline-sniffing antics a few years earlier, it was still a splendidly witty riposte which predictably caused the next day's tabloids to explode in a frenzy of moral outrage. Tossers.

Two days later, it was Richard Dunne's turn to step into the spotlight. West Bromwich Albion had proved to be ideally supine opponents, having mustered not a single threat on David James's goal as we moved towards full-time 1-0 up. When a long ball was punted towards the City goal, James had the situation well covered. Dunne moved across, just to be on the safe side, with Robert Earnshaw the only Baggie in the vicinity. As the back-pedalling Dunne glanced across to check on James's position, the ball clipped the outside of his foot and sped past the onrushing keeper towards the net. The connection was perfect; made deliberately by a striker it would have been feted as a piece of consummate skill. In Dunne's case, it could only be described as an act of abject buffoonery. Earnshaw sprinted as never before in a futile bid to get a touch before the ball crossed the line; West Brom had thus salvaged a 1-1 draw from a game in which they'd not had a single shot on target.

Although results continued to be erratic, there was always a very real prospect that you'd go home from a City game talking about a flash of brilliance from SWP. A mazy dribble and ferocious thirty-yard daisy-cutter against Southampton sealed an important home win to bring in the New Year. Three days later, we travelled to Highbury to face our most testing fixture of the season, against champions Arsenal. By now, Shaun was receiving the media coverage his exploits merited and there was an extra element of intrigue in his visit to his stepdad's old club.

Midway through the first half, Barton's robust challenge allowed him to find Wright-Phillips, almost thirty yards out. A little touch to set himself, then he cut across the ball to deliver a majestic, swerving shot into Almunia's top-right corner. Just stunning. The goal served as an inspiration for the whole team, and we produced the most accomplished performance I'd ever seen from a City side at Highbury. Arsenal pressed ever more strongly, but every City player was contributing and, as we moved into the final ten minutes, a moment of history – for me at least – beckoned. I'd never seen us win at Highbury.

Alas, Arsenal's forward players were always capable of producing something out of the ordinary, and when Thierry Henry's acrobatic overhead kick resurrected an attack which we'd looked to have snuffed out, Freddie Ljungberg was on hand to head home. Eight minutes left and, as they'd done to so many teams, Arsenal went for the throat. This time, though, we held on for a richly deserved point.

Normally, I'd have had mixed feelings about the result, since Arsenal were United's main rivals for the title; with us stuck in mid-table, Arsenal's two dropped points were more valuable to United than our point was to us. But our performance had been such that defeat would have been a real injustice, and I left the stadium beaming with pride at the way we'd played. Central to this was SWP, and not just for the goal. He'd been absolutely magnificent, and even now in my mind's eye I can see him wriggling around then sprinting away from Patrick Vieira, to gasps from the home supporters.

On the tube journey back, we were surrounded by Gooners, and there was only one topic of conversation – Ian Wright's lad. 'What a player! We gotta sign this kid, surely Wrighty can have a word in his ear, what's the point in staying at a dead end club like City?' I smiled to myself, delighted at this rare acclaim for one of our players and also at their presumptuousness. Shaun was City through and through, his newfound status would see him on a healthy package, so why would he move? But as I thought about it more, and the way he'd fit into Arsenal's fluid style of play and penchant for the swift counter-attack, together with the prospect of untold silverware, it became more a case of why wouldn't he move? We just had to hope that his loyalty to City would reflect the years we'd spent nurturing his talents and, in the meantime, be grateful that we'd got an asset that top clubs coveted so dearly.

Arsenal's dropped points appeared less significant when news came through that Spurs had held United at Old Trafford, but delight at this result soon turned to disgust when the facts became known. Roy Carroll had clawed back a shot from Pedro Mendes from so far over the line that it had virtually hit the netting, yet the officials had declined to give a goal. *Cheating fucking bastards.* When I saw the TV highlights, I could scarcely believe my eyes. It was shameful and inexcusable. I made a mental note of the referee's name. A young guy called Clattenburg. Let's hope he gets drummed out of the game before he can do any more damage …

Man Out Of Time

28 FEBRUARY 2005, PREMIER LEAGUE: NORWICH 2 CITY 3

FA Cup third round day fell just three days after the Arsenal game, and sentenced City to a local derby at

Oldham Athletic. Not so long ago, these had been our league derbies as well, and much as I'll always have an affection for Boundary Park, it wasn't a trip I was looking forward to. The ground had changed beyond recognition – the one constant being that it was still bloody freezing – and after expending such energy at Highbury, we were ripe for a serious comedown.

Oldham had been in dismal form, but who wasn't aware that form counts for nothing in the FA Cup? This was their biggest game since their golden age under Joe Royle a decade ago, and they'd be throwing everything at us. I shivered my way down Sheepfoot Lane with a sense of foreboding.

Latics were under new management, another ominous sign, and we conceded a sloppy early set-piece goal. Only as we entered the final stages did we begin to pose any real threat. It wasn't enough. A few close shaves, some heroic saves, and once again we were foremost in the Saturday tea-time headlines as stories of the day's giant killings were trotted out with the usual sadistic glee.

This was a severe blow. The end of the first week in January, and our season was over. Too good to go down, too inconsistent to challenge for Europe, there was nothing to look forward to other than the hope of putting one over United and some more fireworks from SWP. And even that might be counterproductive, as it would cement the resolve of the likes of Arsenal to prise him away from us.

Games already had an end-of-season feel, and even the Eastlands derby was a strangely flat affair. United took the points courtesy of two Richard Dunne own goals, and Keegan's body language had become ever more 'can't be bothered'. Hardly surprising with the team having so little to play for.

Unlike some of our opponents. Our *Monday Night Football* on Sky visit to Norwich City saw us face a team desperately striving to retain their place in the big time.

They'd have regarded our visit as a must-win, and after twenty minutes it looked like they must win it, goals from Ashton and McKenzie giving them the perfect start. Keegan was shrivelled away in his Michelin Man coat on the touch-line, looking like he'd rather be anywhere else.

Norwich, however, weren't accustomed to the dizzy heights of a two-goal lead. A clumsy foul allowed Sibierski to convert a penalty, then some dazzling play from SWP produced a cut-back which Fowler dispatched with the aplomb of days of yore. We reached half-time all-square, with Sky viewers having enjoyed a thoroughly entertaining spectacle. And this was only the warm-up act. Coming back after a brief interlude, Marcus Buckland could hardly contain his mirth as he told viewers that there'd been some strange goings on while we'd been away.

We were then treated to the sight of Delia Smith in the centre circle, yellow and green scarf to the fore, microphone in hand. Clearly unstable and thoroughly lashed up, Delia launched into a passionate and barely coherent speech to her fellow Canaries, urging them to get behind the team. 'This is a message to the best fussball suppoters in the world …We need a twelfth man here! …Where are you? … Where are you? … Less be havin' you! … Come on!' At least the folk in the posh seats now realised why tonight's trifle hadn't had the usual kick.

It was great stuff, but served only to cause the home support to be convulsed in laughter rather than inspiring their team to new heights, and the second half ambled along as if the players knew that nothing could upstage Delia's majestic cameo. Then, two minutes from time, SWP picked up the ball on the right and fired a low cross towards the far post. Fowler, two yards out, moved in for the kill, but got his feet into a right old tangle, managing only to make almost accidental contact with the ball. The inadvertent disguise completely flummoxed Rob Green, who could only watch in anguish as the ball trickled slowly towards and over the line, with barely enough pace to reach the netting. A cruel blow for Norwich, an unexpected lift for us, and all seemed well in Keegan's world as he chatted freely in post-match interviews.

A week later, Bolton were the visitors for a match inexplicably chosen for Sky coverage. City with nothing to play for, Allardyce's gruesome team the epitome of what my dearly departed grandmother would have summed up with: 'If they were playing in me back yard, I'd draw t'curtains.' It was hard to see anyone but the totally committed tuning in. The game fully lived down to expectations, won with a single goal by the despicable Diouf, and Keegan's demeanour afterwards was that of a man due to be executed the following morning who'd just been told that his final appeal had failed.

Despite his promise never to walk away, few, if any, City fans would have been surprised to hear the news of his resignation the following morning. The Cup defeat at Oldham had been a killer, sentencing us to four months of games that didn't really matter. The body language of this most heart on the sleeve character was far more eloquent than the man himself; he knew he'd taken us as far as he could, and that it was time for someone else to have a go.

I suspect most of us agreed with him. Nonetheless, I'll always have a certain affection for the Keegan years, based primarily on the wonderful football we'd played in his first season, when Benarbia and Berkovic enabled us to produce a brand of football which the English second tier had never seen before. One or two teams – and only one or two – might have scored more goals or accumulated more points in gaining promotion, but none can have come close to delivering the thrilling, sophisticated, stylish play that this team produced week in, week out. We'd also had some great days in the final season at Maine Road, not least the epic derby triumph.

Keegan's downfall came with the strategy of recruiting past-their-best wasters like McManaman, Sinclair, Seaman and – even if his form this year had been much improved – Fowler. And his massively over-sensitive nature always made it likely that he'd throw in the towel once the flak started to pour in. Still, three and a half seasons was a pretty decent stint – both for him and for us – and we've certainly had plenty worse.

Call Me The Tumbling Dice

15 MAY 2005, PREMIER LEAGUE: CITY 1 MIDDLESBROUGH 1

Keegan's forlorn departure left little practical alternative other than to let Stuart Pearce take the reins, at least until the end of the season. There was nothing material to play for, the fans were behind him, and with eight games to go it would be a perfect audition to assess his suitability for a permanent appointment.

Pearce's reign began with a narrow defeat at Spurs, but a credible and spirited performance at least suggested a squad of players behind the new man. A week later at The Valley, a vibrant attacking display reminiscent of Keegan's team in its pomp saw us storm ahead, only for a sloppy equaliser to give Charlton a last-gasp point.

The Eastlands' crowd's first chance to express its support for our new leader came at home to Liverpool, a forbidding fixture against a team we hadn't beaten for ten years. The game became increasingly compelling as City fought tooth and nail to get the goal our dominance merited, but of equal note were the antics of Pearce on the touchline. Every pass, tackle and shot was greeted with an exaggeratedly animated response, as Psycho's demeanour made Martin O'Neill look like Jim Royle on sedatives. The crowd were well entertained, but something about it didn't quite ring true. By all means get excited when a shot screams just wide of the post, but surely a ten-yard ball knocked square to a teammate in your own half can be allowed to pass without reaction?

On the pitch, City's energy almost matched that of their new manager but, as the game neared its conclusion, it looked like all we'd get was a point. Then, some smart play down the right allowed Lee Croft some space to pick out a cross, and he pulled it back to the advancing Kiki Musampa. Without breaking stride, an airborne Musampa struck a first-time volley cleanly into the corner for a magnificent and well-deserved winner, celebrated with more gusto than any other goal at the ground all season. The Psycho regime had lift-off.

A four-game sequence of winning at home and drawing away saw us cement our place in the top half, with Fowler belatedly getting close to his Anfield form after two misfiring years. Week after week brought instinctive polished finishing and link-up play, a reminder of what a terrific player he'd been in his heyday. No coincidence that he'd flourished with the departure of Anelka?

With teams above us faltering a little, there was even an outside chance of sneaking into the UEFA Cup if we could win our last two games, both against sides with similar ambitions. The first took us to Villa Park, and a blistering start saw us virtually settle the game within the first ten minutes. The extraordinary Wright-Phillips fastened on to the ball forty yards out, weaved inside two defenders, outside another, then fired a crisp low cross-shot into the far corner for a simply sublime goal. What a magnificent player he'd become. He was one of those rare players that fans of almost all opposing clubs also admired, embodying everything good about the game – enthusiasm, skill, bravery, complete commitment – and showing no inclination towards the dark arts. No diving, no feigning injury, no badgering officials. He looked like a guy who loved playing football so much that he'd do it for nothing.

We'd just about got our breath back when we scored another one almost as good, a lovely build up culminating in Musampa slamming a first-time left-footer into the top corner. Villa never looked like getting more than a consolation goal, and City almost made it a hat-trick of spectacular goals when a brilliant sequence of play ended with Musampa driving against the post.

The jog back to the car was particularly enjoyable, not just reflecting on our 2-1 win but also that other results had very much gone our way; *and* the evil Palace had conceded a last-gasp goal to put themselves in prime position for relegation. Who'd have thought that happy days would be here again so soon? Once the arithmetic was done, the position was pretty simple. Win our final game and we'd be in Europe next season.

When the season's fixtures come out, one of the most eagerly scrutinised is the final match, with its scope for countless what-ifs. What if we need to win to avoid the drop? To get into Europe? To send someone down? To stop them winning the title? Ideally, you want a 'winnable' game, just in case there's something important riding on it. Or a glamour game, a finale to remember throughout the long close season.

This year's final fixture was not what anyone would call a glamour game. Middlesbrough at home. The only thing less glamorous would have been Middlesbrough away. Despite the Ravanelli and Juninho interlude, Middlesbrough would always be a byword for grey, dull and dreary football played by grey, dull and dreary footballers led by grey, dull and dreary managers. Not a prospect to set the pulse racing.

As it turned out, we couldn't have hoped for anything more dramatic. Our direct rivals for the last UEFA Cup spot were Middlesbrough themselves. It would be a final-day shootout. A match which, even a month ago, looked certain to be a meaningless, anti-climactic end to the season, witnessed by a crowd attending more out of a sense of duty rather than with any excitement or anticipation, would now be our most important single game since returning to the top flight three years ago.

The build-up was punctuated by the expected announcement of a permanent contract for Pearce. He could hardly have started more impressively, and his demeanour in post-match interviews, always respectful and never critical of officials, brought a welcome contrast with the increasing tetchiness of Keegan as his enthusiasm for the job had waned. Just one more win and he'd already have cemented his place in City managerial folklore – it would be our first European qualification on merit for over twenty-five years.

A full house assembled at Eastlands incorporating, uniquely in my experience, a full quota from the smog-ridden wastelands. The atmosphere beforehand befitted the occasion, enhanced by the sheer unexpectedness of it all. Who'd have thought that we'd in this position?

The teams came out to a huge fanfare, Pearce picking up his Manager of the Month award – oh shit! – but someone, somewhere had had the bright idea of using this game to advertise our new away kit for next season. Come on guys, this is just not on. We're at home. We play in Sky Blue. That's that. The crass gesture of trying to eke out a few extra summer sales from people who'd have bought it anyway was exacerbated by the fact that the kit was bloody horrible, an ugly, tasteless dark blue abomination.

As expected, Boro are set up to retain what they started with – the point that would see them into Europe. We create a few openings, most notably when Wright-Phillips bursts through in trademark style, but toe-ends the ball just wide as Schwarzer advances. A great chance squandered. But Boro hold on, and the game develops a more attritional feel which certainly suits them more than it does us.

Ten minutes before half-time, they get a free kick some thirty-five yards out. Jimmy Floyd Hasselbaink looks like he fancies it. I'm worried. In all my years watching the game, I've never seen anyone hit the ball as hard as this guy does. And with either foot. With a short run-up and minimal back-lift, he strikes the dead ball with savage ferocity and it sears past the wall, beyond James, and crashes against the underside of the bar. It bounces down and back up to bulge the roof of the net. James saw it all the way and had not an earthly. No one in the world could have stopped it.

We go in at half-time 1-0 down but, within a minute of the restart, a cracking finish from Musampa gets us level. The volume all around is cranked up as the momentum shifts. Boro seldom mount an attack worthy of the name but defend for all they're worth, and the closest we come is when Thatcher's header is cleared off the line. We're heading towards added time, chances are drying up, and we need inspiration.

Pearce provides it. On the far side we see Nicky Weaver being prepared to come on as a sub. Has Jamo hurt himself? No, he hasn't, because the board shows Claudio Reyna's number. In the words so often chanted at a succession of hapless City managers over the years: 'What the fuck is going on?' It soon becomes clear. James comes to the touchline to don an outfield shirt and makes his way upfield. If the definition of a tactical masterstroke is doing something your opponents least expect and would least want, then this certainly fits the bill. We've posed little aerial threat all game; suddenly they've got a 6ft 5in monster of a man to deal with, and there'll be no shortage of balls launched into the box.

The crowd, progressively more frustrated as Boro stifled our attacks with increasing comfort, are now lifted, all smiling and laughing as they roar encouragement to our new striker. Three minutes plus added time remain, and everyone's mood is buoyant and expectant.

James gets his head to a couple of crosses, and also gets the chance to show his skills on the ground, twisting and turning in an attempt to create space for a shot. He resembles a one-man threshing machine, accidentally but brutally scything down a Boro defender as the ball runs out of reach.

Boro are totally unsettled, hacking the ball away desperately and, for the first time, looking disorganised. The crowd by now are in a complete frenzy, everyone on their feet, as City pour forward. Suddenly, we're caught on the break, but Weaver makes his solitary contribution to the season by saving Downing's shot. It could be crucial. We're straight up the other end and Barton fires in a cross towards James at the far post. It gets deflected behind, but the crowd are looking for something more than just a corner. All eyes are on referee Rob Styles. He points to the spot. Quedrue has handled.

This is incredible. It's pretty much the last kick of the season, and everything rests on it. As Robbie Fowler strides up, City fans behind the goal already have their heads in their hands, squinting at the scene through sweaty fingers. I hope Robbie's not looking at them.

He goes for a conventional run up rather than his usual wait for the keeper to make a move technique, and side-foots it to Schwarzer's left. The keeper's gone a fraction early and guessed right. The ball's a foot off the ground, neither struck firmly enough nor right in the corner. It's a comfortable save. Schwarzer is mobbed, Fowler distraught, the fans disbelieving. Just a couple of minutes remain, time for James to cause more mayhem and wipe out another couple of Boro defenders with a sprawling agricultural lunge. An outfield player would have been sent off by now. We can't muster that one final chance, and Rob Styles's whistle sees Schwarzer mobbed and Boro fans dancing in jubilation.

Despite the sickening disappointment, 'Blue Moon' rings round the stadium with as much resonance as it has all season. Yes, it's failure, but glorious, all guns blazing failure. And celebration of a magnificent finish to the season, with a boldly imaginative tactical move which so nearly came off. As I've always said, games don't come much more exciting than Middlesbrough at home.

The next day, Pearce gets some stick for his unconventional substitution. I can't believe it. It had a huge impact on the game, lifted the crowd and the team, visibly rattled a Boro side previously in the comfort zone and got us to within a missed penalty of Europe. It was an inspirational bit of thinking which augured well for the season ahead and for the way in which Pearce would be approaching the job. We might not have too much money in the coffers, but if we could maintain this momentum – and keep SWP away from his big-money suitors – there was still plenty to look forward to.

2005/06

JUST AN ILLUSION

I Don't Like Cricket ...

18 SEPTEMBER 2005, PREMIER LEAGUE: CITY 0 BOLTON 1

Even City fans couldn't have failed to carry a real sense of optimism through the close season. The resurgence under Pearce had been startling. Yet, by the time the big kick-off arrived, fewer than 43,000 turned up to watch the opening match. Yes, the opposition, West Brom, was hardly the most attractive, but there were other forces at work.

Shaun Wright-Phillips, who'd enjoyed such a stellar season, had buggered off to Chelsea in less than satisfactory circumstances. Just a couple of days after allegedly pledging his future to City, there he was, gone. Romantically, you wanted to think that staying at a club where he was truly loved, where he was guaranteed a starting position every week, where he'd figuratively if not physically grown up, where he'd broken into the England team, would carry some weight. He'd struggle to nail down a regular place at Chelsea with Robben and Duff as competition, but the unimaginable increase in wages and the very real prospect of winning medals clearly held sway. Could anyone blame him?

The financial realities of life were something that a club of our relatively modest means would just have to accept. The trade-off for the privilege of enjoying an outstanding performer at his best would always be that someone would eventually make us an offer we couldn't refuse. We got a whopping £21 million for him, but how would the money be spent? The little man had left a huge hole to fill, and Pearce's close season signings of Andy Cole – who even for a United player had always seemed contemptibly arrogant and possessed of a monstrously inflated opinion of his own abilities – and Darius Vassell – lightning quick but not really all that good – weren't exactly the stuff of dreams.

As we moved towards the season's opener, the normal fanfare was noticeably absent. Usually, in a year with no World Cup or Euros to bridge the summer gap, we're chomping at the bit to get back in the swing. This year, the build-up to the big kick-off had been so muted that you'd hardly have noticed that football was imminent. We just weren't ready for it. For the first time in living memory, we were a nation obsessed with cricket.

I've always loved cricket, following Lancashire as well as the England Test team but, when the football season started, City invariably took priority. Not this time. The 2005 Ashes series had already developed into something very special, a gripping saga of heroic deeds, ferocious competitiveness, wonderful sportsmanship and unbearable drama. And by the time the season kicked off, we were only halfway through it.

The day before, I'd been at the real Old Trafford to see England take a grip on the Third Test, the reverse swing of our fearsome four-pronged pace attack and the underestimated spin of Ashley Giles putting us into an unassailable position. I was present and correct at Eastlands for the big kick-off, but my mind was hardly on the game at all. Not that there was much distraction in a flat, dreary, goalless draw, even though Cole and Vassell immediately demonstrated encouraging signs of possessing an intuitive partnership.

Two days later, the Test produced another extraordinary finish, and seemingly every office worker sloped off to their local pub to watch the final session. In a packed to the gills bar at London Bridge, I witnessed Australia's last pair survive 24 balls to secure an unlikely draw, leaving the series level at 1-1 with two to play. The tension was so gripping that football hardly entered my head at all.

City had secured a couple of tidy away wins by the time we went on holiday for a couple of weeks, and it looked as though there'd be plenty of promise for the season when I was ready to embrace it fully. But much of the holiday was spent trying to find out was happening at the end of the Trent Bridge Test and the start of the final encounter at The Oval. We weren't quite yet in the era of mobile phone internet access – or I wasn't anyway – so internet cafes in the south of France were very much the order of the day.

England secured a dramatic win at Trent Bridge, just about managing to withstand Brett Lee's speed-of-light bowling, and when we arrived back home, the final Test was well underway. We needed a draw to bring back the Ashes after an eighteen-year wait. I'd got a ticket for the Sunday, with Australia looking to overhaul England's decent, but not impregnable, first-innings total. A truly heroic spell of bowling from Andrew Flintoff – well on his way to cementing his place in British sporting folklore – saw us secure a miniscule lead. It wasn't the brightest of days, and when the light closed in, England were quick to accept the umpires' offer to come off, with the crowd roaring its approval. For the first time in my life, I found myself having paid good money to watch a sporting event but wanting it to be rained off. Thousands felt the same way.

We went into the final day only needing to avoid being skittled out cheaply. At 126/5 it looked a bit dicey, but an incredible Kevin Pietersen innings saw him announce himself on the world stage and secure a 2-1 series victory. I've been a fanatical sports follower since I was eight years old and this series, without doubt, was the greatest sporting event I'd seen in my life. Its impact on the British public was illustrated by the almost instant awarding of MBEs to every member of the England squad. I didn't expect to witness anything as memorable, that I'd want to watch over and over, that I'd never tire of seeing, ever again. I couldn't imagine it ever being surpassed. On 13 May 2012 it would be. But more of that later.

I'm still coming down from Ashes euphoria as I drive to Eastlands for what feels like the first game of the season. Now we can properly concentrate on the football. Beneath the radar, City have started the season superbly, unbeaten in five games and sitting third in the table. We'd been second going into the previous game, at Old Trafford, but were held to a draw by our plucky little opponents.

Today's visitors, Bolton Wanderers, aren't a particularly frightening proposition, and the Blues are in great voice as Andrew Flintoff is introduced to the crowd, looking remarkably well for a man who's just smashed the UK all-comers' binge-drinking record. Stuart Pearce picks up the Manager of the Month award – his second of the three for which he's been eligible – and we try to forget what a bad omen that usually turns out to be.

City start like a train, and a tremendous diving header from Sibierski rattles the bar, goes twenty feet up into the air and descends flush on to the bar again. When he puts in a superb header from Mills's cross shortly afterwards, Jääskeläinen makes a blinding save, tipping the header on to the bar.

Second half, and Barton hammers in a left-footer which powers past the keeper but comes back off the post. Claudio Reyna is denied by a toe-end save, then Musampa's searing half-volley clatters on to the crossbar. Five times we've hit the woodwork. Some teams don't do that in a whole season. It's still 0-0. It can't carry on like this.

Pearce introduces young Stephen Ireland for his first-team debut. We've heard lots of good things about this lad and he soon shows us why, a crisp half-volleyed snapshot bringing yet another stunning save from Jääskeläinen. He then beautifully plays in Mills for a cross which Musampa blasts inches past the far post. It looks like being one of those days. Then, with just a couple of minutes left, Sun Jihai cuts in from the left and smashes a terrific shot past the keeper ... and flush on to the crossbar again.

Bolton have hardly been in our half but, as we approach added time, Henrik Pedersen is released into the inside left channel. Dunne comes across to cover, Pedersen flicks the ball over his head and Biffer clearly and carelessly swipes the ball away with his arm. You can't not give teams penalties just because they'll lead to a criminal travesty of justice, and Mike Dean does what he has to do. So does Gary Speed, blasting the ball past Jamo to give Bolton all three points.

Is there any other game where this happens? Where one team is utterly superior to the other, yet ends up losing? We couldn't have done more. It's not as if we missed any sitters; every attempt that hit the woodwork was superbly struck and Jääskeläinen had had one of those 'man possessed' days. Frustrated at the injustice as we all were, all anyone could do was leave the stadium with a wry smile. And much as we're all behind Psycho, would he mind just falling short of winning Manager of the Month awards in future?

If You Were Me, Would You Walk Out In Style?

14 JANUARY 2006, PREMIER LEAGUE:
CITY 3 MANCHESTER UNITED 1

Cole and Vassell in the early part of the season had produced moments of genuine class. The form of both of them was a pleasant surprise, most notably Cole, from whom I'd expected next to nothing. The arrogant, selfish, surly individual of Old Trafford had been miraculously transformed into a real team player, a smile on his face, eager to pass on his knowledge to our younger players. It made me wonder how many more of them might morph into decent human beings if they made the trip across from the dark side. Can't imagine it's too many ...

Successive home games against West Ham and Villa both brought some sublime interplay between our new strike-force; intelligent, energetic, selfless movement and exquisite finishing. This wasn't what I'd anticipated at all. An even bigger surprise came in the next home game, in which Everton, as usual, snuffed the life out of the match, leaving those who'd made the effort to get here for the unfathomably early 11.15 a.m. kick-off wishing they'd stayed in bed. With about twenty minutes of an incident-free encounter remaining, Danny Mills picked up the ball on the right, and from thirty yards unleashed a thunderous drive that flew into the far top corner. Fantastic goal. Total fluke.

Next up was a trip to The Valley, just an hour's drive away from home, but even on the morning of the match I wasn't sure whether I'd make it. I was moving house the following day, and still had plenty of packing and cleaning up to do.

Early afternoon was make-your-mind-up time, culminating in the inevitable decision to take a few hours off and leave myself with the prospect of clearing up into the early hours of Monday morning. This had better be worth it …

City started outstandingly, totally dominating the game. Vassell showed superb control to pull down a long ball, weave past a couple of defenders and slip the onrushing Cole through on goal. A cool finish put us one up. Calamitous defending gave Darren Bent the chance to equalise shortly afterwards, but Cole then set up Sinclair for a rare clean strike to send us into the interval ahead.

Barton was lucky to see his feeble penalty parried back out, allowing him to increase our lead, before a screamer from Bothroyd embarrassed James at his near post. Cole then produced another beautiful assist for Vassell to finish cleanly, before following up a poor back-pass to slot home a fifth. He and Vassell had again produced an exemplary display of movement and finishing and, as in all good partnerships, the whole was much greater than the sum of the parts.

City's 5-2 win had given me a perfect send-off from twenty-seven years in Kent, and six days later I hoped for an equally rewarding welcome to Berkshire as I set off on the trip to The Hawthorns. Typically, we fell to a defeat as limp as the previous week's performance had been vibrant.

Pearce hadn't yet been able to eradicate our ingrained inconsistency, but then he was hardly the first, and results overall had been more than acceptable. He still seemed almost unnaturally enthusiastic about the job, his touchline antics often making him the centre of attention. Wigan boss Paul Jewell, when questioned about his own relatively passive touchline demeanour, threw in a comment to the effect that you didn't have to dance around and gesticulate all the time in order to be passionate about the game, clearly intimating that the antics of the likes of Pearce and Martin O'Neill were as much about attention-seeking as being engrossed in proceedings on the pitch. I had to admit that the thought had crossed my mind.

The ups and downs continued, a comprehensive 4-1 win over Birmingham City followed by a 4-3 defeat at Wigan, in which two late goals gave the scoreline a respectability our efforts hadn't merited. Difficult holiday fixtures produced just a point from three games, and for the first time in Pearce's brief reign, we were on a difficult run. Hardly ideal preparation for a visit from the neighbours.

United arrived well off the pace being set by Chelsea, and defeat today would leave them so far adrift that they could forget the title. Roared on by a crowd determined to ram Ferguson's pre-match jibe down his throat – so we're always really quiet, are we? – City tore into them, and a clever little ball from the classy Stephen Ireland allowed Sinclair to swivel and fire home a sweet finish.

Things soon got even better, as Vassell latched on to Cole's flick, manipulated the ball around Silvestre and calmly slotted beneath van der Sar. Half-time, 2-0, a rousing send-off and a real chance to put another one over them. Hold on here, and we'll have our third home win in four derbies.

Victory looked assured when a flying two-footed lunge from a frustrated Ronaldo saw referee Steve Bennett produce a red card. Typically, City looked less effective for a spell thereafter, and van Nistelrooy took advantage of some slack defending to pull a goal back.

Cole had by now given way to Fowler, whose comeback from injury had begun with a League Cup hat-trick against Scunthorpe United. Now, he made the most of his little time on the pitch by sealing the points with a glorious angled strike, before celebrating provocatively in front of the United fans. No one enjoys scoring against this lot more than Robbie Fowler. It was also celebrated with real gusto by Pearce, who allowed himself to be engulfed by the delirious crowd as he savoured his first derby win. And a thoroughly deserved one, with top performances all over the pitch.

Fowler's goal would be his final act as a City player, and he'd certainly had his moments. Unfortunately, moments were all they'd been, rather than consistent displays of the striking prowess which had seen him so revered at Anfield. And the moment above all others for which he'll be remembered is missing the penalty which would have taken us into Europe. Anyone can miss a penalty, but it seemed somehow symbolic that this once great predator's nerve would fail him when we needed it most.

Ultimately I'll always see him as the signing that signalled the start of the decline in our momentum after promotion the previous year, sparking the breakdown in the relationship between Keegan and David Bernstein. Keegan had seemed besotted, playing Fowler even when patently unfit, unable to recognise or accept that the magic had gone. Still, there's a lot to be said for going out on a high …

And Just To Make It Interesting, We'll Have A Shilling On The Side

19 FEBRUARY 2006, FA CUP FIFTH ROUND:
ASTON VILLA 1 CITY 1

The derby win reignited optimism of a tilt at a UEFA Cup place, and Pearce moved to reinforce our striking options with a big-money purchase. Georgios Samaras was snapped up from Dutch side Heerenveen for a cool £6 million and announced his arrival with a classic header in a 3-2 win against Charlton. Lanky and lank-haired, he wasn't exactly a picture of elegance, combining the looks of Freddie Mercury with the gait of Paulo Wanchope. First impressions were that, like both of them, he'd deliver occasional moments of brilliance amid heaps of dross.

Next up was the FA Cup, where a narrow win over Wigan put us into the fifth round draw. Villa away, while not exactly what we'd have hoped for, at least felt winnable. Unfortunately, we'd already arranged a holiday over fifth round weekend, hardly anticipating that City could reach the dizzy heights of the last sixteen. So, I'd be resigned to watching it on the telly – assuming we could find somewhere showing the game.

Madeira was a pleasant surprise. Good food and wine, delightful scenery and no lager louts – well, apart from me, and I'm more of a white Burgundy lout these days – all made for a thoroughly relaxing week. With one exception.

One of the main tourist drags sported a sign, pointing down a side road, to the Prince Albert. 'Pub grub and Live Sport'. This is what we want. I sloped off for a quick reccy, reminding Lindsey of the warnings we'd received about this being a notorious spot for timeshare peddlers, and not to engage in conversations with strangers. Fat chance. She's a Scouser.

The pub was easily located, and the board advertising the forthcoming televisual attractions contained the magical words 'Aston Villa v Man City'. Fantastic. I dashed back to give Lindsey the glad tidings, only to find her in deep conversation with some smiley young chap.

'Would you believe it, this guy's from Jersey!'

'Oh really?'

'Yes, he knows all the bars we go in.'

Hardly surprising. It's not exactly a heaving metropolis. But what's he doing in Madeira? Need I ask.

'Struggling a bit, in all honesty. It would be great if you guys could give me a hand.'

This is looking horribly predicable …

'I get paid for getting people just to come and visit our

property. It takes no time at all, you don't get put under any pressure, but it would really help me out …'

He's done his job well. He's built a rapport with Lindsey which makes her feel almost obliged to say 'oh, go on then'. I glare daggers at her instead of thinking quickly enough to say 'but haven't you forgotten we've got a restaurant booking in twenty minutes?' Oh well, as long as it doesn't take up much time …

He says he'll take us to his office, just five minutes away. We arrive there twenty minutes later, to be greeted by an apologetic lady who says that the car to take us to the hotel is on its way back, and should only be a couple of minutes. OK, we'll hang on. Another twenty minutes and the car arrives.

We reach the hotel and are given a tour by slick, well-rehearsed reps. The hotel is admittedly stunning, state-of-the art facilities, breath-taking views, very classy. The lady is moving into sales overdrive, telling us about some of the famous folk who've already taken out timeshares there, how the remaining places are selling like hot cakes. 'And,' she says, 'the development is part-owned by Cristiano Ronaldo.'

You cannot be fucking serious. I look at her as though she's just murdered my children. OK, I haven't got any children. I look at her as though she's just destroyed my collection of Frank Sidebottom memorabilia. 'I take it you've heard of him,' she says. *Heard of him?* One of Madeira's most famous sons, and certainly its most repulsive, this preening, narcissistic flouncer brings out a level of contempt in me that only Ferguson and Beckham can match. I've wasted three hours of my life, and counting, going through this ridiculous charade. 'Can we leave now, please, we've seen enough.'

The lady says we just have to see the manager, it won't take a minute. I've seen it all before. This is the bit where they go through the process of asking you how much you'd be willing to pay and then miraculously find a way to come up with a deal which matches your price. You're boxed into a corner and then either lose face by backing down or lose a load of dosh by going through with the deal. To be fair, this guy's tactic is a bit different. He's the Honest John of Funchal. 'Look, we don't mess about, we know we'll sell all the slots, this is the price, take it or leave it.' I've no idea what the price was. I wasn't even listening. I wouldn't have gone for it if he had said we could have it for nothing and they'd throw in free flights and limousine transfers every time we came across. I'm not being associated with anything to do with that loathsome oily reptile. Just take us back into town please.

We eventually arrive back at their downtown office to be given our 'gift' – a bottle of cheap sparkling wine, equivalent cash value 0.01p. Scant reward for wasting four hours of our only Saturday on the island. 'I hope you've learned your bloody lesson,' I say to Lindsey, who struggles to suppress a smirk. She knows I'll see the funny side eventually. She's right. I already do. But I'll be milking this in future.

The next day we return to the scene of the crime, making no eye contact whatsoever with strangers, and certainly not talking to them, before adjourning to the pub. It's far from packed, a few folks in City shirts but no visible Villa support. Seems ideal. We tuck into a Sunday roast and await kick-off.

We're on top from the start, moving the ball about with real purpose and creating chance after chance. The best all fall to Darius Vassell, who should be relishing the opportunity to plant a few past his old team. He's got a funny way of showing it. When Barton forces a Villa defender into a clumsy, mishit back-pass, Vassell is clean through on goal. He's got time to look up, compose himself, and pick his spot. Instead, he looks up and becomes totally befuddled. He tries to take the ball around Sorensen, attempting to fool the keeper by executing a couple of step-overs. Sadly, he forgets the golden rule of step-overs. Keep the ball between your feet so that you can take it past the opponent once they've been distracted by your nifty footwork. Vassell is still doing his impression of Michael Flatley being attacked by a swarm of bees as the ball trundles out of his reach, enabling Sorensen to fall gently to the floor, strike a seductive pose, light a cigar and collect the ball at leisure.

A few minutes later, Vassell gets another run at goal. Fatally, he again looks up. It's as if Sorensen has got him hypnotised. *Look into my eyes. Look into my eyes.* Darius falls over his own feet and the ball runs to safety. Distin, Barton and Samaras also pass up very presentable opportunities as we fail to capitalise on a spell of play as good as anything we've produced all season.

We get one more great opportunity before the interval, when a breakaway sees Vassell storm towards two retreating defenders, with an unattended Sibierski surging up on the right. A simple pass will give Sibierski a great chance; instead, Vassell attempts a daredevil pivot to create some space for a shot, and promptly falls flat on his face. It's not been his best half, really. He's had some terrific games this season and scored some cracking goals, but he's one of those players for whom, when things start to go wrong, they never seem to get better. On days like this, he'd be much better off if he pretended to be injured and just got off the pitch before he did himself some serious damage.

We reach half-time and it's been the most one-sided half of football imaginable. The pundits eulogise our tremendous performance, but warn of the danger of not taking your chances when you're on top. As if we didn't know.

Into the second half and, while we're still the better side, Villa are showing more signs of life. I become aware of a guy in a group on the table in front of us urging them on in increasingly vociferous fashion. Fair enough, it's allowed.

Except that, as I tune in to some of their conversations, it becomes clear that he's not a Villa fan at all. He's supporting them because he's got a bet on them to win.

We come close when a prodigious leap from 17-year-old Micah Richards sees him power in a header which Milner clears off the line, but chances are less prevalent than in the first half. Then, the inevitable happens. We should have been out of sight by now, but Villa break and a lucky rico-chet sets up Angel, who blasts first time past James. Villa celebrate, O'Leary is a picture of smugness, City players look stunned and the bloke with the bet on goes berserk. The red mist comes down. It's bad enough going out of the cup in a match you should have won by a street, but to have some twat who doesn't even support them rubbing your nose in it just because he stands to win a few poxy euros really gets the blood boiling. My hackles are well and truly up.

The game becomes scrappy and fractious, Villa happy to break up our attacks by whatever means possible. The camera keeps panning to the smarmy, supercilious O'Leary and I feel like smashing the screen in. The bloke with the winning bet turns round and smirks whenever I yell in frus-tration at another thwarted attack. My mood is not healthy.

Three minutes of added time are signalled. Thanks to an injury-time injury, we're well into the fourth of them when substitute Lee Croft chases an over-hit ball down the right and, with a desperate lunge, manages to play it off a Villa defender for a corner. One last chance. As Barton prepares to take the kick, the cameras show David James coming forward, this time still wearing his goalie's jersey. The ball is flighted over towards Jamo, but it looks a bit too high, even for him.

Thank God for that, as surging in behind him is young Richards, who leaps like a salmon on a trampoline and thunders a header into the back of the net. City fans behind the goal go ballistic, and Richards throws himself into them for a celebration of unbridled ecstasy. Back in the Prince

Albert, I'm screaming, leaping and racing around the pub in a combination of sheer ecstasy and the release of ninety minutes of frustration and increasingly pent-up aggression. The guy with the bet on gets it in spades. Lindsey tells me to calm down. She still doesn't really get football.

The final whistle comes almost immediately, and the cameras stay focussed on Richards as he leaves the pitch in triumph, his face a picture of joy and disbelief. After a brief cutback to the studio, it's back to the ground for a post-match interview with the hero of the hour, a star of the future without a doubt. Richards then faces by far the biggest ordeal of his career so far – an interview with Garth Crooks. The predictably banal questions spring forth, but Richards temporarily deviates from the predictably banal responses. When asked what it felt like, he responds 'fuckin' amazin'', causing Crooks to blurt out a reminder that they're live on air.

Back in the studio, Gary Lineker apologises to those viewers who've accidently tuned in expecting to see *Songs of Praise*, excusing Richards on account of his tender years and lack of experience in front of the camera. Personally, I don't think any apology is needed. Let's face it, if Garth Crooks came up to you, you'd probably swear at him as well. In fact, you'd probably chin him. For reasons best known to themselves, the BBC made him a pundit back in the mid-1980s, and viewers have had to endure his excruciatingly bland and insight-free contributions ever since.

His measured and studious delivery can occasionally lure the uninitiated into thinking they're hearing something deep and meaningful, but any such misapprehension never lasts very long. His ridiculously earnest tones make the most simplistic observations sound profound and stretching, and his vocal inflections are a source of constant bemusement. He employs a wide enough vocabulary, but delivers the words as though he doesn't know what any of them actually mean.

His *piece de resistance* came at the 2002 World Cup, the one where John Motson excitedly and repeatedly envisaged the whole population of England tucking into bacon and eggs while watching the football. England went into their last group game needing a draw against Nigeria to guarantee their passage to the knockout stages. Everyone in the country, nay the world, knew this. The papers were full of speculation as to whether Sven's superheroes would play for the draw they needed, or go for the win in order to ensure they topped the group. England duly secured their point in a 0-0 thriller, and the intrepid Crooks strode on to the pitch to seek out Sven's inimitably illuminating take on proceedings.

'So Sven, *I can confirm* that England have qualified for the knockout phase.' It was as if such qualification rested on results elsewhere having gone our way, rather than the absolute arithmetical certainty it had always been. The laws of arithmetic hold little sway in Garthworld. Eriksson could have been forgiven for responding with 'tell me something I don't already know, you half-witted pillock' but, ever the consummate professional, recovered immediately from an initial and not entirely unfamiliar expression of bewilderment to move seamlessly into his favoured mantra.

'Yes, Garth, first half good, second half not so good.'

At a stroke, one of football's timeless cliches would be changed forever. Managers of doomed relegation strugglers would now provide their fans with a commitment to 'keep on battling until it's mathematically impossible to stay up … AND Garth Crooks has confirmed that we are in fact relegated'.

I'm back home in time for the replay, where goals from Samaras and Vassell give us a win more comfortable than the 2-1 scoreline suggests. The Greek God looks in awesome form. We hope it's not a flash in the pan. The draw for the sixth round has already given us a tie at home to West Ham United. It's the best chance we've had of reaching a cup semi-final in twenty-five years.

Some bizarre fixture scheduling means that the four quarter-final ties are to be played on successive weekday evenings. Ours falls on the Monday, just two days after a home game against Wigan. We're just above mid-table, next to no chance of Europe but none of relegation either. There is little doubt where our priorities should lie. In particular, we'll need Samaras fit and well, so everyone expects him to be rested for the Wigan game. He is, sort of. He's on the bench. When Sibierski gets injured early on, he's on the pitch. Shortly afterwards he's off again, crocked. Out of the cup-tie. Unlucky, yes, but Pearce's logic is difficult to comprehend. You either protect players from injury or you don't.

We create a few chances, but a clean strike from Dean Ashton gives the Hammers the lead. We battle hard, even after Sun Jihai is red-carded for Raising His Arms But Not Doing Anything Even Slightly Aggressive With Them, but a second Ashton goal puts the game beyond us. Musampa hits a late screamer to give us a glimmer of hope, but we can't get the equaliser our efforts deserve.

It is a real sickener, in effect the end of our season, and doesn't it show in our remaining performances. Our final eight league games yield seven defeats and just four goals, and what had looked like being a more than decent season evaporates into dismal anti-climax. And with little or no funds available to bring in summer reinforcements, dismal anti-climax might be as good as it gets …

2006/07

BEING BORING

You're An Embarrassment

21 OCTOBER 2006, PREMIER LEAGUE:
WIGAN ATHLETIC 4 CITY 0

Pearce's signings for the new season weren't exactly eye-catching, with the bulk of our transfer kitty already spent on Gorgeous George The Greek God. Striking reinforcements took the form of a little-known large Italian, Bernardo Corradi, and a well-known small Glaswegian, Paul Dickov. Bobbitt's heroics will and should never be forgotten but they were a long time ago. Other newcomers would have brought a reaction of 'who?' from all City fans other than those with detailed knowledge of reserve team football across Europe – Ousmane Dabo, Hatem Trabelsi, DaMarcus Beasley ...

Transfer fees were either free or 'undisclosed', with the only figures made available being those spent on a couple of new goalkeepers, £2 million for Swedish international Andreas Isaksson and £500,000 for Shrewsbury youngster Joe Hart.

Hopefully, one of these would prove an adequate replacement for the departed David James, although for the opening game at champions Chelsea it was the still jowly Weaver who took his place between the sticks. Chelsea predictably proved much too strong for us, Corradi marking his debut by getting himself sent off.

Three days later, Portsmouth came to Eastlands and any City fans optimistic about the season ahead were soon given a reality check in a turgid, guileless, goalless encounter. There was just one incident of note, and it was a gruesome one; a vicious, cowardly assault by Ben Thatcher on Pedro Mendes. It was on the far side of the pitch from us, and only on TV later did its true brutality become apparent. Thatcher ran at full pelt towards Mendes and floored him, off the pitch, with a forearm smash. This was a man with no place in football, let alone at Manchester City. There've been a few players over the years about whom I've said 'I never want to see him in a City shirt again', but this guy was right at the top of the list. A thug, pure and simple.

We actually got on the scoresheet in the next game, a penalty in off the bar by Joey Barton, and it was enough to give us a surprise and morale-boosting win over Arsenal. The next game provided a real chance to consolidate, away to newly promoted Premier League debutants Reading.

Having just moved to Berkshire, this was now just a fifteen-minute drive from home. You wouldn't really call Berkshire a hotbed of football – or a hotbed of anything other than polo, croquet and posh folk who ponce about in stripey blazers once a year – but Reading's promotion had captured the imagination of the area, with the prospect of international superstars visiting the Madejski Stadium on a regular basis. The game was moved to a Monday evening and the air of excitement and optimism around the town was tangible.

There was a raucous atmosphere inside the ground, the novelty of being in the big time very much in evidence.

It had that cup-tie-at-a-lower-league-club feeling, one of those games where you need to stay firm, let the crowd calm down and then start to assert yourselves. Instead, we let Reading get on top and, amid a constant barrage of noise, they took the lead when a tremendous header from Ingimarsson left Weaver helpless.

Sinclair – how the hell was he still in the side? How the hell had he ever been in the side? – fired ten yards wide from eight yards out, and Samaras and Reyna missed passable opportunities. However, when Dabo made his first notable contribution for the club by getting himself sent off ten minutes from time, the end was nigh. Four games gone, two red cards and it should have been three – Psycho needed to get a grip pretty quickly.

At Blackburn, we managed to keep everyone on the pitch, but still contrived to let in four goals as a promising start faded into disarray. After just five games, alarm bells were ringing loudly. Three days later, they were absolutely deafening and no one could find a way to switch them off. A full-strength City team was outplayed at Chesterfield and dumped out of the Carling Cup. Their winning goal was admittedly a once-in-a-lifetime strike, fit to win any game, but the media were now camped squarely on Psycho's back. Only halfway through September, and the c-word was on everyone's lips. Crisis.

The next game, at home to West Ham, was crucial. Their Cup win was still fresh in the memory, but their general record at City – indeed anywhere away from the comforts of the East End – was dreadful. Gorgeous George well and truly stepped up to the plate, two outstanding finishes securing what even at this stage of the season seemed like a vital three points. It gave Pearce a bit of breathing space and allowed the media to concentrate on making someone else's life a misery.

A richly merited injury-time equaliser from Micah Richards delivered a creditable point at Goodison and the hope that we'd properly turned the corner. A dismal goalless draw with Sheffield United at least extended our unbeaten run to three games, and the visit to lowly Wigan looked like an ideal opportunity to extend the sequence.

Mundane domestic commitments prevented me from getting to this game, and I settled down on the sofa for what I hoped would be a Saturday lunchtime spectacular. It certainly was. Just over a minute on the clock, and Emile Heskey fastened on to a through ball to lash a superb first-time strike into the far corner of the net. Yes, you did read that correctly.

A shocking start got even worse when a Wigan free kick, forty yards out, was arced into the box. Weaver came out to make a routine unopposed catch, only to be somewhat taken aback when Richard Dunne took it upon himself to leap in front of him and plant an unstoppable header squarely into his own net. Four minutes on the clock, two down, one sublime and one utterly ridiculous. Weaver looked at Dunne in the same way as you'd look at an incontinent elderly relative. 'It's OK, I know you can't help it ...'

Despite having eighty-six minutes to recover against a very ordinary side, we never remotely looked like doing so. Wigan's lead was extended when our dozing defenders let Camara nip in and slam home a third. Utterly abysmal. When Valencia was allowed to run into oceans of space to crash in a fourth, I was almost past caring. I'd sworn so much during the previous eighty minutes that I'd run out of expletives.

We had been thrashed beyond recognition by Wigan Athletic. *Wigan Athletic.* The first time we'd ever played them was in January 1971, and I'd stood on the Kippax as we squeaked through an FA Cup third round tie. We'd won four trophies in the previous three seasons and were one of the best teams in Europe; they weren't even in the Football League. Thirty-five years is a long time in football ...

A Quick Half And I'll Be Off …

30 DECEMBER 2006, PREMIER LEAGUE: WEST HAM 0 CITY 1

The only consolation after the Wigan drubbing was that we were still unbeaten at Eastlands. Even so, our fans had hardly been getting their money's worth – six games, four goals for us, none for the opposition. Attendances were drifting down towards, and sometimes below, the 40,000 mark – and even these were exaggerated by counting in the increasing number of season ticket holders who couldn't be bothered to turn up. What we needed was a game against totally hapless opposition, who'd defend like dustbins and make life so easy that even we couldn't fail to bag a few goals. Step forward Fulham FC.

Fulham's defence was so porous that even the hitherto hapless Bernardo Corradi managed to hit the net – not once, but twice. After each goal, he ran to the corner flag, hoisted the pole out of the ground and used it as an imitation sword to knight Joey Barton. It was a bizarre sight, but strangely amusing nonetheless. With hindsight, it would have been preferable if he'd been able to locate a real sword and used it to lop Barton's head off, but at this stage Joey was by some margin our most important and influential player.

Sir Joseph responded to his newly exalted status by strolling through Fulham's alleged defence to slot home a third. The move had started with a hoof upfield from our own corner flag, which suddenly left us with a two against one counterattack. Sunday park teams don't defend like this but no one, other than the two men and a dog comprising Fulham's away support, was complaining. We'd been treated to three City goals in a single half. Fans went out for their half-time cuppa wondering whether they'd come to the wrong ground by mistake. Fulham grabbed a consolation in the second half, but a comfortable win maintained our unbeaten home record and kept our heads above the drop-zone water. What we needed now was to get off the mark away from home.

No chance of that in the next game, away to Liverpool, but at least the margin of defeat was respectably slight. Four days later a trip to one of our happier hunting grounds, Villa Park, offered more realistic prospects. And 'horses for courses' came up trumps again, as we produced our best display of the season so far. Vassell atoned for his catalogue of misses in last season's Cup tie by drilling home a crisp volley to give us a thoroughly deserved lead. If he'd done that last year, it would have spared us all a lot of agony, but then we'd never have got to witness Micah swearing at Garth Crooks.

We looked dangerous every time we attacked, and a Samaras cut-back was smartly slotted in by Barton to put us in the uncharted, but fully merited, territory of two goals up away from home. Corradi dragged Barton off to the corner flag – Christ, how many knighthoods can one man take? – but instead used the pole as a makeshift guitar, as the two of them grooved to the latest imaginary Italian rock classic.

Out of the blue, McCann pulled one back, but we soon killed them off with an outstanding goal from an unlikely source. When Distin brought the ball out from defence, we expected a ball upfield and a return to his natural position. Instead, he played the ball out to Samaras and stormed forward onto the instant return pass. Now in Villa's half, he turned on the afterburners to sear past the last defender and advance on goal. As Taylor came out, Distin calmly stroked the ball past him for a magnificent goal, putting the seal on a tremendous team performance. Surprisingly, Corradi didn't think this superlative effort worthy of a knighthood.

The Villa game was as good as it got. An abysmal goalless draw at home to Watford was hardly the best preparation for a trip to Old Trafford, and when Rooney scored in the first few minutes we looked set for a hammering.

It's hard to find words to describe the defending. Absolutely fucking diabolical will do for now. A hopeful diagonal ball from Ronaldo should have been intercepted twice, but was instead allowed to pass through to Rooney, eight yards out. We responded with spirit, coming close a couple of times, but then contrived to give away an even worse goal, complete haplessness allowing United to break down the left and Louis Saha to bundle home. Giving away comedy goals at Old Trafford doesn't generally get you very far.

Hatem Trabelsi then made his first meaningful contribution in a City shirt by firing in a screaming twenty-yarder, but hopes of a comeback were dashed when a third comic cuts goal – a heinous miss-kick from Richard Dunne, who hadn't had his most co-ordinated afternoon, giving Ronaldo a tap in – put United in the clear. We hadn't played too badly overall, but conceding even one of the goals we let in would have been enough to make any manager homicidal. Three of them – well, it's amazing that Psycho didn't butcher half the team. They ought to have been bloody nervous when they got in the shower.

Two straight home defeats followed and, almost in the blink of an eye, we were back in crisisland. The Boxing Day visit to Sheffield United was billed as a relegation six-pointer, but Stevie Ireland, in and out of the team despite showing enormous promise, crashed home a stupendous late half-volley to deliver a priceless win.

Next up, a trip to The Boleyn Ground. It's a bloody horrible day, a howling gale, lashing with rain, the sort of day where you wouldn't leave the house at all if it wasn't for City. We take our places in the ground, the wind and rain stinging our faces. Even before the game starts, it's a wretched experience. And it just gets worse. The quality of play in the first half, from both teams, is abysmal. There isn't a goalmouth incident worthy of the name, both sides content to lump it forward aimlessly time after time. Even our justifiably feted away support find it beyond themselves to generate any enthusiasm. It's dire.

The half-time whistle blows. Thank God for that. Staring out at the groundsmen tending the pitch will be more entertaining than what we've had to put up with. I've never even thought about leaving a game at half-time before, let alone done it, but this has been truly the most miserable forty-five minutes of football I've ever witnessed. I've had enough. I look at Lindsey with a pained expression. 'I'm not sure I can take another half of this.' She doesn't exactly argue. Had she said 'don't be hasty, we might get a crucial win with a brilliant individual DaMarcus Beasley goal' then I might have reconsidered, but my mind's made up. We trudge out of the ground and back towards the tube station.

It feels absolutely like the right decision. Common sense has for once prevailed. I'm not going home to beat the traffic, I'm not going home because the game already looks won, or lost, I'm going home because I'd rather boil my head in oil than watch any more of this dross. If you went to the cinema and couldn't get into the film at all, you'd leave. If you went to a gig and hated the music, you'd leave. Even allowing for the essential unpredictability of sport, there seems no possibility of either of these teams producing anything remotely worth sticking around for. And, apparently, they didn't. Apart from a brilliant individual DaMarcus Beasley goal …

Passionless, Pointless

11 MARCH 2007, FA CUP SIXTH ROUND: BLACKBURN 2 CITY 0

A New Year's Day victory over Everton made it three wins in a row, putting us in surprisingly good heart for the start of a new Cup campaign. Last year's quarter-final had been our first for fourteen years, a pretty lamentable record, but some decent draws gave us the chance to repeat the achievement. Sheffield Wednesday succumbed in a replay, Southampton were seen off fairly comfortably, and a fifth round visit to Preston North End gave us every opportunity to secure another last-eight place.

Falling behind to a first-minute goal wasn't the ideal start, but we gradually clawed our way back, and the seal on a fine 3-1 win was set with another marvellous finish from Stephen Ireland, running on to a looping ball to crash a sensational volley into the net. This boy looked like he had everything it takes to become a really top player. The next day's draw was eagerly awaited, but delivered not the best news – Arsenal or Blackburn, away.

The two had drawn at the Emirates, where a typically dour, defensive, physical display from Mark Hughes's side had secured a goalless draw. An indignant, frustrated Cesc Fabregas taunted Hughes afterwards, incredulous that the architect of such joyless, cynical football could ever have played for Barca. Hughes had the last laugh, as the replay saw his team earn a surprise win. So, a trip to Ewood Park beckoned – not exactly easy, but certainly preferable to the alternative.

You couldn't say we were going into the game in tip-top form; we'd picked up just one point – and one goal – from the last five games, all against mediocre opposition. The goal was a rare strike from Bernardo Corradi, who by now had become a figure of ridicule, labelled 'Bernardo Cribbinio' by our *City Till I Cry* fanzine. It looked like bringing us a point at Portsmouth, but a familiar late defensive blunder gifted Kanu a winner. It was hard to deny that some sort of moral justice had been served, as Portsmouth's first goal had come by way of a superb strike from Paulo Mendes, happily now fully recovered from Ben Thatcher's appalling early season assault.

At least Thatcher had been offloaded during the transfer window, the first real opportunity Pearce had had to wield the axe. His only new signing of any note was the Belgian international Emile 'Needles' Mpenza, who I'd always thought looked pretty useful even if he was now past his heyday. We might not have the wherewithal to bring in real top stars, but at least we could boast some of the greatest nicknames in football history, with Needles proudly joining 'Chris' Musampa in our hall of fame.

Despite our shocking league form, I travelled to Ewood with a weird, inexplicable, completely atypical feeling of confidence. Maybe the memory of that epic promotion day back in 2000 was playing tricks with my subconscious. I wasn't alone. Chatting to Dave and Tom, respective editors of our two fanzines, they too were strangely upbeat. Most weeks, this lot had played like the worst City team in living memory – how 'typical City' would it be for them to reach our first semi-final for twenty-six years?

With a huge contingent of Blues roaring the side on, the game had the feel of a really big occasion. But the team never showed up. We started reasonably enough, with Vassell looking as though he might be on for one of his better days, but subsided feebly after conceding a soft goal to Mokoena. Even with an hour to go, there was never any suggestion of a comeback, and the lack of spirit was summed up by an angry exchange between Barton and Corradi. Those happy knighthood days seemed a long time ago.

When Mokoena saw red midway through the second half, we naively thought that the team would redouble its efforts; instead, our tentative, unimaginative, passionless performance brought about a mood of increasing anger. A late breakaway gave Matt Derbyshire a simple chance to extinguish our hopes good and proper, and ignited the first rumblings of 'Pearce out' among the fans. Coming out of the ground I felt incredibly let down. My pre-match optimism may have been somewhat irrational given our recent form, but surely Psycho should have been able to get us up for this one?

Another joyless season. Usually, there are a few memorable moments to look back on, but this time there'd been less entertainment than I could ever remember. Our lack of attacking ambition, even when trailing, was startling, and though we all accepted that the tools at his disposal weren't exactly the sharpest, there was an increasing sense that Psycho wasn't getting the most out of them. His dejected, almost desperate, demeanour after the match suggested that he just didn't know where to turn. When the next game brought defeat at home to Chelsea, we were starting to look nervously over our shoulders. Just a couple of points off the drop-zone, in an appalling run of form, and three of the next four games away from home.

The positive side of 'typical City' had failed to turn up at Blackburn; it had been saving itself for the league instead. Incredibly, all three away games were won, with Needles playing a starring role. He grabbed the first in a surprise 2-0 win at Middlesbrough, followed up with the only goal at Newcastle and was then instrumental in a crucial 3-1 win at relegation-threatened Fulham. The prospect of a nervy finish to the season had been nipped in the bud. Forty points on the board with six games left at least meant that we could 'look forward' to Premier League football next season. And wonder whether there would ever come a time when our ambitions might be just a bit loftier than that.

Blank Generation

5 MAY 2007, PREMIER LEAGUE:
CITY 0 MANCHESTER UNITED 1

With those nagging relegation fears banished, at least I could now concentrate on the important things in life.

These have always included catching up with pals and enjoying a few glasses, and I was looking forward to a nice industry dinner towards the end of April. On arriving at our table, Ian, our host, asked me whether I'd like to say hello to our special guest. I glanced across; he looked vaguely familiar. I looked more closely; he was very familiar. Sir Geoff Hurst. And Ian had kindly arranged for me to sit next to him.

I do a bit of mental arithmetic and estimate that Geoff must have been, say, 25 in the 1966 World Cup, which would make him a good 65 now. Jesus Christ! He looks fitter than most 40-year-olds and can hardly be a pound heavier than when he was putting the Germans to the sword. Takes himself a bit seriously does Geoff, but I suppose if you're the only man in history to have scored a World Cup Final hat-trick then you can do what you bloody well like.

I'm looking forward to having a good old natter with a fellow Ashton-under-Lyner, and reflect that it's the second time I've met a man with three World Cup Final goals to his name. The first was Zinedine Zidane some seven or eight years earlier. In a hotel lift, on the morning of the Euro 2000 final. I was on my way down to breakfast when the door opened and in walked the great man himself. I can recall our conversation to this day:

Me: Bonjour (*Hello*)
Zizou: Bonjour (*Hello*)
Me: Bonne chance pour ce soir (*Good luck this evening*)
Zizou: Merci (*Thank you*)
Me: Vous avez de la confiance? (*Are you confident?*)

As banal small-talk questions go, even allowing for my dismally limited French, this one takes some beating. He's the greatest player in the world, one of the best of all time, and in the form of his life. Of course he's going to be bloody confident. Even Garth Crooks wouldn't have asked him something as inane as that.

At this point, fortunately for Zizou, the lift door opens and some other hotel residents get in. Zizou gives me a little nod of bemused acknowledgement and scarpers out, even though I suspect he hasn't yet reached his intended floor. Much better to walk down the stairs than continue with this kind of ordeal. What will the English buffoon ask me next? Am I looking forward to the game? Will I be happy if we win?

Anyway, I fare a bit better with Geoff as we have a long chat about his playing days, and I manage to avoid lapsing into the 'did it cross the line?' question he would have heard twenty million times before. We talked about West Ham's win at City in 1970, famous for Ronnie Boyce's forty-five-yard volley into an empty net after Joe Corrigan had cleared from the corner of his penalty area and meandered obliviously back towards the net. After the game, Geoff asked Joe what had happened, and our gentle giant apparently replied: 'Well, I was strolling back towards goal when I noticed this ball in the back of the net. I thought "fuck me, there must be two balls on the pitch! How the hell did that happen?"'

Geoff has to make a short speech and is staying stone-cold sober, in marked contrast to most of us around him, and I can't help but start laying into all things United. Geoff is too smart to be drawn into slagging anyone off, but I eventually manage to get a reaction when I claim that Bobby Charlton was the most over-rated player in the history of football.

'How the hell can you say that? He scored 49 goals for England!'

'But Geoff, they were all against Luxembourg.'

We chatted about lots of his old teammates, and he was visibly surprised at my contempt for Alan Ball, based wholly on his time as City manager. Clearly, he'd been one of Geoff's favourite players. When I woke up the following morning, I switched on the news to find Alan Ball very much in it. He'd passed away during the night. I could hardly have felt worse. It would be hypocritical to suggest that he was anything but an unmitigated disaster in his time at City. But he was obviously a true football man, a fantastic player whose place in history is assured forever, and his early demise was terribly sad.

Meanwhile, City's performances continued to veer between disappointing and desperate, and more often than not desperately disappointing. Hopes that April would prove to be Eastlands' *Month Of The Goal* were dashed when Aston Villa held out for a clean sheet in their 2-0 win. By now, we hadn't scored a home goal since New Year's Day, a run of seven consecutive barren matches. Pearce's team was hopelessly short of ideas, invention and confidence, and the manager's own demeanour reflected the circumstances. The days of haring up and down the touchline, kicking every ball, making every tackle, seemed like years ago. In a similar way to Keegan, the body language that once exuded confidence, enthusiasm and belief now displayed resignment, disillusionment and despair. We were nowhere near good enough, and Pearce clearly felt powerless to do anything about it.

Our final home game, the last chance for the players to send us into the summer with at least a goal to remember them by, was the derby. And the circumstances were bleakly familiar. For us, it was a game with nothing resting on it, other than the chance to bloody the nose of our nauseating neighbours. For them, it was a crucial match, as they sought to wrest the title back from the *nouveaux riches* upstarts of Stamford Bridge.

We at least gave a decent account of ourselves, competing well from the start, even though United's general superiority was painfully evident. The vile Ronaldo strutted about in his usual fashion – has there ever been a man more in love with himself than this guy? – and the day's biggest cheer came when he was left writhing after a challenge from Michael Ball. Replays would show that Ball deliberately stamped on his chest – absolutely indefensible, he should have gone for the face – but the referee elected to turn a blind eye. No such leniency just before half-time, though; when Ronaldo fell over Ball's stationary foot, the inevitable spot-kick resulted. The repulsive brilliantined pansy duly converted to give them a half-time lead and it looked like that was that. We hadn't scored here for the last 693 minutes, why should the next forty-five be any different?

The first thirty-five weren't. Much huffing and puffing, but little to trouble van der Sar. Then, with just ten minutes to go, Ball surged into the area and went tumbling after a challenge from Wes Brown. It looked a tad theatrical, but Rob Styles pointed to the spot. A golden chance not just to score a goal, but also scupper United's title bid. The season might have a happy ending after all. After the usual moaning to the referee and all-round petulance, the stage was set. Darius Vassell stepped up. I'd only seen him take a penalty once before, when his shoot-out miss helped put England out of Euro 2004. I wasn't flush with confidence.

Vassell went for power, hitting the ball straight down the middle in the expectation that the keeper would dive one way or the other. Van der Sar indeed did so, but the ball struck his trailing leg and flew over the crossbar. Groans all around, but nobody was really surprised. It just summed up the season.

Seldom can we have gone into a summer break as low as this. Sure, it's grim when you get relegated, but at least you can start to think about coming straight back up, with lots of wins against lower quality opposition. All we'd got to look forward to was the same old turgid football, a manager who'd lost his mojo, and players who weren't good enough to lift us any higher. We had bugger-all money to change the situation and looked like perennial also-rans. Nobodies. Anonymous. In my forty years of following City, we've always been newsworthy. Not always for the reasons we'd have preferred, but enough to make us a central topic of sporting conversation nonetheless. But now, if we fell off the face of the earth and ceased to exist, nobody but City fans would notice we'd gone. And even some of us would take a while before we realised ...

2007/08

THE BOGUS MAN

The Luckiest Man Alive

19 AUGUST 2007, PREMIER LEAGUE:
CITY 1 MANCHESTER UNITED 0

Things had to change, and they did. The sacking of the hapless Pearce was predictable and welcome, the refreshing honesty and exaggerated enthusiasm a distant memory. He'd been horribly exposed as uninspiring and unimaginative. Yes, we were hardly stinking rich, but not a single goal in eight consecutive home games was testament to Pearce's tactical inflexibility. In some games we didn't manage a single shot on target – in one, we didn't manage a single shot at all. I wasn't upset to see him go, but equally wondered how we could attract anyone much better. The cycle of mediocrity looked set to go on and on.

Suddenly, as the media speculated on who Pearce's replacement might be, there was a dramatic development. The one thing that might see us achieve a step change.

A rich benefactor. A seriously rich benefactor. Allegedly. Thaksin 'Frank' Shinawatra, former Prime Minister of Thailand. The man to lead us to the promised land or, at least initially, enable us to compete in the transfer market for slightly better players than Bernardo Cribbinio and Gorgeous George. As the stories began to circulate about his background and how exactly he might have come by his riches, it was rare to see his name mentioned without the accompanying expression of 'human rights violater'. Did we care? Not really. Don't believe everything you read in the papers. All that mattered to most of us was the loot. And who he selected to spend it.

Frank's riches enabled our managerial shortlist to be upgraded a tad, and at last the opportunity to recruit a proven winner was there to be grabbed. Instead we went for a proven conman. Sven-Goran Eriksson's period in charge of England had seen some of the most depressing and uninspiring performances possible, characterised by his complete inertia as games evolved, most notably in the 2002 World Cup quarter-final against Brazil. His infatuation with Beckham, and the attendant celebrity roundabout, had led him to select the monstrously over-rated one-trick pony even though patently unfit. So it was that Beckham's self-obsession and selfishness together with Sven's stupidity led to the vacuous clothes-horse shirking a routine tackle as a prelude to Brazil's vital equaliser. Then, 2-1 down against ten men, the team passively let the sands of time run down without raising a single threat to the Brazil goal. Thirty-six years of hurt and counting.

Same again in Euro 2004 against Portugal, where the distance between midfield and lone striker Owen was so great that we were reduced to lumping fifty-yard Hollywood balls in his general direction and scarcely mustered a worthwhile attack. The initiative was duly handed back to the hosts, as Sven sat around and did nothing, doubtless daydreaming about his potential conquests for the evening ahead. In 2006, he gave up a crucial squad place by taking along a 17-year-old just for the ride, and another series of dismal performances led to a lucrative termination of Sven's contract. Undoubtedly his happiest day as England manager.

What had initially been regarded as coolness under pressure, a calming influence for the players, was now recognised as absolute indifference. Maybe his reserves of passion had been exhausted in his high-profile amorous liaisons, joyously reported in and ridiculed by the tabloids. A complete charlatan, a cynical mercenary beneath contempt, and the only consolation for those of us sick to the back teeth of the simplistic interviews, the benign vacant smile and the laid back to the point of being comatose attitude was that he was surely destined never again to hold a managerial position of any credibility ...

The news of his appointment left me absolutely gutted, so much so that I saw the optimal outcome to be for us to lose the first four or five games, enough for Frank to dispatch Sven with his (allegedly) customary alacrity before too much damage had been done. Then we could get a proper manager and build for the future. I'd never felt as low as this at the start of a season. I vowed never to go again while he was in charge.

Sven wasted no time in bringing his pal Hans Backe to the club to help him source new talent, and it was easy to visualise his first scouting report:

'So Hans, what have you been looking at today?'

'Well, Sven, I've had a complete review of our existing talent pool.'

'Excellent, excellent! So what have you found?'

'Julia, receptionist, slim, blonde, large breasts, peachy bottom, mid-twenties, single, looks a real good-time girl; Karen, ticket office, bit older, fuller figure, but very pretty, nice and chatty. Married but bored. Might be interested; Emily, marketing, nice personality but a bit flat-chested and complexion like stale Ryvita; Sandra, finance

department, looks hot but big burly possessive boyfriend. Best to steer clear.'

'Hmmm. First half good, second half not so good.'

Sven's secondary priority saw him assemble an eclectic mix of foreigners that most of us had never heard of. Elano Blumer from Shakhtar Donetsk and fellow Brazilian Geovanni; young Italian striker Rolando Bianchi; Spanish full-back Javier Garrido; allegedly promising Swiss youngster Gelson Fernandes; Croatian defender Vedran Corluka; supposed Tottenham target Martin Petrov and his compatriot Valeri Bojinov, labelled the 'Bulgarian Wayne Rooney'. Sven was widely mocked for supposedly having made all of these purchases on the back of videotape viewings; apparently, he hadn't seen any of them play live.

The season's opener took us to West Ham, normally a favourite trip; instead I chose to watch the mighty Maidenhead United, admittedly with the radio tuned to the live commentary from Upton Park. It's one thing telling all and sundry that I actually wanted us to lose, but when it came to the crunch the reality was different. That familiar rush of excitement was present and correct on hearing Bianchi fire us ahead, and what sounded like an accomplished performance was rounded off with a late Geovanni goal.

All the new recruits performed well, and Sven wore a contentedly smug expression on that night's *Match of the Day* as he gently berated his critics over his supposedly remote purchasing strategy. He may not have seen all of them live, but his trusted, knowledgeable coaching staff certainly had. And how could the press be so stupid as to doubt the methods of a proven, internationally experienced manager? Round one to the Scandinavian Love Machine.

The next game saw the visit of newly promoted Derby County, and a super goal from new homegrown starlet

Michael Johnson not only broke City's 2007 Eastlands' goal drought, but also brought another three points. A 1-0 win against a team which would go on to become, statistically, the worst team in Premier League history may not have been too much to write home about, but no one could argue with six points out of six – and United to come at the weekend.

Now, when I said I'd never go again while Sven was in charge, what I actually meant was I wouldn't go again unless I changed my mind. It was derby day. I had to be there. It didn't mean I'd changed my mind about Sven.

City lined up with the same mix of new recruits and homegrown talent as in the previous games, most notable among the latter the nation's third most famous Schmeichel in goal. Stylistically reminiscent of his dad, though bearing not quite such a strong resemblance to Chesney's dog, Kasper looked about 14 years old at the most and simply not imposing enough to withstand the onslaught sure to come his way. Still, at least he had the formidable pairing of Biffer and Micah Richards in front of him.

The game soon settled into a familiar pattern, United having more of the ball, certainly carrying the greater threat, but Dunne and Richards looked rock-solid and Schmeichel had hardly been called upon. Sadly, the same couldn't be said of City's medical staff, as a seemingly innocuous early challenge saw Bojinov stretchered off. Five minutes into its second Saturday, his season was over.

Though secure at the back, we hadn't threatened van der Sar's goal at all until midway through the half, when Elano found Geovanni in space. With Vidic half-turning away, Geo fired in a low thirty-yarder which took a faint touch off the Serb's calf and flashed low into the bottom corner. After the usual pandemonium, we were 45,000 people with minds as one. How the hell can we hold on for almost an hour?

I'm still not sure how we did. Dunne and Richards were immense, with Richards defending like a man possessed, the very definition of 'they shall not pass'. What a find he looked to be. Schmeichel also more than played his part with some vital saves, one of them featuring his dad's famous 'star jump'. He was obviously a more than capable shot-stopper, but coping with crosses was a different matter. Every ball in the air brought a sense of panic, but there was always someone there to clear the danger.

Every now and then we'd get a release from the pressure, usually by getting the ball to Petrov on the left. The epitome of the flying winger, Petrov would play the ball twenty yards ahead then sprint furiously after it, looking for all the world like an aphrodisiac-fuelled Rigsby in rampant pursuit of Miss Jones. Like Rigsby, he never quite managed to nail his target, but he was enough of a menace to keep United's defence honest and discourage them from over-committing.

We survived unbreached until, with just seconds to go, a near post corner was flicked on to Tevez, a couple of yards out. As his header flashed goalwards, Ferguson was up from his seat in aggressive jubilation, only to shrink back in disbelief as the net failed to bulge. Somehow, the hapless Argie had managed to put the ball wide – for all the hype and controversy surrounding him, anyone could see that he'd never make a decent Premier League striker ...

The guy next to me had been in a state of apoplexy throughout the whole half, constantly looking at the scoreboard clock and bemoaning how slowly the minutes were passing. He continued to count them down aloud, almost one by one, until the board for additional time went up. I kept telling him to stay calm, pretty rich for a man with my track record, but also indicative that the last couple of years had lessened the part City played in my life. Not by much, but enough to notice a difference. Five years ago, in the last Maine Road derby, I'd been just like him, probably even worse. Now, I was still tense, fraught, but not quite so all-consumed. It still mattered, just not quite as much.

We held on for an unlikely win, and even I had to admit that nine points from nine, top of the league, no goals conceded and a derby win under his belt constituted a pretty good start for Sven. And seven points – count them, seven – ahead of United. Round two to the Scandinavian Love Machine. It is, however, a marathon not a sprint ...

Oscillate Wildly

27 OCTOBER 2007, PREMIER LEAGUE: CHELSEA 6 CITY 0

A narrow reverse at Arsenal is scant reward for another strong performance, but mundane defeat at Blackburn evokes the sound of bursting bubbles. Michael Johnson's lovely goal is enough to beat Villa, and some tabloids ludicrously start to refer to him as a new Colin Bell. Give the lad a chance. He's promising, but not that promising. Martin Petrov announces his true credentials in the next game at Fulham, two goals in a dynamic display not quite enough to overcome some sloppy defending in an entertaining but ultimately disappointing 3–3 draw.

The next home game is a Saturday lunchtime encounter with Newcastle, as we look to extend our 100 per cent home record. It turns out to be our best and most entertaining performance since the days of Benarbia and Berkovic. Elano, Johnson and Ireland produce some wonderful intricate passing to cut through the Newcastle defence time and again, and Petrov's pace and direct approach give us real menace on the flanks. Is there more to Sven than I'd given him credit for? For sure, his England teams were never remotely as entertaining as this.

We fall behind to a rare Newcastle attack, but equalise with a smart Petrov finish before a glancing header from Needles gives us a richly deserved lead. We're completely on top as we reach added time, and a free kick over thirty yards out allows us the chance to at least run the clock down, even if it looks a bit too far out for a realistic shot at goal. Oh really? Elano steps back, and puts his instep right through the ball. It sears goalwards, and a full-stretch Shay Given can't get anywhere near it as it crashes into his top right hand corner. It looks spectacular enough first time round, but when you see it from behind the line of the shot it's truly staggering. The ball flies true as an arrow, no dip, no swerve, as it passes the wall and reaches its target – an inch beneath the bar, an inch inside the post. It's a feat of sheer geometric precision, and from the way Elano struck it, there's no doubt that he intended to put it precisely there. Bloody hell, this guy is seriously good.

The next week brings Middlesbrough to Eastlands and, if anything, Elano is even better. Two goals, a lovely twenty-yarder and a delicate, curling free kick – in contrast to the howitzer he'd unleashed last week – confirm him as a huge talent and propel us into the top three.

A third successive home game brings yet another win and yet another Elano goal, against Birmingham City, and while the performance is less spectacular, the three points put us up to second and make the following week's trip to Stamford Bridge a must-see. But for me, a couldn't-see. A trip up north for a friend's fiftieth has long been scheduled, so I'll just have to settle for radio commentary while we drive there. The media have been building up our chances all week, conveniently ignoring the fact that we haven't won away since the opening day of the season. Nevertheless, the eyes of the football world are upon us, and it's a welcome change.

It sounds like we start brightly, creating a couple of chances and giving as good as we get. But Essien gives

Chelsea the lead and though we come close to equalising, Drogba gets a second before the interval.

We need a quick start to the second half to have any chance, but Drogba and Joe Cole add two more within fifteen minutes. They're cutting through us almost at will. When you're getting hammered like this, listening to the radio makes it seem even worse, as the commentators reiterate your failings time and again with what sounds like undisguised glee. They keep telling us it'd be even more if it wasn't for Hart, but it soon is anyway, as Kalou and Shevchenko complete a humbling rout. It's a horrible feeling, but I keep telling myself that it's nowhere near as painful as an unlucky last-minute defeat. And at least I've had plenty of time to get over it by the time we arrive at Linda and Martin's.

It's a Halloween fancy dress theme, and lack of preparation time coupled with innate stupidity means that the best that I can do is turn up in a Frank Sidebottom papier-mâché head with a witch's hat stuck on top. It's a high-impact outfit, but suffers from some serious practical drawbacks. You can't eat, you have to drink through a straw, you can hardly see anything and it's so hot that you feel as though you're about to pass out within ten minutes of arriving. Other than that, it's bloody brilliant.

The party is great fun, and at least temporarily wipes away the memories of the painful soundtrack to our journey to get there. Returning home the next day, a glance at the papers brings it back very quickly. A week ago, our unconvincing win over Birmingham brought out the old cliches along the lines that winning when not playing well is the sign of a top team. A week before that, 'Manchester now has two teams capable of challenging for the title', according to *The Guardian*, no less. Now, this one result proved beyond doubt that our position in the table was a false one, and the 'told you so' flak poured in from all sides.

As if we didn't know. It was only our home form that had got us up there in the first place, and some of those wins had come in tight games which could easily have had a different outcome. Equally, we were nowhere near as bad as the Chelsea game had made us look. But even among the allegedly 'quality' papers, realistic assessments don't make for good reading. From title contenders to flash-in-the-pan mediocrities in the space of ninety minutes. Build 'em up then knock 'em down. The only language these guys understand.

99 Blue Balloons

27 JANUARY 2008, FA CUP FOURTH ROUND: SHEFFIELD UNITED 2 CITY 1

City responded to the battering at the Bridge by registering two narrow home victories, each won with Stephen Ireland volleys. The first saw off Sunderland and prompted a bizarre celebration, with Ireland dropping his shorts to reveal a pair of Superman underpants. A warning from the FA followed, as did the regular refrain of 'Ireland is Superman' from his increasingly enraptured fan club. This guy clearly had some serious talent, even if it was becoming equally apparent that he didn't quite have all his chairs under the table.

Wanting to spend a bit of time with his girlfriend, he'd made up a story about his grandmother having just died in order to get out of a Republic of Ireland friendly. The lady in question was a bit surprised to read about her own demise in the press. 'Oops, sorry, I meant my other grandmother.' She too publicly professed herself to be alive and well. 'No, no, no ...what I meant was the new partner of my recently divorced granddad.' Didn't take the press long to dig holes in that one as well.

Not a man of towering intellect, young Stephen, but then I suppose that's not what we look for in our footballers. What we do look for is the ability to hit a first-time twenty-yard volley into the top corner to give us a last-minute winner and maintain our 100 per cent home record. That's what he did against Reading, with a truly stunning goal. The scope to improve further, to become the main man in the team, was there in abundance; so was the potential for everything to turn pear-shaped in no time. Which way would Stevie go?

We threatened to improve our dismal away record, but could never quite manage it. Joe Hart's superb display at Portsmouth, an early indication of his quality and potential, earned us a point; then, we took the lead at both Wigan and Villa without being able to capitalise fully. We reached Christmas having won every single home game, but just the one away from Eastlands. Boxing Day brought the visit of Blackburn and the end of our perfect home record, with Roque Santa Cruz scoring his second equaliser a couple of minutes from time. We'd deserved to win this one comfortably, but had ridden our luck in enough of our earlier wins and couldn't complain too much. But when two more unimpressive home league draws followed, it looked as though Sven's Midas touch was starting to desert him.

Maybe he could deliver some cup magic? The Carling Cup had looked like a decent proposition, with a home quarter-final against Tottenham Hotspur a decent enough draw. An offside Defoe scored early on, but we got a real boost when Zokora saw red for a two-footed lunge. Steed Malbranque's challenge shortly afterwards was even worse, but referee Bennett chose to take no action. We put the Spurs goal under siege, were denied a clear penalty, and salt was rubbed into the wound with a breakaway clincher by Malbranque, who by then should have been showered, changed and on his fourth glass of wine in the players' lounge. We felt hard done by, but Dimitar Berbatov's performance had been so spell-bindingly brilliant that you could make a case for a Spurs win on that account alone.

The FA Cup third round produced a goalless draw at Upton Park, and a diving header from Elano saw us scrape through the replay to earn a fourth round trip to Championship strugglers Sheffield United. I'd be missing this one, as we'd booked a holiday to Cape Town. Oh well. I'd just have to hope I could find somewhere to watch it.

It turned out to be harder to find somewhere you *couldn't* watch it, as every bar seemed to be showing wall-to-wall football. An afternoon spent transfixed by the magnificence of Table Mountain or a few hours in a boozer glued to a TV screen? No contest. Seen one mountain, seen 'em all. By the time our game kicked off, just seven Premier League teams remained in the competition, so the incentive was there. A good win today, a couple of kind draws, and who knows?

The mood wasn't improved by witnessing the end of the United-Spurs tie, won by United after some criminal refereeing gifted them a ridiculous penalty and a scarcely believable sending-off, enthusiastically received by a group of boisterous Reds in the bar. Worse still, this lot were clearly intent on sticking around to watch our game, roaring their approval when Blades' manager Bryan Robson appeared on the screen. Despite the fact that Robson's trademark managerial skills had led his team inexorably towards the drop-zone, I felt a deep sense of foreboding as kick-off approached.

City were at full strength, emphasising the importance Sven was attaching to the Cup. I couldn't argue with that. Robson, however, had chosen to rest a few of his regulars in view of a forthcoming league game three days later. All grist to the mill for our red companions: 'If you lot can't beat Sheffield United reserves ...'

City fans had travelled in vast numbers, and the teams' entry was greeted by the release of hundreds of balloons, many of which were still nestling in Joe Hart's goalmouth as the game kicked off. I have never understood what it is that possesses people to do this. Hart cleared a few of them away, but subsequently decided he'd be better employed concentrating on the game.

After ten minutes or so, United got a man free down the left, and a scuffed low cross trundled towards the six-yard box. Michael Ball prepared to make a routine clearance, but as he drew his foot back, the ball's path deviated slightly after colliding with a couple of balloons. Ball made contact only with thin air, and the ball bobbled on to the unmarked Shelton, who just about managed to suppress his mirth for long enough to take a touch and prod the ball home.

My, how our red friends laughed, especially when replays showed the true extent of the role played by the balloons. Deep inside, I knew that the goal shouldn't have been allowed, that the balloons should have been cleared away before the game had started. But how pathetic would it sound to complain about it? And they'd been released on to the pitch by our own fans! Another of those moments where you shake your head, grin and bear it, and say 'it could only happen to City'. Hart furiously stamped on the remaining balloons, fuelled by the anger that he hadn't done it sooner.

In another ten minutes we were two down and, even against such moderate opposition, it looked a long way back. Elano was getting increasingly ratty, and Sven brought him off at half-time to be replaced by the promising Danny Sturridge. Within a couple of minutes, Sturridge buried a superb volley to halve the deficit, and the comeback looked inevitable. 'You've got 'em now,' said the Reds. But we hadn't. We never established the sort of momentum we needed, and United had as many chances to kill the game off as we had to draw level.

Full time, out of the Cup, and the patronising words from the Reds just made things worse. 'Unlucky there, that goal should never have been given, still you're doing much better under Sven than anyone could have thought.' Well, are we *really*? What I wanted to say was 'shut the fuck up you smug bastards, just wait until we get you at Old Trafford in a couple of weeks, we'll see who's laughing then'. Yeah, right.

Silence is Golden

10 FEBRUARY 2008, PREMIER LEAGUE: MANCHESTER UNITED 1 CITY 2

Here it is again, the fixture I await with trepidation. United at Old Trafford. I prefer to have it right at the start of the season, just to get it out of the way. This year it's in February. It 'coincides' with the fiftieth anniversary of the Munich air disaster. Do people honestly think this is a good idea?

United are going to mark the anniversary in a big way. Fair enough. It was an horrific accident, which has become part of the fabric of the club. But it was fifty years ago. The vast majority of people inside the stadium wouldn't have been alive when it happened. Of course a tribute is right, but the copious media coverage in the build-up to the game makes it feel more like something on the scale of Remembrance Day.

Naturally there'll be a minute's silence, and it's been revealed that both teams will wear shirts free from sponsors' logos, recreating the image of 1958. They stop short of insisting on hobnail boots and leather caseballs. However, as the day gets nearer, there's increasing speculation that City fans will be incapable of honouring the minute's silence. A trawl round our fan forums isn't encouraging. There are plenty of knobhead keyboard warriors out there, bragging that they'll be in the ground giving it the 'Munich' chants. It's profoundly depressing. I'm not going to the game. I don't even want to watch it on TV. It's going to be a horrible day. Just one utterance from a pissed-up City fan – or someone masquerading as one – and the rest of us will be pariahs for years to come.

City Supporters Club is worried, and suggests to United that, in keeping with a growing trend, the minute's silence should be replaced with a minute's applause, thereby drowning out any misguided idiots. United quite reasonably refuse, saying that it wouldn't be in keeping with such a solemn occasion. The press pick up on it, claiming that City have 'tried to get the minute's silence for the Munich victims cancelled'. The possibility – or in their eyes the certainty – that our disgraceful yobbish fans won't be able to respect the victims sends the press into a frenzy of indignation, and City fans are condemned even before the trial. We're the lowest of the low. And yet, in the preceding week, attempts to hold a minute's silence at Wembley and Croke Park internationals are cut short less than halfway through. Must have been City fans there as well.

Both clubs do everything they can to hammer home the need for good behaviour. We're reminded that one of our own, Frank Swift, also perished in the disaster, and posters with Frank's image are put up in the away fans' concourses. Outside the ground there's a massive poster showing the Busby Babes lining up before their final match prior to the crash. It's undeniably poignant. Except for the massive AIG logo in the bottom right hand corner. The Munich air disaster, sponsored by AIG. Denied from having their logo seen on United's shirts, they had to make sure they got in on the act somewhere. Unbelievably crass. An outfit like that deserves to go bust …

The teams come out, Sven and Ferguson lay bouquets in the centre circle and the referee's whistle blows for the minute's silence to begin. Every fan has been issued with a scarf and, as the camera pans round the ground, it's a sea of red and white with just a small corner of blue and white. Every single fan is static, silent, with scarf raised aloft. It's a very moving sight, a stadium united in respect for the fallen. There's even a coincidentally proportionate mix of colours, the pocket of sky blue representing the memory of Frank Swift, with the vast bulk of red honouring the Busby Babes. You could hear a pin drop until the referee's whistle signals the end of the minute.

I breathe a huge sigh of relief. Ferguson turns towards the City fans and applauds. It really shouldn't be necessary to congratulate people on achieving the prodigious feat of staying quiet for a whole sixty seconds, but fair play to him. Now we can get on with the game.

Even on TV you can tell that this is anything but a derby atmosphere. The overwrought ceremony and our fans' exemplary behaviour have seriously muted the home support. With so much potential venom ready to be unleashed on City fans if they'd so much as rustled a programme page, their emotional energy is spent even before the game starts. United's 'ticker' banner has been removed for the occasion. There are none of the usual chants of hatred and mockery from one set of supporters to the other, instead just support for their own team. No bad thing in general, but in a derby? Just not right at all.

City benefit from the almost surreal atmosphere, finding it easy to get an early foothold and taking the lead when Vassell sweeps home the rebound after van der Sar parries his first shot. United can't get going at all, and we go further ahead when Benjani glances home a header from Petrov's cross. *He comes from Zimbabwe, he scores on derby day …*

In the second half, we're happy to hold on to what we've got, and United make little impression until a late goal from Carrick gets the nerves jangling. Even then, we

negotiate Fergie-time with relative ease to record our first
Old Trafford win since Denis Law's backheel and our first
double over them since 1970. Say what you like about Sven,
but he does seem to have the sign over Ferguson.

Of course I'm delighted with the result, and massively
relieved that our reputation as fans has been enhanced
rather than demolished, but there's something about the
day that feels a bit hollow. It's been like a phoney war, a
match during which the usual enmity and aggression has
been temporarily suspended, and nothing like a real derby
at all. Winning at Old Trafford should mean silencing the
hostile hordes, sending Ferguson's face beetroot red with
anger, standing up to an onslaught from a team desperate to
cement their position at the top of the table and to keep us
in our place. But this was a memorial service first, a football
match second.

I'm more glad to get rid of this game than any other I can
remember. Munich was a shocking tragedy, and it's hard to
imagine what it would have been like to live through it at
the time. But it was a very long time ago, and United and
their fans' self-righteousness regarding the tragedy, and the
behaviour of other fans towards it, really gets my goat. Of
course mockery of the victims is unacceptable, and it's good
to see that it seems to have at last faded away.

But had it happened to say Liverpool, Leeds or us, are
we to believe that United fans wouldn't have behaved in
the same, or an even worse, way? United fans, the inven-
tors of English football hooliganism in the mid-1960s?
United fans, the first to get a match abandoned by invading
the pitch? The first to get their team banned from playing
European matches at home? Who've openly mocked the
deaths of Shankly, Revie, Mercer et al? Who've sung about
Heysel and Hillsborough – '96 was not enough'? Who
regaled Cardiff fans in the mid-1960s with charming ditties
about Aberfan? Who constructed 'Istanbul Reds' banners to

taunt Leeds fans about the death of two of their supporters? Give it a fucking rest, boys.

And what about the club itself? On a human level, the loss of great players and the immediate impact on the team was devastating. As a means of generating long term wealth for the club, its impact has been incalculable. Quite understandably, it immediately spawned a legion of Manchester United Supporters All Around The Globe Who Don't Know Very Much About Football, and a major part of their worldwide support can be traced back to the tragedy. And as a means of ensuring a continuous flow of new supporters and the associated income, hammering home the story ad nauseam is as powerful as any trophy win.

Meanwhile, the tales from survivors and families of the deceased have been consistent, persistent and well-documented; they say the club's attitude towards them was penny-pinching, unsympathetic and sometimes simply callous. Embittered, impoverished victims selling their stories for a few quid, or the stark facts? I know where my money is …

Same As It Ever Was

22 MAY 2008, FRIENDLY:
HONG KONG INVITATION XI 3 CITY 1

The derby win is cause for huge celebration, but everyone's focus is more on the behaviour of our fans in the stands than the performance of our team on the pitch. 'We are impeccable!' becomes a regular chant, reflecting Ferguson's comment after the game. Hang on a bit. Is it really that hard to stand in silence for one minute? If you were asked at an interview to describe your proudest achievements, you probably wouldn't say: 'Well, I once stood silently for a whole sixty seconds so that I didn't tarnish the memory of the victims of a tragic air disaster.' So why all the fuss?

Because expectations were so low. Because so many people had genuinely feared, or expected, or hoped, that our fans would disgrace themselves on this most publicly solemn of occasions. Instead of feeling proud, we should have felt insulted. Yes, of course it was a relief that our fans had behaved so well, but as people fell over themselves to compliment us on our behaviour, it just felt ever more demeaning.

At least we could now get back to the straightforward business of 'normal' football matches, and hope that the derby win would signal an upsurge in form. Instead, we won just one of the next seven, slumping down the table, and even sparking rumours that Sven's tenure might be coming under threat.

A bizarre game at Sunderland briefly stopped the rot. Every now and then, you get a match where you think: 'How the hell did we win that?' You'd prefer these to be vital cup-ties or promotion or relegation deciders rather than meaningless late-season encounters, but they're welcome just the same, especially when the victims' manager is Roy Keane.

We'd had not a single shot at goal when Sturridge clearly fell over his own feet inside the Sunderland area, ten minutes from time. No one appealed, but the referee pointed instantly to the spot. Elano put the penalty away, only for Sunderland to come back almost immediately and equalise. The home side then laid siege to our goal, but a sudden breakaway put Vassell through. He scuffed his shot horribly, scarcely imparting any pace on the ball whatsoever, but Craig Gordon had been completely wrong-footed, and the ball trundled apologetically into the corner of the net. Keano wasn't happy. Couldn't have happened to a nicer person.

A comfortable win over Portsmouth seems to quell speculation over Sven's future, and when we take an early two-goal
lead over Fulham, we look set to sign off from Eastlands
on a high. However, the miserable capitulation that follows
not only retains Fulham's hopes of avoiding the drop, but
re-ignites the Sven rumours. A few days later, suddenly and
unexpectedly, the rumours turn into fact. It's official, at least
according to a BBC source. Thaksin has told Sven that he'll
be sacked at the end of the season.

No tears from me. Maybe the great start raised Frank's
expectations to unrealistic heights. Or maybe Sven really
isn't that good a manager at all, a charlatan who just gets
a bit lucky now and then. That's where my money is, and
always has been. Let's hope Frank's next choice of manager
is a bit more palatable.

In the meantime, I've received an invitation to do a couple
of slots at a conference in Hong Kong. It'll be a four- or
five-day jaunt, it's after the season finishes and it sounds too
good to be true. I've never been there but people tell me it's
an amazing experience. I accept immediately.

For the last two games, morale in the camp – with so many
of the squad having been bought by or given their chance
by Sven – is at rock bottom. Fans sign petitions to 'Save Our
Sven' and placards are displayed during our drab 1-0 defeat
at Anfield. There are more protests on the season's final
day, when a desperate, given up the ghost performance at
Middlesbrough results in a humiliating 8-1 defeat. Hardly the
sort of memory you want to be taking into the close season.

There's a strange hiatus. Sven's departure has still to be
officially announced by the club, yet all and sundry seem
to know that he's on his way out. We really aren't managing
this very well at all. Sven gives a few interviews to the media,

and doesn't appear overcome with disappointment. In fact, as ever, he doesn't appear to show any emotion whatso-ever. Strange old stick, the Scandinavian Love Machine. Still, once again he'll be walking off into the sunset with a bumper pay-off, and the perceived harshness of his dismissal will no doubt make it easy for him to stroll into another job. With a nice long-term contract, and another big pay-off when results don't match expectations. Nice work if you can get it. *Caveat emptor.*

The delay in formalising Sven's exit means that he won't actually depart until after the club's post-season Far East tour. The club website mentions that there'll be two games, the second in Hong Kong. The date looks familiar. I check my diary and find that the match will be played while I'm over there – on the day I fly back home but well before departure time. I'll be able to watch it. Spooky.

Tony and I fly over on FA Cup Final day, and we watch in a Heathrow bar as Portsmouth take the trophy. My mate Collina is a lifelong Pompey fan; he's at the game and it's the first time he's seen his team bring home any meaning-ful silverware. I'm pleased for him, and for them – they're a proper football club and they deserve it for taking out the Scum in the quarter-final – but I can't help reflecting on how many supposedly smaller clubs have won things since City last tasted success. And how many more there'll be before we do so again. If we ever do.

Hong Kong is exhilaratingly vibrant, we have a fantastic time, and I wish I could have stayed for longer. Folks at the conference are well aware that City are in town and I tell them that I'll be going to the game. They think I must be some sort of superfan as opposed to the beneficiary of the most freakish coincidence. We head off to the stadium well in time for kick-off. We're playing against a Hong Kong Invitation XI. The opposition for Sven's last game in charge of Manchester City will be a team of part-time

Chinese dustmen. The crowd is sparse to start with but builds up steadily, as this game is the first of a double-header, the second featuring AC Milan. City field a team with a good sprinkling of first-teamers, and the familiar languid figure of Sven meanders along the touchline in front of us.

City are well on top in the opening phases, and take the lead with a nice volley from Didi Hamann. The dustmen equalise before half-time, but City still look much the stronger team. In the second half, our commitment level noticeably diminishes, and the dustmen score a couple more goals to secure a comfortable win. The teams trudge off, and Sven disappears into the tunnel, his final act as manager of Manchester City. As I head off in a taxi towards the airport, I can't help but reflect that he's been consistent to the last. First half good …

WELCOME TO MY NIGHTMARE

Little Frank Hasn't Even Got A House On The Old Kent Road ...

31 AUGUST 2008, PREMIER LEAGUE: SUNDERLAND 0 CITY 3

9am, 4 June 2008. I'm just contemplating the start of the working day when I receive a text message from Paul, my business partner. He's a United season ticket-holder. I'm not sure how I cope. The message reads: 'You've got a Fatarse.' Normally this would provoke a response along the lines of: 'Speak for yourself, you fuckwitted lardbucket.' It's this kind of dynamic, intelligent, inventive repartee that sets us apart from our competitors. As far apart as they can possibly get. However, I know that the lack of space between 'fat' and 'arse' is not accidental. My heart sinks, the rumours are true, and what is very close to my worst nightmare has come to pass. Mark 'Fatarse' Hughes is the new manager of Manchester City.

In my eyes, Hughes has no redeeming features whatsoever. I hated him as a player, so typical of United, overly aggressive, always in the referee's face, forever thrusting elbows into defenders and backing into them, reacting with outrage on the rare occasions he was penalised, a truly horrible piece of work. And I hate him even more as a manager, the unapologetic architect of Blackburn's brutal approach, vying with Allardyce for the crown of overlord of anti-football, happy to embrace thugs galore in his ranks. Then there's his constant bitter whinging to the media after every game, the same old barely coherent rant about how hard done by his lads had been, how referees always favour the 'big boys'. What the hell do you expect if all your team does is kick the shit out of them for ninety minutes? And he's got the personality and charisma of a housebrick. Christ, even Jack the Ripper didn't have a crime sheet this long.

It's a black day, one of the very blackest, and I'm plunged into a morose mood. I've usually managed to come to terms with former United players coming to City and, if they perform, even been able to execute the mental gymnastics required to embrace them as our own. But a manager is different. He's the figurehead of the club, the man always fronting up on TV and in the press. There'll be no place to hide from the reality that we are 'Mark Hughes's Manchester City'. I can almost hear Sven cackling from beyond the payoff: 'Be careful what you wish for …'

But how did it happen? After a few purely medicinal glasses, I drift off to sleep and my subconscious provides the answer …

7am, 17 May 2008. A sprightly, sharp-witted pensioner is jolted awake, as so often, by the snorting beast beside her. As she prises

her eyes open, she catches sight of a luminous red glow and is over-come by panic. 'Alex!! Alex!! Wake up!!! There's a fire!!'

As her husband stirs from his slumbers, she realises it's a false alarm. It's that bloody nose again.

'Alex, the state of that conk of yours. You know what the doctor told you but you never listen, do you? I suppose you were lashed up again last night?'

'Give over, woman, I just had a few drinks with an old friend of mine. We can't have had more than six bottles of red.'

'Don't be ridiculous. You haven't got any friends.'

'Oh, just shut up if you can't say anything sensible. You're worse than that blind frog bastard.'

'At least he's educated and civilised.'

'You don't need education to win trophies.'

'Good job for you, isn't it.'

'Look, I've got things to do, go back to sleep for a while. How about ten years?'

'You'll be lucky, I wouldn't miss your funeral for the world.'

'Miserable bag!'

'And I wonder why that is? The thought of dancing on your grave is the only thing that keeps me going.'

'You'd never do that!'

'Aye, I suppose you're right – I'd get killed in the rush.'

How the hell had he put up with this woman for so long? Still, he had more important things to attend to. He painstakingly manipu-lated himself out of bed and lurched his way down the stairs. But the voice behind him was still there.

'Mind you don't fall and break your neck – you're too heavy for me to shift on my own.'

Tottering into his study, Alex fumbled around for his mobile. The special one. He had got wind of some seriously bad news and had a very important call to make. He brought up the contact list and his shaking, gnarled fingers scrolled through the names.

There it was. Fatarse. A man who'd always coveted the United job, and would do anything to improve his chances of getting it.

Slow-witted as they come and easy to manipulate. The perfect choice to put in place his masterplan. Let's nip that Sky Blue project in the bud. At the fifth attempt, he managed to dial the right number.

In his luxury country pile, Mark Hughes was up early as usual, busy with his kids' jigsaw puzzle. He'd been grappling with it for three days and had at last got all four corner pieces into position. All he had to do now was work out where the other five pieces went. Suddenly, his trance-like concentration was interrupted by the sound of his mobile phone. He looked at the screen. It read 'BACONFACE calling'.

What the hell did Taggart want at this time of the morning? If he thought he could prise one of his Rovers players away, he could forget it. Next season they'd be going for the treble – record number of fouls committed in a Premier League campaign, record number of yellow cards and record number of red cards. So no way would he let any of his midfield enforcers go. Or his defensive enforcers. Or his attacking enforcers. That only left Roque Santa Cruz, and no one in their right mind would take a risk with a crock like that.

'Hello Sparky, how're ye doin'?'

'OK, thanks, Sir Alex, to what do I owe this honour?'

'Well, I'll get straight to the point. I've got a proposition for ye.'

'But you know I'm already married.'

Jesus, this guy doesn't get any brighter, does he? *'Not that kind of proposition, Sparky, I mean a job proposition.'*

Bloody hell, he's retiring at long last! This is it! I'm going back to Old Trafford!

'That's brilliant Sir Alex, I always knew you thought I was the man to take over. It'll be great to get back to Stretford!'

'No, Sparky, that's not what I mean. Not yet anyway. But you're close though – I'm talking about the City job.'

'What, Manchester City?'

'Yes, Manchester City. Those useless bitter blue bastards. Thirty-two years and they're still there. I need someone to make sure it gets to forty years. Someone I can rely on to screw it up for them.'

'Hey, that's not fair! I don't screw things up! Look at my record with Rovers – eleventh, ninth, twelfth – it's fantastic. Everybody says so!'

'No, I mean deliberately screw it up, you blockhead! I've heard on the grapevine that they're coming into serious money.'

'But they've already got serious money, haven't they, with that Human League violater fella, Frank Sinatra or whatever they call him.'

'Human rights violater, for Christ sake! But not him, no, some-one new. Some bloody Sheikh. Got mega-billions. Makes the Glazers look like they haven't got two- ha'pence to rub together. Even richer than Michael Knighton.'

'So how do you know all this?'

'Well, I was at a bloody charity dinner with their PR guy, Garry Cook or whatever his name is. Full of crap. Can't understand half the stuff he says. "We're a business whose core competency is foot-ball," he said to me. What the fuck is that meant to mean? Anyway, he should have said "core incompetency". This guy just can't stop shooting his fuckin' mouth off, and he was bragging about these new investors coming in. Deal'll be done in a couple of months. Reckons it's a certainty. More money than everyone else in the Prem put together. So they're looking for someone who knows how to spend it. And if they get the right man, we'll all be fucked. So that's where you come in.'

'So you're saying I'm not the right man?'

'No, Sparky, you just don't get it, do you? I want you to go in there and deliberately screw it up. You know, sign a few overpriced, prima donna injury-prone muppets, use tactics that no-one can understand, make ludicrous mindless substitutions, all that kind of stuff. They'll lose interest soon enough, then bugger off and put their money somewhere else.'

'So what's in it for me?'

"Big fat contract, big fat pay-off. Set you up for life. And the lifelong pleasure in knowing that you helped to keep those bitter blue bastards down.'

'And what makes you think they'd give me the job?'

'Well, I told Cook about how you're being groomed for the United job, how I thought you were the best young manager in the country. So he'll think he's got a right result if he gets you on board, that he's really got one over on us.'

'But he will have got one over on you, won't he, if it stops me coming to United?'

'Course he bloody won't, you'll only need to be there a year or two, then it'll all be over and you'll be a free agent again. Agent Hughes. Yes, I rather like that …'

A few days after Hughes's appointment, I'm gently recuperating at home, watching one of the group games in Euro 2008. A tasty match it is too, Italy v Holland. Feet up, nice glass of wine, very civilised. Holland look really good, and about twenty minutes in they spring Italy's offside trap to put van Nistelrooy through on the right. Buffon comes out and dives at his feet, but Horseface nicks the ball away. Buffon's arms come into contact with the striker's feet. We've been here hundreds of times before. Down he goes, ref points to the spot, big argy-bargy about whether it's a red card for the keeper.

Not this time. Van Nistelrooy stays on his feet and attempts in vain to recover possession before the ball goes out of play. I'm absolutely flabbergasted. I couldn't have been more shocked if Katie Price had burst through the TV screen, thrust her ludicrously inflated, scarcely concealed mounds of silicon in my general direction and said: 'Come on Steve, you know you want to.' Obviously I'd have replied: 'Piss off you botox-infused publicity junkie, you epitomise everything that's wrong with this country today and I wouldn't touch you with a surgically sterilised bargepole.'

But that's not really the point. In that situation, in his United career, van Nistelrooy wouldn't have gone down nine times out of ten, he wouldn't have gone down ninety-nine times out of a hundred, he'd have gone down absolutely every single time, 100 per cent guaranteed. So why the extraordinary change in behaviour? An ingrained sense of respect for Italians? He'd found God and seen the light? Didn't want the Dutch to be portrayed as a bunch of divers? Bit late for that with Robben in the team.

When the same thing happened again in the next match, there was only one conclusion to be reached. Despite the overwhelming evidence to the contrary throughout his Old Trafford career, van Nistelrooy was not after all programmed irreversibly to cheat under all possible circumstances. So where had his hitherto despicable behaviour come from? A long and unfortunate series of accidental falling over incidents? Playing when so much under the influence of traditional Dutch recreational substances that his ability to stay upright was impaired? Some sort of hearing defect which had affected his sense of balance, and had only just been corrected? Or acting under managerial instruction? Makes you wonder, doesn't it ...

As the season came upon us, the papers were full of how Frank's assets had been frozen, how the authorities were closing in, how there was no money for us to spend. With no shortage of schadenfreude, there was speculation that we might have to sell some of the players we already had, that we might even be heading for bankruptcy, and how it all served us bloody well right for getting into bed with a somewhat less than fit and proper person. Why do we never get it right?

The Hughes regime began with a 4-2 defeat at Villa, a nine-minute Gabriel Agbonlahor hat-trick deciding the match.

We got some points on the board the following week, where a typically flimsy West Ham were comfortably seen off at Eastlands.

Then, a very strange thing happened. With just over a week of the transfer window left, our club with no money spent £9 million to bring Shaun Wright-Phillips back from Chelsea. Where had the dosh come from? Maybe the papers had yet again been full of crap. Whatever the financial machinations behind the scenes, I was delighted to see Shaun back. None of us had wanted him to go, but Chelski's filthy lucre had proved irresistible. He'd his moments during his time at the Bridge, but not too many of them, and there was a real sense that he was coming back home. Despite the nagging mantra of 'never go back', I thought that this was a tremendous piece of business. Less high-profile was the signing of a defensive midfielder from Hamburg, Vincent Kompany, and an unheard of Brazilian striker, Jo. Brazilian striker – how can you possibly go wrong?

SWP's second City debut was at Sunderland, and his two goals in a 3-0 win were ecstatically received. Much more of this and I'd have to think about getting properly back into the fold. And, if Frank's financial position wasn't as bad as had been reported, maybe we'd sign one or two more before the transfer window closed ...

The Day The World Turned Dayglo

13 SEPTEMBER 2008, PREMIER LEAGUE: CITY 1 CHELSEA 3

We return from holiday, and it's a delight to see the recorded highlights of the win at Sunderland. It's as though Shaun has never been away, and the joy on his face, and those of the travelling masses after his goals, is great to see. I still feel a bit nervous about it though – if Frank's in the financial dire straits he's reputed to be, how the hell did we find the money? And is everything going to go tits up in an instant? But maybe it's just paper talk.

The very next day, a brief statement is issued by the club. It sparks a frenzy of media comment. We're in discussions with regard to a possible takeover by the Abu Dhabi United Group. 'In discussions.' Could mean anything. I don't get too excited. I'll believe it when I see it. Nevertheless, the way everyone's talking suggests that these 'discussions' we're in are seriously advanced.

Tuesday 1 September. Transfer deadline day. I can't imagine we'll be doing much business. Frank's broke and we're still only 'in discussions' with our new suitors. I go downstairs, get some breakfast and put on *Sky Sports News*. The first thing I notice is the breaking news ticker running along the bottom of the screen. My bleary eyes follow it across as it reveals: 'Tottenham accept £30m offer for Dimitar Berbatov from Manch ...' I don't need to see the rest. Yet again, the Scum will be breaking the bank to recruit another big name. I'm a huge fan of Berbatov; last year, in Spurs' Carling Cup win at Eastlands, he gave one of the greatest individual displays I've ever seen. His skill in tight spaces under severe pressure was astonishing, his vision almost supernatural. Nobody could ignore his virtuoso performance; on the way back into the city centre, he was the only topic of conversation. And now he'd be signing for *them*. Except ...

The ticker rolls on to reveal 'Manchester City'. Am I hallucinating? I watch its next crossing more diligently. It really does say Manchester City. What's going on? I turn the sound up. The takeover deal's as good as done. There's serious money to spend. Bloody hell! I'm installed on the sofa for the duration. Not much work will be getting done today.

It soon becomes clear that we're not the only ones after Berbatov. United are also in the hunt. But rumours emerge through the course of the morning that we've got an alternative target in our sights – Robinho, from Real Madrid. *Sky Sports* reporters track down Mark Hughes. He's on the golf course and appears to have not the slightest clue about what's going on. Or the slightest clue, full stop.

As the day rolls on, it becomes clear that Ferguson is hell-bent on securing Berbatov from under our noses, going to meet him personally at Manchester airport and kidnapping him before he can get to Eastlands. But the Robinho story gathers ever more momentum, and by the end of the day, both clubs have got their man. City sign Robinho, United sign Berbatov. But they, and he, must wonder what's going on. A £30 million signing would normally dominate the headlines. Not today. All anyone wants to talk about is the Robinho deal. And what it portends.

Our new owners are unfeasibly rich. And enormously ambitious. There's no concern about the provenance of their wealth. If they stay around, we'll have greater resources than any other football club. Anywhere. The watching world is appalled. We've hardly done anything yet, just brought in a marquee signing, but the wise words of every football pundit under the sun are united and unequivo-cal in their condemnation. Already we're ruining football. We'll be distorting the transfer market, paying unrealistic, unmatchable wages, acquiring a bunch of mercenaries just to deny them to other teams, ripping off our supporters to finance it all, destroying the club's soul. It's crass, vulgar and just not right. But we'll learn soon enough that you can't buy success …

The international break means that there's a blank week-end before the 'new' Manchester City can be paraded before its public. By one of those quirks of the fixture list, we're at home to Chelsea, who suddenly look like Old Money. And now not even enough money, as Robinho had been hotly tipped to sign for them until we came along. In the build-up to the game, Robinho's soundbites tell us how delighted he is to be at City, which stretches credibility just a bit. It's probably the last place a man of his ego expected to pitch up. When asked about his targets, he talks about wanting to prove himself as the best player in the world. I don't like this one bit. Footballers always talk about the team coming first, even if their actions often reveal otherwise. Robinho is flagrantly and unashamedly a 'me first' type of guy. It doesn't bode well.

Still, it's a bit early for misgivings. It's a lovely sunny afternoon and a real carnival atmosphere. Street vendors more usually proffering scarves and baseball caps and doing a roaring trade in tea-towels and elastic bands, as the hordes descend on 'Middle Eastlands' determined to honour our new owners in their own special way. Nobody can believe our luck. It sounds too good to be true. Which usually means that it is. But the noises coming from those supposedly in the know have been resoundingly positive. These guys really are in it for the duration. It's a genuine long-term project. All the rest of us can do is wait and see.

For now, all eyes are on Robinho as the teams take to the pitch. He's very slight, and the thought of what he'll be like on a freezing February night at Stoke inevitably crosses the mind. But this is a balmy September evening in beautiful Beswick, a perfect playing surface, an expectant full house, millions glued to their TV screens and an occasion just made for this aspiring superstar to make his first statement.

The game starts at a bright pace, City giving as good as they get against a clearly very accomplished Chelsea. After fifteen minutes or so, we get a free kick, about twenty-five yards out, nicely central. There's not much doubt as to who'll be taking it. Robinho struts up, chest puffed out, all set to seize the moment.

He steps back carefully, waits for the whistle, ambles up to the ball and strikes it languidly towards goal. The ball clears the wall, soars beyond Petr Cech's reach and caresses the top corner of the net. It's a wonderful sight. Robinho exults in a 'yes, I really am that good' kind of way, and we all go berserk. Bloody hell, maybe he genuinely is something special. Only when we see the replays is the truth revealed. The ball took a huge deflection off Frank Lampard's head, but for which it would have been swallowed up by Cech as easily as a routine back-pass. Jammy sod.

The euphoria lasts for a full three minutes, three minutes in which we can dream of a brilliant new dawn, in which we'll start to put big teams to the sword, where the Temple of Doom will become a distant bad dream. Then, City fail to deal properly with a corner, Terry's header rebounds to Carvalho, and the ball is crashed emphatically into the roof of the net. Still, no more goals before half-time, City competing well against an obviously superior team, with Robinho showing some nice touches and working hard to impress. So far, so good.

The second half sees Chelsea show some real quality, a slick move ending with Lampard firing a sweet cross-shot into the corner of the net, but City get a potential lifeline when Terry is sent off for a professional foul on Jo. It looks a bit harsh at the time; with hindsight it looks absolutely ridiculous. It would soon become apparent that there were no possible circumstances under which Jo could be regarded as having a 'goalscoring opportunity'. Hughes had somehow succeeded in signing the only living Brazilian bereft of the slightest trace of natural footballing ability.

Any renewed optimism following the sending-off is quickly quashed, as a clinical counter-attack ends with a composed finish from Anelka, and Chelsea see time out with relative comfort. They're a class act alright, and there's no real sense of disappointment at the final whistle. City have performed really well, Robinho has shown some promising touches and Wright-Phillips has played like he's never been away. Indeed, his duel with Ashley Cole has been one of the game's highlights, both players going at it hammer and tongs for the full ninety minutes, but in the best possible competitive spirit. It's great to have SWP back; how much better would things have been for us – and maybe also for him – had he never gone away in the first place?

The next day's papers tell of how it's business as usual, how all the money in the world can't bring overnight success. Tell us something we don't already know. No one expects us to be challenging for silverware just yet; what we do expect is signs of real progress as the season goes on, that we're heading towards that top four, that we're a proposition good enough to attract players of real ambition as well as cynical mercenaries. As Garry Cook never tires of reminding us, we're undertaking a long-term project here, and everyone needs to be patient and realistic. Natural characteristics of all football fans ...

Around The World In Eighty Hours

27 NOVEMBER 2008, UEFA CUP GROUP STAGE: SCHALKE 0 CITY 2

One consolation from Sven's brief tenure was that City had focussed on trying to play nice clean football, and our lofty placing in the Fair Play League table was sufficient to get us into the UEFA Cup. Well, into the first qualifying round, anyway. A trip to the Faroe Islands before the season had even begun in earnest was probably less than ideal preparation for what lay ahead, but a 2-0 win, replicated in the second leg, saw us safely through to the next hurdle.

This time, an unheard of and unpronounceable mob from Denmark – FC Midtjylland – stood in our way, and when we lost 1-0 at home in the first leg, we assumed that the burden of a raft of UEFA Cup games wasn't high on Hughes's agenda. The second leg remained scoreless until injury-time, when an incredibly stuffy own goal brought us back level on aggregate, ultimately leading to a penalty shoot-out. Two superb saves from young Joe Hart saw us squeeze through to the next stage of what was already starting to look like a never-ending saga.

Next up were Cypriots Omonia Nicosia, 2-1 victories in each leg seeing us through to the group stage. At last we might get to play some proper teams. The draw grouped us with FC Twente, Schalke, Paris Saint-Germain and Racing Santander. Some nice looking trips there, but this was the era when you only got to play each team once, the luck of the draw determining whether it would be home or away. Our aways were Schalke and Racing, and it was the former which captured the imagination.

For those of us of a certain age, Schalke would forever be associated with one of Maine Road's most glorious nights as the City of Bell, Lee and Young tore apart our highly rated opposition to storm into the European Cup Winners' Cup final. I'd been there, 12 years old, standing on the Kippax, and it remains one of the most evocative occasions I've experienced in well over forty years of watching City. I've looked out for Schalke's results ever since, and now I'd get the chance to see a re-match. Better still, my great pal Bob had family with Schalke affiliations living close to Gelsenkirchen, and was really keen to get to the game.

First though, Twente at home, and the visit of newly deposed England manager Steve McClaren, replete with ridiculous faux Dutch accent. But at least no umbrella, as the teams took the field on a nice dry Manchester evening. They're more common than people think.

It took us two minutes to stamp our authority on the game with a cracking goal from Wright-Phillips, only for an out-of-the-blue break to bring Twente level. Robinho then produced a majestic curler from the corner of the area to put us back in front, and Benjani added to our tally to get us off to a perfect start.

Next up, the trip to Germany. To be absolutely sure of getting tickets, Bob used his local contacts to get a couple of seats with the home fans. It was a great excuse to head back to Kent, revisit a few old favourite watering holes, before catching some kip and heading off to catch the early morning ferry. A nice, hearty breakfast, a smooth crossing, and we were on the road.

Gelsenkirchen isn't exactly party town, but there were enough bars around to slake the thirst of even the most hell-bent on inebriation blues, a few of whom looked as though they hadn't slept for days. With good reason. Some guys had managed to get flights here for just £1. Now that's what you call a bargain. Except they weren't really flights here. They were via Dublin, Paris, Vienna, Munich, and God knows whatever convoluted routes. Five flights, four changes. You could have walked here quicker. The same route going back. Adventure maybe, but a bargain?

With Bob's local knowledge, we were able to find a nice direct route to the magnificent Veltins Arena, where we had superb seats, just below the press box, and no fears about letting our allegiances show. Not all Blues had been quite so lucky, with the sold out away end only half-full as the game started, congestion problems causing severe delays. Honestly, you travel halfway around Europe to follow City, then end up missing the kick-off.

City start well, Daniel Sturridge and Ireland especially prominent, but there's no breakthrough until just before the interval. Then, some terrific play from Sturridge allows him to fire in a low cross, which is haplessly allowed to pass through to Benjani at the far post. Our European and derby day specialist sweeps the ball into the roof of the net to give us a half-time lead, still not witnessed by a full contingent of travelling fans. German efficiency, eh?

The second half brings a composed, confident, mature performance and a second comedy goal. Ireland chases after a lofted pass as Neuer comes out to meet him. Stevie just gets there first, and prods the ball goalwards along the ground. For some reason anticipating a chip, the keeper leaps in the air, allowing the ball to pass beneath his feet and trundle into the net.

We never look like letting it slip, cruising to a fully merited win and making qualification for the last sixteen almost certain. A few celebratory beers back in town and a memorable day is complete. European football? Piece of cake.

Shameless

30 NOVEMBER 2008, PREMIER LEAGUE:
CITY 0 MANCHESTER UNITED 1

Back in the league, results remained inconsistent and as November came towards its close we were still in the bottom half of the table. Grist to the mill for the many mockers desperate to see the lottery winners fall flat on their faces: 'All that money and you're still behind Hull and Wigan.' But even the Hughes haters – and I was certainly foremost among them – recognised that he'd need time to have any chance of delivering.

There were, however, some constants, notably the hugely improved form of Stephen Ireland, who'd harnessed the talent obvious to all since his first cameo appearance to a much enhanced athleticism and work-rate. He was finding the energy not just to get into scoring positions but also to accept them with aplomb, and had become the heartbeat of the team. A real Superman. On the other hand, Jo had still shown no signs whatsoever of being remotely competent, and it looked as though Hughes had picked up an absolute turkey. Still, at least Christmas was coming.

The big talking point remained Robinho. A few eye-catching performances and moments of exquisite skill were counterbalanced by total anonymity when the going got tough. The impression remained that he was a marquee signing, a 'present' from the owners, and a player that Hughes would never have bought of his own volition. Despite his obvious skills, I just couldn't warm to him. Even Rodney Marsh wasn't as self-obsessed as this guy.

He scored a hat-trick of clean, precise finishes against Stoke, played quite majestically against Portsmouth in a 6-0 drubbing, but in tighter, more demanding games, the contribution just hadn't been there. Not only did we have a lousy away record, we'd also started to falter at home, losing to Liverpool and Spurs despite having been ahead in both games. Maybe not a full-blown crisis yet, but the next two home games had the potential to turn it into one.

Arsenal were always eagerly awaited opponents at Eastlands, even if recent meetings hadn't produced the fireworks and flowing football which the last few Maine Road encounters had delivered in abundance. Good thing for us, as it was usually Arsenal doing the delivering. This one was also rather underwhelming to begin with, but a mix-up just before half-time allowed Ireland to put away what was becoming a typically assured finish.

In the second half, Arsenal started to find more fluency, but were undone by a breakaway goal of sheer majesty. Shaun collected the ball in his own half, waited for Robinho to make his move, and played an inch-perfect defence-splitting pass to set the Brazilian through on goal. As Almunia advanced, Robinho put his foot beneath a ball rolling away from him and scooped it gently over the stranded keeper. Absolutely breathtaking. One of the most sublime pieces of skill ever seen at the ground was greeted with part rapture, part wonderment, part disbelief. It was certainly enough to see off the Gunners, who never looked like getting back into it. Sturridge's late penalty sealed a 3-0 win, at least confirming our status of an 'on our day, we can beat anyone' sort of side. United were next up; we could do with another of our days.

The press was full of the usual drivel as the big match build-up intensified, most of it emanating from an inevitable source. This week's attempt to get into the mind of the match officials concerned the treatment meted out to the Precious One himself, Cristiano Ronaldo. According to Ferguson, teams had adopted cynical premeditated tactics to ensure that they could reduce his impact without incurring the wrath of the referee. Systematic fouling, players taking it in turns to hack the prancing tart down so that the worst punishment anyone could receive would be a yellow card. Using this rotational approach, teams might get away with ten or more fouls on Ronaldo without having their numbers reduced, and it was time referees got wise to it. A clear message, then, for Howard Webb, the man in charge.

City came into the game buoyed by the wins over Arsenal and Schalke, and with last season's derby double still fresh in the mind. The stance from our opponents was disdainfully dismissive. This isn't a big game for them, we're not proper rivals, Liverpool is their real derby, etc., etc. Good of them to turn up, really.

As Sunday afternoon's entertainment unfolded, the redoubtable Mr Ferguson's worst fears were realised. The capacity crowd indeed witnessed a disgraceful display of cynical rotational fouling, dealt with all too weakly by Mr Webb. Events unfolded as follows:

Nineteen minutes: Foul by Fletcher on Wright-Phillips. No action taken.

Thirty-three minutes: Foul by Evra on Wright-Phillips. Advantage played. Foul by Fletcher on Wright-Phillips. Fletcher booked.

Fifty-three minutes: Foul by Berbatov on Wright-Phillips. No action taken.

Fifty-nine minutes: Foul by Ronaldo on Wright-Phillips. Ronaldo booked.

Sixty-six minutes: Foul by Evra on Wright-Phillips. Evra booked.

Eighty-four minutes. Foul by Carrick on Wright-Phillips. Carrick booked.

Fergie's right again. This sort of thing really does need to be stamped out.

City fans left the game disappointed at a narrow 1-0 defeat and frustrated at the cynical treatment meted out to our most threatening player on the day. There was the small satisfaction of seeing Ronaldo sent off for a deliberate handball, although he should have been admiring himself in the mirror long before that, after responding to his first booking with overtly sarcastic applause for the referee.

United had been on top in the first half, but City had responded well and wasted a few good chances to equalise. We would have had a lot more had it not been for cynical, rotational fouling, but then that's all you can expect from teams with no sense of fair play. Or self-awareness.

Another Nail In My Heart

3 JANUARY 2009, FA CUP THIRD ROUND: CITY 0 NOTTINGHAM FOREST 3

We don't exactly bounce back in style from the derby defeat, failing to hold on to an early lead at Fulham, then giving up a last-minute goal at home to Everton to fall to a fourth home reverse in six. We're dangerously close to the relegation zone and defeat in our next game – away to bottom club West Brom – will put us squarely into it.

It's a grey day and a grey match to go with it. Both sets of fans have voted with their feet, preferring Christmas shopping to the spectacle of two out-of-form sides struggling to string three passes together. During the most turgid of first halves, most of those who bothered turning up must have wished they were wandering aimlessly round John Lewis, looking for some overpriced novelty item to leap out from the shelves. It might not be just what they always wanted, but it'll do.

City looked a little more interested in the second half, but were suddenly caught in possession and exposed to a counter-attack. Luke Moore, who hadn't scored all season, was put clean through on Hart, and slotted home with ease.

Desperate times. With just four minutes left, an improvised back-heel from Felipe Caicedo took a tortuous route via West Brom goalkeeper Scott Carson, the post and Carson again before trickling over the line. Oh well, a draw at the bottom club is hardly ideal, but it could be worse. A few minutes later, it was. A long diagonal cross found Bednar in total isolation six yards out, and his header looped over the stranded Hart to give the Baggies an unlikely win. We'd spend Christmas in the bottom three. Definitely not what we always wanted.

Boxing Day finds us at home to newly promoted Hull City. At the start of the season, most people would have expected this match to feature a team in the relegation zone, but few would have got its identity right. Hull have been a revelation, sitting comfortably in the top half of the table and boasting great wins at Arsenal and Spurs. Another one today, and Hughes will be under serious pressure. I can't be the only City fan who thinks that defeat might not be too bad an outcome in the long run.

Instead, Hull display a naivety we could never have expected, giving space to Ireland, Robinho and Wright-Phillips and allowing us to play to our strengths. Ireland is stupendous, providing two superb crosses for Caicedo to convert as well as a delightful assist for Robinho. Hull are way too open, but the way we're exploiting it is clinical and very easy on the eye.

It gets better still when SWP produces some vintage trickery to set Robinho up for a fourth. At the interval, City come off the pitch to a standing ovation; Hull don't come off it at all. They're stopped in their tracks by perma-tanned manager Phil Brown, who sits them down in the area in front of their own fans and gives them a right royal ticking off. It's very, very funny. They know when they've been tangoed.

The second half is flat by comparison, but features a slick and richly deserved goal for Ireland, whose display has been outstanding even by the standards he's set for himself this season. The 5-1 win emphasises just what we're capable of, and makes you wonder how a team with so much talent can possibly be flirting with the relegation zone.

Two days later, a trip to Blackburn, new occupants of bottom place. We've visited two previous basement dwellers this season and lost both times. Surely the impetus from the Boxing Day massacre will see us avoid a third?

With four minutes to go, we're 2-0 down. Another shambolic, spineless away performance. Then, as we move towards added time, a loose ball falls to substitute Sturridge, and his cleanly struck volley gives us a glimmer of hope. Almost immediately, Sturridge picks the ball up on the right, beats a couple of men, and slides a diagonal ball into the mysteriously unmarked Robinho. He's done nothing all game. Blackburn away in the wind and rain is not his bag. He cushions the ball perfectly as Robinson comes to narrow the angle, before caressing the ball effortlessly past the keeper into the corner of the net. It's a beautiful, composed finish with virtually the last kick of the game.

It's only a point against a team we should be wiping the floor with, but it feels like a win. It gives us some momentum going into the New Year, and we'll be sure to be splashing the cash in the transfer window. It's a win–win situation. Either we pull away from the lower reaches of the table or Hughes will be sacked. Ideally both.

There's also the small matter of the FA Cup, and the third round draw is kind, bringing Championship side Nottingham Forest to Eastlands. Struggling Championship side Nottingham Forest. I wasn't planning to go, but I woke up on Saturday morning with that irresistible urge. I've always loved the Cup. It's my age. For folks of my generation, the Cup Final was the only live club game televised all season, and the images from those days will live with me for ever. The league was the gauge of quality, but the Cup was where legends were made. A quick phone call to reserve a ticket, and I'm off on a 400-mile round trip to witness the first step on the road to Wembley.

We rest a few players, but it's still a very strong side that takes the field. Ireland injured, Robinho given a break, but still internationals in most positions. With Forest battling against a drop to the third tier, it should be a formality. It is, but not for us. Forest are sharper from the outset, roared on by their 6,000 fans, and they soon take the lead when Richards' headed clearance is met with a stunning volley from Nathan Tyson. A great goal, but not what I've given up half my weekend to see.

A few minutes later Zabaleta carelessly loses possession. The ball is pulled back and a mishit shot screws across goal. Robert Earnshaw – if you don't know the answer to a footy trivia quiz question then it's usually him – is the only player in the vicinity and he fires home before somersaulting away in delight. We're pathetic, and leave the pitch at half-time to a chorus of boos. It's the first time the home fans have made any real noise all day.

We improve a bit in the second half, but Forest wrap it up with a hideously self-inflicted third. Hamann goes into meltdown and throws the ball straight to Garner in our own area. The youngster looks up and drills a shot inside Hart's near post to complete a miserable day.

There's simply no excuse. Yes, two of our creative main-stays were out, and we lost a third, SWP, to an early injury. But the lethargy and lack of effort against a team struggling to avoid relegation to the real Division Three was disgrace-ful. We've had decades of knowing we're not good enough to win a title. Every year, a major aspiration is that we might have a decent cup run to brighten the season up. To toss the opportunity away with such disdain is unforgivable.

Hughes has only been here for four months, but he's get-ting towards his ninth life already. Every time the pressure's really on, we've turned in a performance to get him out of jail, but it's never yet been a catalyst for real improvement. We're in the transfer window now and he needs to get it right.

Hate To Say I Told You So

14 FEBRUARY 2009, PREMIER LEAGUE:
PORTSMOUTH 2 CITY 0

Transfer windows don't come much more important. The squad needed more depth, steel and commitment and these at least were characteristics which 'typical Mark Hughes players' generally possessed. He'd already snapped up Wayne Bridge, and soon acquired Nigel de Jong, an alleged midfield enforcer, from Hamburg. Never heard of him. A few days later came the news that Craig Bellamy would also be joining the ranks. I'd definitely heard of *him*. And I didn't like it one little bit. How could this walking tantrum possibly help to galvanise our disparate bunch of misfits?

The next four games all looked winnable. We delivered the goods in the first one, a narrow victory over Wigan achieved via a Zabaleta goal and an astonishing miss from Zaki. Next up were Newcastle United, in the bottom three and there for the taking. They had Barton in their side, we had Bellamy in ours. Plenty for both sets of fans to jeer about. Nigel de Jong made his debut and, with Bridge also included, we were getting closer to seeing what Hughes's vision of the future would look like. We were also encouraged by Shay Given's absence from the Newcastle side – he'd been strongly linked with us and his absence tonight seemed to cement the rumours that he'd soon be on his way.

Newcastle were simply dire. Every now and then you see a side and think 'this lot are going down'. This lot were going down. We took the lead when smart play from Robinho set up SWP, and Bellamy sealed the win and capped a tremendous, energetic display with a fine goal fifteen minutes from time. Some horrific defending from Bridge – unimpressive throughout – gave Newcastle the chance to pull one back, but they never got close to an equaliser.

Two wins on the trot, and I was already eating my words about Bellamy. It was immediately obvious that he was a bloody good player, quick, skilful and committed. He also played with his head up, aware of where his teammates were. Much, much better than I thought he was. Clearly one of those that you hate if he plays for anyone else, but you love if he plays for you. And marking his debut with a goal against a former club was a great way to start, although if he didn't score goals against former clubs, he'd never score at all.

Three days later, a trip to Stoke City. It's horrible. All long throws, hard tackles, total commitment and baying neanderthals. Rory Delap is sent off for lashing out at SWP but we still can't cope with it. James Beattie scores just before half-time and we seldom look like recovering. It's their first win in eleven, and a perfect chance to build some momentum has been squandered.

The only good news is that Shay Given has at last put pen to paper, and he makes his debut at home to Middlesbrough. We're desperately poor and Boro have a hatful of great chances. Given saves the lot of them. It's a fantastic performance, and three of his saves from Alves are breathtaking. Bellamy bags a smart goal from one of our few opportunities and we somehow end up pilfering the points. Hughes's new signings have made an instant impact. Now, how about an away win?

The trip to Portsmouth has been re-arranged for FA Cup fifth round day, in itself a painful reminder of the Forest debacle. But that was before Given, Bellamy and de Jong. Pompey are in dire straits, no win in nine, and a new caretaker manager just appointed after the dismissal of Tony Adams. We all know never to underestimate the impact of new manager bounce, but this is just a temporary appointment from within. Surely, *surely*, we'll be good enough to take care of this lot?

Pompey dominate the first half, but don't look as though they have anything like the quality needed up front to get past Given. We've got the quality up front alright, but it's not exactly putting itself out in a bid to make itself felt. Robinho in particular just doesn't want to be there. Minute by minute I get more aggravated with his indolence and lack of effort. Elano isn't a whole lot better.

In the second half, Pompey continue to huff and puff and the crowd as ever are right behind them, sensing a win against the big spenders. With twenty minutes to go, Glen Johnson bursts through, sees his first shot blocked, but fastens onto the rebound to strike it cleanly into the top corner. Huffing and puffing has had its reward.

Huffing and puffing is an alien concept for Robinho. Why run when you can walk? Why walk when you can get someone else to carry you? His display today has been an absolute abomination, an insult to fans who've spent valuable time and hard-earned cash to come and see it. Never have I seen an exhibition so clearly state 'I couldn't give a toss'. We've had some right prima-donnas over the years, the Rodney Marshes, Giorgi Kinkladzes et al, but I've never witnessed anything to compare with the brazen disdain shown by this alleged superstar. Lots of forward players struggle to track back, but this was on a different scale. No effort to reach simple passes, no attempts to run into space, no concentration on the rare occasions he did receive the ball, no interest in proceedings whatsoever. Why the hell had Hughes left him on for so long?

When Robinho at last got the hook, plenty of the away supporters joined in the jeers. It had been an utterly disgusting performance, disrespectful to his teammates, to Hughes and to the fans. The fears I'd had ever since I saw this self-obsessed glory-hunter strut on to the pitch for his debut had proved well-founded. I never wanted to see this twat put on a blue shirt again.

We could only improve after the substitution, but almost immediately an unmarked Hreidarsson powered in a header from a corner. Game over, though there was just enough time for David James to produce a fantastic late save to deny Ched Evans. A goal, less still a point, would have been much more than we deserved.

It was a very angry drive home, and I received a text from Collina saying 'looks like your players want to get Hughes the sack'. I couldn't argue with that. Robinho had been the worst by far, but the whole side had showed so little stomach for the fight. Wasn't this supposed to be a characteristic of Hughes's teams? And if he couldn't even get this out of his players, what hope was there?

Istanbul, Istanbul, We're Not Coming

16 APRIL 2009, UEFA CUP QUARTER-FINAL:
CITY 2 HAMBURG 1

The UEFA Cup saga continued. Six qualifying matches and four group games had seen us through to the last thirty-two, and the draw was kind – FC Copenhagen. A beatable team and a great place to visit. We arrived in Denmark for the first leg to find a city covered in snow, and it continued to fall before, during and after the match. They're used to this kind of thing here, though, and there was no danger of the match being called off. Despite the crippling cost of a pint of beer, a full contingent of City fans were suitably lubricated and boisterous as the game kicked off in a stadium full on three sides and with an artist's impression of a full stand behind the goal to our right.

It was almost a replay of the Schalke game, City looking comfortable from the off and taking the lead with a soft goal just before half-time. Nedum Onuoha's rare sortie forward ended with a shot more like a back pass, but the Danish keeper somehow allowed it to trickle past him and over the line.

Copenhagen came out strongly in the second half and grabbed an equaliser, but when SWP conjured up a low cross from an impossible position, Ireland was on hand to sweep it home. The Danes were rocking now, but Robinho's casual failure to convert a one-on-one kept them in the game, and a last-minute equaliser was a real dampener.

Two smart finishes from Bellamy saw us through in the second leg, and another trip to Denmark beckoned, to face the lesser-known Aalborg. Our 2-0 home win looked more than sufficient, the second leg remaining goalless with just a few minutes to go. Then, a soft late goal was followed by a last-minute penalty and, after looking in no trouble throughout the whole tie, we were suddenly on the rack. But Given kept us afloat during extra time, and his two crucial saves saw us prevail in the penalty shoot-out.

Our quarter-final opponents were Hamburg, and a classy finish from Ireland gave us the scarcely believable boost of a first-minute away goal. Hamburg simply carried on as though nothing had happened. By the time they equalised just seven minutes later, Given had already made two stunning saves and we were being completely overrun. A harsh handball against Richards saw them take the lead from the spot and we'd all have settled for keeping it at 2-1. We couldn't quite manage it, incessant pressure telling with what looked likely to be a decisive third goal.

We had it all to do. Being 3-1 down was tough enough, but Hamburg had looked way better than us. The club acted quickly and commendably to at least ensure a noisy full house in the second leg, slashing prices to a fiver and encouraging fans to create a real party atmosphere.

It worked. Roared on by a crowd as partisan as any experienced at Eastlands, City tore into the Germans, only to suffer a massive setback after just seven minutes when some sloppy defending was punished in full. The night looked as though it could go very flat very quickly; one more for them, and we'd need five. Instead, we pressed them back, and when Elano's shot was blocked by a Hamburg defender, the referee pointed instantly to the spot. Harsh, lucky, but almost a replica of the one given to them in the first leg. Elano dispatched the spot-kick with aplomb, and we threw it all at them in a bid to get another before the break. Elano so nearly delivered again, but his bullet of a free kick from thirty yards smashed against the crossbar.

The roar of encouragement as we came out after the interval was spine-tingling. *Come on, we can do this!* We ripped into them, and were soon rewarded when some unusually deft footwork from the bulky Caicedo gave him room to slot home. *Just one more and we're level!* Soon, another free kick, another chance for Elano. This time going for placement over power, he bent it over the wall with the keeper rooted to the spot. The ball thudded against the post and was hacked clear. So agonisingly close, but still plenty of time. The force was with us.

A great save led to a corner, and Elano's mishit low delivery looked meat and drink for the keeper. Instead, he allowed it to bounce past him towards the unmarked Caicedo, just five yards out. Not anticipating the keeper's error, the big man just couldn't sort his feet out and the ball rebounded from his shin and spooned over the bar.

We continued to batter them, and a marauding Richards powered through down the right but couldn't maintain his composure at the vital moment. Hughes inexplicably brought on the hapless Gelson Fernandes – I've never seen anyone who looks less like a footballer than this guy – and when he made his next substitution five minutes later, I was screaming for him to take Fernandes off again. Biffer got a red card for a second booking, but Hamburg were by now showing so little attacking intent that it hardly mattered.

As the minutes ticked by, our energy levels gradually dropped, and for all our possession we couldn't create that one clear chance we needed. At full time, the Germans sank to their knees in relief, and the crowd gave the players a rousing ovation. A sickener, but team and fans couldn't have given more, and at least we'd all had a taste of what big European nights can be like.

The rest of the season petered out with mixed results, and a final league placing of tenth. Mid-table mediocrity at extravagant cost. Sven's team had come eighth and accrued more points, and he'd been rewarded with the sack. Our new owners had a big decision on their hands.

2009/10

BEGINNING TO
SEE THE LIGHT

He's Lost Control Again

12 SEPTEMBER 2009, PREMIER LEAGUE: CITY 4 ARSENAL 2

The summer break saw plenty of transfer activity. From Arsenal came Emmanuel Adebayor – moody, unpredictable but, at his best, close to unplayable. His teammate Kolo Toure arrived too, a player who seemed to have lost his way a bit, but still one of real pedigree and experience. Experience of winning things. On the face of it, two decent signings, but clouded by the niggling feeling that Wenger doesn't voluntarily let players go without good reason.

After a long and fractious pursuit, we also landed Joleon Lescott from Everton for a ludicrous £24 million, seriously hacking off David Moyes into the bargain. No one could remotely suggest that we'd got value for money, but value for money isn't what we're about anymore. The only question is whether he's better than what we've already got.

Hughes clearly felt so, spelling the end for Richard Dunne, soon shipped out to Villa. Biffer had had his accident-prone moments, but with four player-of-the-year awards to his credit, was he really past his sell-by date? Definitely, according to Garry Cook, in a chilling exposition of where the club's priorities now seemed to lie: 'Richard Dunne doesn't sell shirts in the Far East.' And Joleon Lescott does? And, more importantly for those of us deluded enough to think that what happens on the pitch still matters, is he any better than Biffer?

However, much the most controversial and exciting signing saw Carlos Tevez relocate from Trafford to Manchester. What made it so sweet was the fact that none of them wanted him to go. A major fan favourite – 'Fergie, Fergie, sign him up' – Ferguson had tried everything to keep him, if only they could afford to. Hats off to the World's Greatest Football Club Owners. I don't normally care too much for Americans, but the Glazers are a shining exception.

It was a major coup for City, who celebrated by commissioning a giant Sky Blue poster of Tevez, showcased in the city centre, bearing the legend 'Welcome to Manchester'. A lovely touch of humour, executed with real style. 'Childish and stupid' according to Screaming Lord Baconface. How dare we poke fun at the mighty, untouchable Reds.

So, how long would it take for the new boys to gel? Approximately 110 seconds, the time it took Adebayor to thrash home a twenty-yarder to put City ahead at Blackburn. Superman sealed the points to get the season off to an ideal start, then Tevez and Adebayor combined for the latter to hit the only goal against Wolves. Off to Portsmouth next, where a towering header from Adebayor was enough to win the game, and topped off a superb display from the striker. He'd hit a hot streak straight away, and would hardly lack incentive to keep it going in the next game – at home to his former employers.

You don't often get a match so eagerly anticipated so early in the season, and it was with no little angst that I was unable to get to it. It clashed with a long-arranged trip to stay with friends in Guernsey. Still, there are worse places to visit; it's small, quiet, friendly and scenic, and there's not much to do other than drink. Something the residents are extremely good at. The main priority for the weekend was to locate a pub to watch the game live, and this proved easy enough. The only problem was being surrounded by Gooners, but hopefully it wouldn't be too contentious a match …

Adebayor gets a hostile reception from the away fans, and the Gooners in the pub mimic their counterparts at the game, more concerned with giving Ade grief than encouraging their team. We eke out a lead when Richards's looping header creeps home via the post and the hapless Almunia. Midway through the half, a nasty challenge on Ade from van Persie sees the two of them get in a bit of a tangle. The Dutchman gesticulates in familiar fashion, and 'get up, you tart!' is the general consensus from everyone in the pub, a fair reflection on the fragile nature of a man who makes Darren Anderton look like Charles Atlas. No one thinks any more of it until a few minutes later, when the all-seeing Sky cameras show a replay of the incident, highlighting Adebayor's stray foot coming down perilously close to van Persie's head. Little, if any, contact but the more you saw it, the worse it looked.

We reach half-time with our noses in front, but the tension builds as the second half progresses. Arsenal press us back and eventually get their reward, as van Persie extracts his revenge, taking full advantage of Lescott selling himself like a whore to turn and drill a precise twenty-yarder low into the corner. The locals, if that's what they are, rather like it.

The pub is rocking. I'm not enjoying it, and no amount of Guinness helps. Still, with Bellamy and SWP, this team is built for counter-attacks and, with twenty minutes left, we hit them with a classic sucker-punch. A slick break ends with Richards cutting the ball back to Bellamy, whose clean, confident first-time strike flies unerringly past Almunia to put us back in front. This guy is a seriously good finisher.

Now the match is completely open. Clever play from Wright-Phillips sees him get past Clichy to find some space on the right. His cross is perfect for Adebayor, who's got between the two central defenders and can attack the ball with a clear run. He meets it with a classic downward header to leave Almunia helpless.

I'm leaping with joy again, but my celebrations are nothing compared with Adebayor's. He's completely lost control. All eyes are glued to the screens as he hurtles towards and then down the touchline, his face contorted with ecstasy. He carries on sprinting at full pelt, like Usain Bolt on a bad hair day, none of his teammates coming close to catching him.

By now, I'm laughing out loud as he surges on and on, way past the halfway line. Then I realise where he's going. *Shit!* He's heading for the Arsenal fans. Another couple of seconds and he's almost there, knee-sliding towards them and opening his arms in a 'what do you think of that, then?' gesture. The Gooners aren't slow to respond. They hurl debris towards him and dish out dog's abuse. His teammates usher him away before things get really ugly.

It's absolutely hilarious, one of the truly great goal celebrations, but no doubt the sappy health-and-safety brigade will condemn him for trying to incite a riot. The usual suspects from Her Majesty's Gutter Press call for a lengthy ban. What a load of cobblers. When you've had seventy-five minutes of 'his dad washes elephants, his mother's a whore', you're entitled to give a bit back. There were no offensive gestures, just a polite reminder of how much they'd missed his happy, smiling face.

Things just get better and better. Bellamy plays in SWP in to sprint unopposed towards goal and, as Almunia goes to ground, Shaun delicately dinks the ball over him for a delightful fourth. Arsenal almost immediately get one back – and immediately almost another – but it's City's day. And, outstanding as Bellamy and SWP have been, it's Adebayor's day. He's started his City career on the hottest of hot streaks, goals in each of his first four games due reward for his skill, strength, speed and commitment. He had spells like this at Arsenal as well. The big question is for how long he can keep it up. And for how long he'll be banned, as the media witch-hunt cranks into overdrive.

The FA deem that he had indeed intended to stamp on van Persie. Three-match ban. At least there's no further punishment for the goal celebration. Quite right too. But he'll be getting one hell of a reception when we visit the Emirates ...

It Ain't What You Do

19 DECEMBER 2009, PREMIER LEAGUE:
CITY 4 SUNDERLAND 3

The first match of Adebayor's ban could have come at a better time, as we made the short trip to the Theatre Of Hate. Still, with four wins from four and Tevez and Bellamy looking sharp and dangerous, we travelled with genuine hope. Most of the media build-up focused on the return of Tevez, and the prospect of him ramming it up Ferguson was almost too delicious to contemplate. 'Welcome Back to Trafford' banners were conspicuous by their absence as the teams took the field.

City get off to the most slovenly start, once again exposed by a quickly taken throw-in. When would we learn that the opposition isn't obliged to wait until you're ready? Rooney capitalises on a catalogue of cock-ups to prod United ahead, and a long afternoon seems in prospect, if not quite as long as it ultimately turns out to be. Tevez scurries here, there and everywhere, making a nuisance of himself in the style which United fans had come to love. Whatever they say now in their attempts to rewrite history as only they can, he'd been hugely popular at Old Trafford. After twenty minutes, he hassles van der Sar into a blunder which leads to Gareth Barry coolly converting our first opportunity of the game.

Terrible marking allows Fletcher to restore their lead, but Bellamy soon equalises with a phenomenal strike from the corner of the area, the ball searing across van der Sar and into the top corner. Not dissimilar to Franny Lee's 'look at his face!' goal, and celebrated with much the same gusto. Again, we can't hold on, and yet more lax defending gives Fletcher the chance to re-enact his earlier effort. This time it looks terminal and, as we enter four minutes of Fergie time, defeat seems inevitable.

Then, with customary arrogant complacency, Ferdinand tries to scoop a fancy dan showboating ball forward but succeeds only in gifting it to Petrov. The ball is promptly fed to Bellamy down the left, with a clear run towards goal. As the keeper comes out, Bellamy just manages to drag the ball around him and, from an oblique angle, nudges it into the net for an unlikely equaliser. We've got out of jail, and a point will do very nicely, thank you very much.

The four minutes of added time pass by, as does a fifth. Martin Atkinson shows little inclination to bring proceedings to a close. *What the fuck is going on?* United get a free kick forty yards out, but it's cleared with ease. Surely that's it? No it isn't. Still no full time whistle. Ryan Giggs gets the ball and slots it through to a criminally unmarked Owen, Richards having gone completely walkabout. With the clock showing 95.34, Saint Michael fires past Given to give United the points.

My God, it hurts on so many levels. Losing in the last minute is one thing, but losing after the last minute is more painful still. The *Verministi* aren't slow to remind us that the indicator board represents the *minimum* amount of added time, and that our substitution and goal celebration occurred after the board had been raised and should, therefore, have been taken into account. And they're absolutely right. But how often does it actually happen in practice?

Our defending has been woeful throughout, with every single goal eminently avoidable. Of course, so were two of ours, but that's not the point. At Old Trafford of all places, concentration on the job is essential, and to lapse so often is a massive concern. Hughes has brought in plenty of attacking talent, but we won't be winning anything anytime soon unless he sorts the defence out. He's been here more than a year, but we still look more porous than ever.

And then there's the identity of the scorer. Michael Mother Bloody Teresa Owen. Even when he first burst on the scene as a teenage sensation, I could never warm to him. A real Little Miss Goody Two Shoes, the press forever turned a blind eye to his frequent simulation on the pitch and his gambling excesses off it. Pretty much every other player would have been pilloried. He seems just right for United, that underlying but unmistakeable smugness enabling him to fit smoothly into the array of contemptibles that now surround him.

The press predictably label it 'The Greatest Derby Of All Time', which is stretching it a lot, but no one can deny it's been one of the most dramatic. When City bounce back with a comfortable win at home to a flouncy-as-ever West Ham, it looks as though there's no harm done to morale, and five wins from six still represents a highly impressive start.

Two months later, the record reads five wins from thirteen. Seven successive draws, mostly against teams who'd regard a mid-table finish as a major success, saw us tumble down the table and started the whispers about Hughes's position being put under scrutiny.

At least a comprehensive win against Arsenal in the Carling Cup quarter-final boosted spirits. I'd brought my business partner and rabid Red Paul to the game and, ever game for a laugh, he agreed to pose in City scarf and sky blue Santa hat against a backdrop of the stadium. This was too good an opportunity to pass up; our corporate Christmas card went on to feature the photograph, providing our clients and friends with the reassurance that we were a company 'committed to promoting good and renouncing evil'.

Carling Cup progress was all well and good, but Hughes needed league wins – and fast – to have any chance of surviving. Next up were Chelsea, and the pressure was on. We got off to a shocking if unlucky start, when Drogba's shot led to a series of ricochets and an unwitting own-goal from Adebayor. This time, we scrapped as if our lives depended upon it and grabbed a lucky and similarly messy equaliser, giving Ade the distinction of scoring at both ends.

In the second half, a Tevez free kick sped past an unsighted Cech to give us the lead, but mounting Chelsea pressure provoked a rash tackle from Onuoha, and an obvious spot-kick. Lampard, so often our nemesis, stepped up but Given plunged to his right to make a brilliant save. We held out for the last few minutes and celebrated a vital win, none more so than Mark Hughes, who had once again seen his team produce a get-out-of-jail performance when the chips were really down.

Four days later, we were off to White Hart Lane. Not exactly a happy hunting ground in the past and tonight an utterly miserable one. We were abysmal. Had things improved at all under the Hughes regime? Every time we thought we'd turned the corner, we'd put in a shocker and be back to square one. But these were Hughes's players, it was his team. He no longer had any excuses. He cut a forlorn figure in the interviews after the game. Most of us had had enough of forlorn.

Saturday brought Sunderland to Eastlands, and I was delighted to see Paul's photo featured in the match programme, accompanied by text describing how I'd brought him to the Arsenal game as a special treat, for his first proper game of football. Bless. But more serious issues were afoot. Even before the game began, there were rumours that Hughes's sacking was imminent, and they intensified as the match progressed. The team started as if nothing were amiss, two early goals giving us what seemed a comfortable lead before the same old defensive failings resurfaced.

By half-time, Sunderland were level; I was also receiving texts saying that Roberto Mancini would be taking over from Hughes. I hadn't followed Italian football for many years, and had no idea what his credentials were. And I'd also long since stopped giving any credence to rumours. Let's just win the game first, eh? Bellamy put us ahead, another sloppy concession pegged us back before a final goal from Santa Cruz sealed a 4-3 win that was actually far less exciting than the scoreline suggests. It was as if the match was secondary to events behind the scenes. At full time, Hughes gave a little wave to all corners of the ground, widely interpreted as a farewell. I raced back to the car to get chapter and verse.

Five Live confirmed everything. Hughes had been sacked, Mancini was taking over. It turns out his credentials weren't too bad at all: three Serie A titles and tons of cups. Sacked by Inter Milan for not winning the Champions League. We could just about live with not winning the Champions League for a while, I think. The drive home was accompanied by a soundtrack of increasingly sanctimonious drivel from pundits and former players, all expressing outrage at the way Hughes had been treated.

It was disrespectful, dishonourable and above all bloody stupid – had our mega-rich owners learned nothing from the mistakes of the past, that chopping and changing managers never got you anywhere?

The stats were gleefully trotted out, that Mancini would be City's 765th manager over the period during which United had had just one, and just look at the respective trophy hauls. There was nothing but sympathy for this decent and honourable man and absolute contempt for the way he'd been treated. And, most of all, a transparent sense of real spite, a passionate hope that Mancini fails, that we fall flat on our faces, that our owners get fed up and go off to find a new plaything, and that we plunge back into the abyss. It'll be just what we bloody well deserve.

What a bunch of absolute wankers. How many City games had any of them actually seen during Hughes's reign? Did they know what his record was? Played fifty-five, won twenty-two, drawn thirteen, lost twenty. Mediocre mid-table stuff. Mediocre mid-table stuff, with the huge financial resources and talent at his disposal? With a team made up of his own players? An away record of just four wins from twenty-eight games? Decent and honourable maybe, nowhere near good enough certainly. If our owners had made any mistake at all, it was in not getting rid of him sooner.

A press conference is called to unveil our new manager. Mancini doesn't speak much English. It's a bloody good job, or else he'd have got the next flight home and passed the whole thing off as a bad dream. It's an absolute PR disaster, fuelling outrage and mockery, and once again stars Garry Cook. Tetchy and irritable from the off, he clearly hasn't bothered to make sure everyone has got their ducks in a row about the sequence of events. When was the decision to sack Hughes made? When was Mancini first approached? When did he accept the job?

The answers didn't stack up, the questioning became ever more aggressive and the whole thing descended into farce. Hughes was sacked because we had 'fallen behind the target points trajectory'. What was this? Seventy points. But win the next game and you'll be back on track! Yes, er …

Why couldn't everyone tell it as it was? It wasn't just the results, but the performances, the inability to see out winning positions at home, the lack of gumption and commitment in so many away games. And of course Mancini would have been approached before Hughes was axed, we'd hardly want to leave ourselves managerless for a vital chunk of the season, would we?

When Joe Royle was sacked by David Bernstein, Kevin Keegan was unveiled as the new man the very next day. Had Bernstein met Keegan, got him to agree terms, and sign on the dotted line from scratch in the space of twenty-four hours? I doubt it. That's how things work in successful operations. And, apparently, some very unsuccessful ones. Only get rid of the incumbent once you've got his successor lined up.

Cook and the club were rightly pilloried for their shambolic performance. Though none of this was his fault, they'd all be queuing up to get their knives into Mancini at the earliest opportunity. Even those of us delighted to see the back of Hughes despaired of the way in which it had been handled. Cook may have done lots of great things for the club behind the scenes but he should never, ever have been allowed out in public. Seldom can a new manager have been appointed anywhere against such a backdrop of critics so eager for him to fail. We could only hope he proved to be a man who enjoys a challenge …

These Boots Are Made For Licking

19 JANUARY 2010, CARLING CUP SEMI-FINAL FIRST LEG:
CITY 2 MANCHESTER UNITED 1

The Mancini regime gets underway with a Boxing Day game at home to Stoke. Just how often have we played Stoke on Boxing Day over the years? Probably no bad thing, as a hangover numbs the grim reality of how excruciating they are to watch. City are workmanlike, competent and secure a comfortable, if unspectacular, 2-0 win. We certainly don't look like giving much away at the back. It's a very Italian beginning.

Two days later, a trip to Molineux, a favourite ground which evokes plenty of memories. With all the relocations to identikit characterless bowls, there aren't too many left. It's a bitterly cold and clear night, just as it should be, and City fans are really up for it. So are the players. We start well, take the lead with a slightly fortunate goal from Tevez, but in the second half produce easily our best away performance since … since … I honestly can't remember. Certainly before Mark Hughes darkened our doorways. Garrido bends in a superb free kick, and a crisp twenty-yarder from Tevez seals a comprehensive 3-0 win. Mancini is up and running, and has already bought himself some breathing space. How the media men must hate it.

A tricky FA Cup tie at Middlesbrough is safely negotiated before Birmingham are battered 4-1 at Eastlands, courtesy of a sparkling Tevez hat-trick. Mancini is disproportionately angry about the concession of Brum's consolation goal. He clearly takes this kind of thing very personally. He's even more angry next week, as a robust and feisty Everton over-power City at Goodison Park, with Fellaini running the show. No complaints from Mancini, he's still learning about the squad, and in any event everyone's focus has switched to the game coming up in three days' time. The Carling Cup semi-final first leg, at home to United. 1969/70 revisited.

The war of words has well and truly broken out. Ferguson says he'll continue his policy of resting players. He's not that bothered about the Carling Cup, even less bothered about City. We're still a small-time club with a small-time mentality. That Tevez poster is still needling him. He was perfectly happy to let Tevez go, he says, ever prepared to rewrite history. Gary Neville also wades in, questioning his former teammate's motives in moving to City. Mind your own business and stick to what you're best at. Scaring children. Tevez hits back, calling Neville a boot-licking moron. It's great stuff, just like the old days. It feels like we're back in the big-time.

City do everything they can do to crank up the atmosphere as kick-off approaches, dimming the lights and projecting images of giant blue moons on to the stands. United fans had got wind of this, and let off an array of red flares. Far from diluting the effect, it just builds the anticipation levels even further.

Fergie's been telling porkies yet again. United are at full strength. No one is remotely surprised. City are forced into a change in central defence, young Dedryck Boyata coming in to replace the injured Kolo. It's a cagey opening, but United suddenly create some space down the right. Given can only parry Rooney's shot, Giggs rolls the ball home and it's the worst possible start.

We're still behind as the interval approaches. Then, Bellamy gets free down the left and takes on Rafael. The full-back makes a grab for Bellamy's shirt outside the box, but the Welshman shrugs it off and powers on. Rafael has another tug at the shirt and this time Bellamy goes down. Mike Dean points immediately to the spot and is surrounded by furious United players. They're insistent the foul was outside the box. Dean's response is so clear and explicit that we can even make it out in the stands. He's given it for the second offence. He saw the first one but played advantage, as Bellamy had continued to surge towards goal. It was the second foul which dragged Bellamy down, and that was inside the area. It's an outstanding piece of refereeing. Would he have been brave enough to do the same thing at Old Trafford?

It's Tevez to take the penalty, and the pressure couldn't be higher. He has to wait an inordinate amount of time for United's protests to subside. Plenty of their players, Rooney to the fore, are in his ear as he tries to compose himself. He sprints forward and smashes the ball high past van der Sar, before setting off towards the United bench, ear cupped towards Ferguson and Neville. It's a perfect time to score, and gives us all the momentum going into the second half.

We soon make it count, and when Kompany keeps an attack alive by hooking the ball back into the goalmouth, Tevez reacts like lightning to nod the ball past the keeper. It's another ecstatic celebration, on the pitch and in the stands. *Fergie, Fergie, sign him up!* You know you wanted to.

We're at the pivotal point of the match. Does Mancini stick or twist? Taking any lead to Old Trafford will put us in with a real chance, but a two-goal margin would make us clear favourites. We don't push for it too much, but still have one great opportunity, when SWP's snapshot is blocked by van der Sar. United increasingly dominate possession, and Rooney is everywhere, dropping deep to pick the ball up and posing a constant threat. Time and again we just about manage to crowd him out, but there's a sharp intake of breath every time he gets near the ball.

As the minutes tick by, we'd all settle for a 2-1 lead going into next week, and even those far, far too young to have been around at the time will be aware by now that this was exactly how the first leg ended up all those years ago. Good omens always help in times of stress.

At last, the final whistle blows, and we can all look forward to a week without much sleep. It's going to be a tumultuous night at The Theatre Of Hate, and even my longstanding passionate aversion to the place and its residents won't keep me away. Some games you simply cannot miss.

Church Of The Poison Mind

27 JANUARY 2010, CARLING CUP SEMI-FINAL SECOND LEG: MANCHESTER UNITED 3 CITY 1

In one of those inexplicable errors of judgement that we all make every now and again, I've decided to take the train to Old Trafford. Maybe it's the memories of getting the train there to watch Lancy in their 1970s John Player League pomp. Maybe it's the fact that I've not been there for years and can't remember the bus routes. Maybe it's because it feels like the safest option. Whatever, it's not the best decision.

Anyone doubting the existence of life on other planets need only get themselves down to Platform 14 at Manchester Piccadilly station, two hours before kick-off for a United home game. It's tucked away around the corner from the main station, so that businessmen, tourists and normal folk aren't exposed to this alien life-form. They'd never come back to Manchester otherwise.

Slowly, the platform becomes populated with an ungodly assortment of oddballs, spanning every race, colour and creed. They do, however, have two things in common. They're all wearing United colours and there's a disturbingly vacant look about each and every one of them. I'm distinctly uneasy.

They board the train in silence, coalescing into a seething mass of sub-humanity, a grotesque array of slobbering neanderthals. There's no evidence of the influence of drink or drugs, yet not a single pair of eyes reveals the slightest light of intelligence. They break into a low monotone drone, bereft of tune, like an ancient pagan chant. 'United Roooooad, take me hoooome, to the plaaaaace, I beloooong, to Old Trafford, to watch United.'

I feel very uncomfortable, much more so than on the many other occasions I've found myself surrounded by opposition fans. Ever since I was a little boy, I've had a fear of dogs. This is entirely rational. They have sharp pointed teeth and you can't tell what they're thinking. It's a dangerous combination. This lot are the same. They could turn in an instant. I keep my head down, trying to avoid eye contact, but I briefly catch a glance from a guy of a similar age, with a little girl who I hope is his daughter. My look asks him: 'What the hell are you doing subjecting her to this?' His look says: 'I know you're not one of us, but your secret's safe with me.'

The journey takes forever. At last the Theatre Of Hate comes into view and, for the first time in my life, I'm pleased to catch sight of the ugly monstrosity. I escape from the train, breath a massive sigh of relief, vow that Platform 14 will never see me again and get into the away fans' concourse as quickly as humanly possible. A quick pint, as much to cope with the ordeal just passed as the one about to come, and I take my seat in what I'll always call the Scoreboard End, ready for a night of death or glory. It's a bit noisy.

City look completely comfortable, early possession is even, and there are no real scares. After about twenty minutes, we put together a decent attack which ends with Tevez trying to outstrip Ferdinand in the box. The two go down in a heap in front of the Stretford End, and from our distant vantage point it looks a decent penalty shout. The ref gives a goal kick, and there are no real protests. When I watch the replay the following day, I'm amazed. It's an indisputable penalty, and I can't understand why we didn't make more of it.

We continue to give as good as we get, and Tevez and Ferdinand soon clash again deep in United's half. Tevez crashes to the ground as if poleaxed by a flailing elbow. This time there are protests aplenty. Replays show Ferdinand looking round to locate his opponent's whereabouts before arming him off. It's a minimum yellow, borderline red. Not here it isn't. No card whatsoever. We're playing well, but let no one doubt the size of the task ahead of us. Howard Webb at Old Trafford is as fearsome an opponent as they come.

Bellamy's having a feisty duel with Rafael, and has got him for pace. We need to isolate them one-on-one. After half an hour, we do just that and Bellamy gets to the line and cuts an inviting cross back to the unmarked Tevez. His header bounces up off the turf, but isn't far enough into the corner, and van der Sar claws it away. It's the best chance for either side in the first half, and we've held our own as well as we could ever have hoped. Forty-five minutes to go, and we're still one up. But the kitchen sink will soon be coming our way.

Initially, United don't really step up the pace, and a storming run by Richards ends with a twenty-yard left-footer that van der Sar struggles to get round the post. Then, we attack down the left and win another corner. It's a corner which changes everything.

As Bellamy comes to take it, he's pelted with missiles from the mob, a mob which has been told that tonight is zero tolerance, that United will be doing all they can to prevent and stamp out trouble. He's struck by a coin, and as he doubles over, a full bottle of cider fizzes past his ear. No alcohol to be brought into the ground? Quality stewarding, lads. The referee comes across to Bellamy's aid as, ostensibly, does van der Sar. However, the keeper's real objective soon becomes apparent, as he sweeps away the debris onto the surrounding track, getting rid of the evidence. What a nice chap.

A shaken Bellamy is understandably reluctant to go back into the morons' den, and Barry comes over to take the corner. Oh well, at least he's more expendable. It's a shocker of a corner, easily headed clear towards Rooney, near halfway. He out-manoeuvres de Jong near the touchline, before looking up and playing a long diagonal ball into the space where Giggs is hurtling at full pelt. The man tracking him is Shaun Wright-Phillips; he's got the pace for the job, but not the height, and the ball just clears his desperate leap and sets Giggs clean through on goal. His first touch is heavy, and Given manages to force him wide. It looks as though we might get away with it, but reinforcements have arrived fast and the ball eventually finds its way to Paul Scholes on the edge of the area, who drills the ball low into the corner to score what feels like his 957th career goal against City. Fuck, Fuck, FUCK!!

As I stare blankly out, three things cross my mind. First, how can we give up a goal from our own corner? Then, that we would never have scored a goal like that, not just because we don't have Rooney in our side but also because we never leave anyone up when defending a corner. It's a tactic I've never understood. And thirdly, had Bellamy taken the corner instead of being physically assaulted, how different would the outcome have been? The intervention of the mindless thugs had made an impact, alright; still, if we lose the tie, I'm sure we'll be able to put in an appeal. Yeah, right.

The goal changes the tempo and pattern of the game completely, and United go straight for the throat. We've got to survive this spell if we want to go through, but after two or three near misses we're breached again, a messy sequence of play ending with Carrick slotting home. The night is alive with the sound of boneheads, and it feels like a long way back.

It isn't really. Just one goal and we're level. We start to get a spell of decent possession, with Bellamy to the fore. He crosses from the left, and Tevez hustles to get in front of

Ferdinand, before contorting his body to execute a perfectly timed mid-air back-heel. The ball slots between van der Sar and his near post for a breathtaking aggregate equaliser. It's a sublime piece of instinctive skill. We're right back in it, and don't we let our gracious hosts know it. 'Fergie, Fergie, sign him up.'

Though wholly different in physique, the way Tevez manoeuvred himself into a position where he could get in an attempt at goal with a single touch is reminiscent of the great Denis Law. And what we've just seen provides a fleeting reminder of the last time a City player back-heeled a goal at that very same end, by far the classiest moment ever witnessed within the walls of this hideous cesspit.

There's a real shift in momentum as a new sense of belief courses through team and fans alike. Bellamy again outstrips Rafael, and his cross looks ideal for the unmarked Adebayor, twelve yards out. He's got a free header to become an all-time City legend. But he's nowhere near as good in the air as people think he is. Static as he heads the ball rather than running on to it, his feeble attempt loops harmlessly wide and his chance to make history has gone. We soon get another chance, when Ade puts Tevez through with a clear sight of goal. Crucially, he takes one touch too many and allows a desperate Ferdinand to slide across and block.

We're heading for extra time. Just three minutes of added time to negotiate. United have sprung back to life. It's as if they need to score now or they're out. A cross comes into the near post, where Fletcher is unmarked. His header looks like a certain winner, but Given miraculously gets the ball around the post. Relief and disbelief in equal measure. *Will we ever stop giving them free headers six yards out?*

Apparently not. A short corner yet again catches us dozing, and Giggs crosses for Rooney, unmarked, right in front of goal. He nuts it goalwards and even Given can't react in time. It's not as if we hadn't been warned.

It's a crusher, and there's no time to respond. I walk towards the exit, only to find the stewards blocking the way. We're locked in, a sea of silent glum faces, surrounded by the cavorting masses. Their celebration goes beyond mere ecstasy; it's absolute hysteria. Contorted, gurning faces leer in at us from all sides. It's a celebration way beyond that befitting getting to just another little old Carling Cup Final. It shows how much beating us matters to them.

Suddenly, music emerges from the tannoy. It's singalongam-oron time. The sound of a sickly sweet voice fills the night air. Bloody hell, it's Doris Day and 'Que Sera Sera'. How naff is that? But then I start to pick out some of the lyrics, telling of how 'Fergie's Red Army' went down in the first leg, but triumphed in the end. It's been specially recorded just for this one evening. They've actually commissioned someone to sing these words, in the style of Doris Day, just so it can be played for this two minutes, and never again.

This is beyond naff. It's fucking unbelievable. It's so utterly crass that I can't stop myself breaking into a smile. I'm not the only one. Three minutes ago, we were denied our first Wembley final for twenty-nine years. We should be distraught, devastated and angry. Instead we're smiling. *You can win as much as you like. You'll always be wankers.*

Ferguson is his usual spectacularly graceless self in victory, saying that United could have had six or seven. Yes, they could, if they'd got all their chances on target and we hadn't had a goalkeeper. But what about us? We had plenty of chances of our own, should have had a penalty, could have seen them reduced to ten men, and saw their yobbo fans exert a critical impact on the outcome. But coming away from here feeling hard done by is a way of life for visiting teams. If Cloughie was resurrected and went on to replace Ferguson, his first words to his new charges would have a familiar ring. 'You can chuck all your medals in the bin, you haven't won any of 'em fairly.'

As I stroll back to catch the bus, I'm still wearing a wry smile. It gets a bit wider when I see a road sign directing traffic towards 'Manchester'. Not 'City Centre', but 'Manchester'. I'm nowhere near as gutted as I ought to be. The two matches have been fantastic occasions, both played out in cauldrons of noise and excitement. It's felt like football as it used to be, and there's the promise of lots more of it to come. Playing in games that really matter is where we want to be; what we need to do next is start winning them.

A Song For Europe

5 MAY 2010, PREMIER LEAGUE: CITY 0 TOTTENHAM 1

The FA Cup looks a decent proposition, with a fifth-round tie at home to Stoke. A comedy goal from SWP sets us well on the way, but the dreaded Delap long throw is headed directly home by Fuller for an infuriating equaliser. Shay is one of the great shot-stoppers, but dominating his box is not a strong-point. The same thing happens in the replay, as ten-man City are overcome in extra-time.

Just one priority now – getting into the Champions League. But sometimes, especially at home, we were so passive as to make you think we were the away side. Having racked up an impressive win at Fulham three days earlier, we all expected Mancini to continue in an attacking vein for the visit of our most obdurate of opponents, Everton. Instead, focussing on nulling their strengths rather than playing to ours, he selected a side to go toe to toe in midfield. It never looked like working, as the visitors wrapped up a 2-0 win, the manner of which left us wondering whether Mancini really was 'too Italian' after all.

As we reached the business end of the season, successive games against Burnley and Birmingham looked like banker wins. At Turf Moor, we reached half-time 5-0 up, yet still wondering if we'd get the points. An already sodden pitch was turning into a quagmire and, if it carried on lashing down, the game might be abandoned. It could only happen to City.

Indeed it already had, almost fifty years ago, when Denis Law's six goals at Luton Town ultimately counted for nothing. I was counting the minutes, hoping we'd reach the stage where the referee would find it impossible to act, but at last the rain relented and the threat subsided with it. We won 6-1, and a few days later almost did the same against Birmingham, who at least managed to keep us down to five.

Not much talk now of an Italian mentality, and ideal preparation for the next assignment – United at home. For a change, it was a vital game for both sides, with them needing a win to keep on Chelsea's coat-tails and us to keep our noses ahead of our fourth-place pursuers. And how we owed them one. Amid unrelenting tension, a cagey game was played out with very few real chances. United had more of the ball, but seldom looked like doing anything telling with it. Belatedly, and perhaps deliberately, we started to press for a winner as we got to the last few minutes, and for the first time all afternoon looked the more likely to break through.

Into Fergie time, and we're pressing hard. Bellamy receives the ball, attempts an ambitious crossfield pass, but it's cut out and United have time for one more counter-attack. Evra gets the ball on the left, and plays a hopeful ball into the area. Strolling into space, unattended, is Paul Scholes. You'd think our lads would recognise him. Little ginger bloke, specialist subject scoring goals against City. He powers in a free header. It's a horrible, slow-motion moment. Given's at full stretch, and you can see he's struggling to get there. *Please don't be on target!* It is. United fans cavort in glee. I close my eyes, praying I'm in the middle of a bad dream. I open them and feel sick to the pit of my stomach.

Three times, *three times*, they've scored injury-time winners against us in the same season. And this one hurts the most. Maybe it's the cumulative effect. Maybe it's the fact that their title hopes would have been all but over had they not won. Maybe it's the fact that it's here rather than at Old Trafford, where you always fear the worst. Maybe it's the sight of the loathsome Gary Neville taunting our fans. An unedifying sight at the best of times, Neville surpasses himself by kissing Scholes full on the lips. What happened to the Public Indecency Act?

It's the bitterest of pills to swallow. United are graceless and gloating as ever, claiming they'd 'passed us to death' and dominated the game. The stats show that, other than the goal, they'd mustered two shots on target, neither of which troubled Given. Real domination, that.

It takes me a good few days to even start to get over this one. United have inflicted more pain on us this season than in any other, more pain than anyone should have to bear. You'd like to think that, one day, we can give them a taste of their own medicine. My God, they and their nauseating supporters deserve to suffer. It seems inconceivable that we could conjure something up which would eclipse the pain of three injury-time derby defeats in a single season. But football's a funny old game ...

A trip to the Emirates is next, and Mancini wisely keeps Adebayor on the bench. When he does emerge late in the game, he gets almost as much stick from City fans as from the Gunners. What the fuck does he look like? He's got his hair in bunches! *In bunches!* Never can any footballer have looked such a complete wanker. The Hoddle and Waddle mullet? The Keegan perm? The Seaman ponytail? The Jason Lee pineapple? Not a patch on the Adebayor bunches.

We emerge with a creditable point, especially as Given crocked his shoulder early on. With Hart out on a full-season loan to Birmingham, we're given special dispensation to recruit a new keeper for the final three games. We manage to get Marton Fulop from Sunderland reserves, and he's thrust straight into the side for the next, crucial, game at home to fourth-place rivals Aston Villa.

Nothing but a win will do. We start brightly, but Villa strike on the break when Carew's weakly hit shot finds a route between Fulop's legs. We build momentum and camp in the Villa penalty area. Clattenburg is besieged by penalty shouts. Foul on Zabaleta. Waves play on. Handball by Warnock. Nothing doing. Tevez flattened by Dunne. Fair challenge. Johnson tripped by Warnock – at last, the bastard points to the spot. Halle-bloody-lujah. Tevez steps up, blasts straight at Friedel, but gets lucky as the ball ricochets into the net.

Almost immediately, Carew pivots to smash a shot against the bar. We go straight back on the attack, and Johnno shows tremendous composure to set up Adebayor for a simple tap-in. It's been a cracking game, and the second half carries on in the same vein. Eventually, SWP produces some vintage magic, slaloming past two Villa defenders before playing Bellamy in. Bellamy looks up, and plants a lovely curler into the top corner. He never looked like doing anything else. Three vital points in the bag.

Villa are now out of the race. It's between us and Spurs, and we meet in three days' time. With both of us having final matches against opponents with nothing to play for, the team in fourth after this game would be almost certain to reach the promised land for the first time. We need to win; a draw would do Spurs. The media hype would do justice to a title decider, with the biggest game in Eastlands' short history being at the epicentre of British sporting attention from the minute Saturday's final whistles had blown.

As kick-off approaches, Andy Morrison and Paul Dickov are wheeled out on to the pitch to a tumultuous reception – a symbolic gesture of how far we've come from the dark days of being 2-0 down at Wembley in the third-tier play-off in 1999. From the jaws of anonymity to the Champions League. What a story it would be. I just wondered whether it was a tad presumptuous, and a gesture better suited to a game after we'd actually qualified.

We start on the front foot, pressing Spurs back and bossing the midfield. Tevez is all action, one barnstorming run seeing him get through on Gomes, only for the keeper to parry for a corner. Crowd noise tumultuous, tension unbearable, intensity of effort unsurpassable. As an occasion, it's living up to the hype; as a game it's not bad, but there's too much at stake for anyone to really enjoy it.

We continue to dominate possession, but it's Spurs who create the best chances. Crouch heads against the post, then the ball drops to Bale just ten yards out, and he flashes it inches wide. The collective sigh as the ball crashes into the advertising hoardings instead of the rigging is almost deafening. We counter with a sweet Johnno strike which forces Gomes into a flying save.

Half-time, and the tension is such that breathing is a real challenge. We all stand up to shake out those taut muscles and the PA system floods the air with a selection of special Mancunian tracks for this special Mancunian occasion. 'Love Will Tear Us Apart', 'There Is A Light ...' and 'She Bangs The Drums'. Utterly fantastic. Criticise our football all you like, but nobody does half-time music quite like we do.

Into the second half, and there's a clear and disconcerting change in momentum. Spurs have taken our best punches, and re-emerged with real attacking purpose. We struggle to get within a sniff of Gomes's goal, whereas their attacks seem more and more menacing. Fulop saves brilliantly from Defoe, and even a full-stretch Crouch isn't quite long enough to reach a low cross.

We're hanging on, and Spurs go for the kill. A draw will do them nicely, but they want to get the job finished here and now. Kaboul picks up a loose ball and makes ground down the right. He gets past Bellamy's limp challenge and fires in a near post cross. It's deflected towards goal, and all Fulop can do is push it out towards Crouch. He cranes his neck and heads into the empty net. It's been coming.

We never look like recovering. The visiting supporters are dancing in jubilation long before the end, and the game peters out tamely, along with our Champions League hopes. On tonight's evidence, Spurs deserve it. They got better and better as the game wore on, sensing their chance as the effort of so many testing games in quick succession eventually caught up on us.

As the long walk down the spiral staircases and beyond begins, the familiar strains of 'Heaven Knows I'm Miserable Now' emerge from the PA. What can you do but smile? Yet even before Morrissey reaches the end of his beautiful, witty masterpiece, he gives way to the strains of 'Glory, Glory Tottenham Hotspur'.

For us, it's an evening of massive anti-climax and disappointment, yet we still help the victors celebrate their moment of triumph. Now that's class. It's a small touch, but our ability to act with dignity, grace and a bit of wry humour at a time of acute disappointment illustrates perfectly the difference in culture and values between us and *them*. I'm as gutted as anyone, but can't help smiling, and feeling proud, that the new regime is staying true to our traditions, and treating those two imposters just the same. With Mancini now able to recruit his own type of players over the close season, the chance to experience triumph rather than disaster can't be far away.

2010/11

RIP IT UP

Baby You're A Rich Man

Much of the summer was spent following the World Cup in South Africa. The best holiday I've ever had, the worst football I've ever seen. England were abject from start to finish, and Rooney's foulmouthed tirade at fans who'd saved for months, if not years, to come and support the national side – and understandably felt a little bit let down by the White Pele performing more like a beached white whale – was completely despicable.

Our internal flight to Port Elizabeth was packed with England fans, together with a sprinkling of pundits, one of whom was a very approachable Graham Taylor. I couldn't resist asking him whether Alan Green was as big a twat as he seemed. 'No,' said Graham. 'He's much worse.' Did I not like that.

The trip also contained a moment of terrible sadness, as a mate texted me with the news that Chris Sievey – the man behind Frank Sidebottom, a comedy creation of absolute genius – had passed away. I'd got to know Chris a bit over the previous couple of years and was absolutely devastated. Frank's gigs always made me cry with laughter, and a small but important corner of my life had been taken away. Chris was a big blue and clearly loved to be inside a costume, a combination which made him a perfect choice for his role as the original Moonchester. His gestures and mannerisms gave the mascot a personality all of its own, one which subsequent incumbents have been completely unable to match. I got back home in time to attend a tribute evening, a hugely appropriate, surreal and well-attended event. Rest in peace, Chris. But Frank will never die.

As ever, the World Cup meant that close season signings were deferred until very late in the summer, allowing speculation to build to fever pitch. Which mercenaries would our untold riches enable us to attract? The two biggest names turned out to be Yaya Toure from Barcelona and David Silva from Valencia. Jerome Boateng, who'd starred in Germany's impressive World Cup run, also joined the ranks, along with Aleksander Kolarov from Lazio and James Milner from Villa. The press remained sceptical, with Silva and Yaya both featuring prominently in lists of the players expected to be the season's biggest flops.

There was also a particularly and personally troubling development over at Old Trafford. Back in the 1990s, I spent six years working with an outfit called Bacon and Woodrow, a firm of actuarial consultants. Thoroughly professional, but about as exciting as they sound. I then saw the light and moved to work with the world's largest purveyor of alcoholic beverages. Shortly afterwards, Bacon and Woodrow were taken over by a global firm of consultants called Hewitt.

A few years later they themselves were swallowed up by a mob called Aon. The very same Aon that had just been

announced as the new shirt sponsors of Manchester United.
It goes without saying that Aon is an American company.
Had I stayed at Bacon and Woodrow, I'd now be employed
by a firm whose name had immediately become synony-
mous with Manchester United, and which was pouring
millions of dollars into its coffers. Except, of course, that
I wouldn't. Hand on heart, I'd have resigned on the day the
deal was announced.

The news was a horrible shock. This was a company
that I still had close ties with, having worked with them
on mutual clients and on several occasions appointing
them to provide advice to companies I was involved with.
I had some good friends there. The stories coming out
were harrowing. On the day of the sponsorship announcement, every single employee walked into the office to find
a Manchester United shirt on their desk. In the reception
area of each of their main UK offices, life-size cardboard
cut-outs of Giggs, Rooney and Ferdinand sporting Aon-
logoed shirts greeted their clients and visitors. It was unbelievable. Aon employs some really nice people. And some
really talented people. And even some people who are nice
and talented. These people just don't deserve this. I've never
been to any of their offices since.

The impact on staff may have been small – in a profession
whose intake comprises primarily folks who find accoun-
tancy too exciting, interest in professional football is generally restricted to statistical analysis, such as compiling lists
of all-time leading scorers of second-half headed goals for
away teams wearing black shorts on a Tuesday when there's
an 'r' in the month – but how many of their clients would
have been seriously hacked off? No middle ground with
this team. You love 'em or you hate 'em.

Shortly afterwards I received an invitation. Would I like to
attend a dinner to celebrate Aon's link-up with Manchester
United? At Old Trafford. With the chance to meet

'Manchester United legends'. This has got to be a wind-up. If it was, it certainly worked:

'Thank you for your email of last week. Please accept my apologies for the delay in responding; it's taken me quite some time to recover sufficiently from the shock. While normally delighted to accept your hospitality, I'm afraid that the specific event you are proposing is utterly preposterous and misguided and I can't imagine that any right-minded person would be even remotely inclined to attend.

'Firstly, your global partnership and sponsorship agreement with Manchester United is absolutely nothing to celebrate. I find it amazing that such a highly professional and well-regarded outfit as yourselves should choose to associate with this morally bankrupt, corrupt and wholly objectionable institution.

'Manchester United stands for Greed is Good, and has ruthlessly and shamelessly exploited its supporters for many years. It cares nothing for the impact of its actions on fans, the broader community or even its former employees, the latter evidenced by the callous disregard for the families of the Munich air disaster victims, while the club itself has made, and continues to make, enormous financial capital from the tragedy.

'Winning is everything, no matter what lengths they have to go to, what rules they have to break, in order to achieve it. This "we have a divine right to victory so it doesn't matter how we get there" mentality is exemplified perfectly by the despicable Ferguson. Their spectacular arrogance and gracelessness, both in victory and defeat, is something truly sick-making and a repulsive example to set before the public, especially the many children who are coerced by their mindlessly selfish parents into following this vile team. What sort of value sets will these poor souls grow up with?

'Do you really want your clients and other contacts to think that you approve of the tawdry methods employed by this loathsome outfit, or worse still conclude that you yourselves must therefore use similar underhand tactics, deceit and bullying in your own business?

'I must also make a couple of observations on the language used in your e-mail. You describe the cesspit that is Old Trafford as "one of the world's great sporting theatres". Are you under the influence of some kind of hallucinogenic drug? This revolting, brash, eyesore tells you everything you need to know about its owners, garish neon lights blaring out as if to say look at us, aren't we bigger and more important than you? There is no aesthetic quality whatsoever to this grotesque arena, inside or out, just a huge ugly tasteless monstrosity whose only saving grace is to be situated well outside the City of Manchester, so as not to cast a blight on God's own country.

'You then go on to threaten potential guests that they will meet "Manchester United greats". Exactly what treats do you have in store for your victims? Perhaps Eric Cantona, the celebrated kung-fumeister, will put in an appearance and allow guests to leave with personalised studmarks in their chests as he recreates his finest moment?'

The potential antics of Messrs Robson, Charlton, Blackmore and O'Shea were also ruminated upon, though in terms possibly not appropriate for reproduction in a book of this nature.

Aon's forerunner was an outfit that took pride in its speed of response time. Three years later, I'm still awaiting a reply. How standards have fallen.

We're not exactly afforded an easy start to the new campaign, an away trip to Tottenham followed by the visit of Liverpool. White Hart Lane is sunny and buoyant, the home fans understandably celebrating their forthcoming Champions League campaign at our expense. Silva starts but, right from the outset, the play seems to pass him by. Fears – or, for many, hopes – that he's not physically robust enough for the Premier League get some early support.

Yaya looks off the pace, and in the first half we're absolutely overrun.

Fortunately, Joe Hart is hell-bent on vindicating Mancini's decision to give him the nod over Shay Given, and he delivers an absolute masterclass in goalkeeping. His save from Defoe's close-range volley is breathtaking, and there are half-a-dozen other top-drawer efforts to go with it. We reach half-time all-square; had we been three or four down, none of us could have complained.

We make a bit more impact in the second half, but the 0-0 outcome looks inevitable from about twenty minutes out, as both teams tire in the late summer heat. A point at Spurs is a point more than we usually get, and it's a content bunch of Blues that exits the stadium.

Four days later, it's the first chance for the home crowd to get a sight of our new signings. Silva is given a rest, presumed absent on an urgent mission to devour five steaks a day, but Milner starts along with Yaya and Boateng. It's also an Eastlands debut for Sheikh Mansour, who receives a predictably ecstatic welcome. He looks so bloody young! How does this work, exactly?

City recognise that this would be an opportune occasion to put on a decent display, and dominate from the start. We get a first real glimpse of Yaya's attacking potential as he takes up more advanced positions than in his Barca days, and certainly looks the part. We're terrific going forward, and take a deserved lead when a delightful, incisive move between Johnson and Milner frees Barry to slot home a clean finish.

The second half sees us continue our dominance, duly rewarded when Tevez claims a touch on Richards' header, which finds its way past Reina. Only now do Liverpool spring to life, and when a Gerrard piledriver comes back off the post, Hart further cements his position with blinding saves from two follow-up efforts. Shay did a top job for us, but this guy just looks unbeatable.

Johnno wins a soft penalty, duly despatched by Tevez, and the 3-0 final score sends all but the Scousers away very happy indeed. Yaya has looked imperious, Milner hugely impressive on debut and it's been Barry's best game since he joined us a year ago. Business as usual for Tevez, a keeper apparently possessed with superhuman powers and, for sure, one very happy and impressed owner. Four points in the bag from two of our toughest fixtures, and it's a very mellow stroll indeed back to the city centre. Early days, but we know, and Sky's watching millions know, that we're on the right track.

Please Allow Me To Introduce Myself

7 NOVEMBER 2010, PREMIER LEAGUE: WEST BROM 0 CITY 2

The euphoria and optimism generated by the comprehensive win over Liverpool was quickly pricked by defeat to a last-minute penalty at Sunderland. Still, best to get performances like that out of the way early on, and there remained plenty to get excited about. Mancini had made his final signing of the transfer window, and it was the most intriguing of all – Mario Balotelli from Inter Milan. This boy's reputation well and truly went before him, an intoxicating mix of brilliance, moodiness and madness, branded as 'unmanageable' by José Mourinho.

How could Mancini hope to succeed where the Special One had failed? Perhaps because he'd done it before, bringing Balotelli to Inter Milan at the age of seventeen and giving him plenty of game time. Mario had been an important figure in three successive Serie A triumphs, and was only just 20 years old. No one in football knew him as well as Mancini. So why all the fuss?

Balotelli announced himself with a late winner in our Europa League qualifier in Timosoara, but an injury a few minutes later meant we'd have to wait a while before seeing him in the Premier League. City had started to impose themselves, with David Silva in particular beginning to make his influence felt. Chelsea were beaten at Eastlands for the second year running, as Tevez secured the points with a breakaway strike. A narrow win over Newcastle was then followed by a trip to Blackpool, where we rode our luck to come away with a 3-2 win. Tevez weighed in with another two goals, both of which could easily have been disallowed, but the highlight was a fabulous effort from Silva, slaloming through the Blackpool defence before curling in a beautiful left-footer for his first league goal.

Next up was another Europa League tie, at home to Lech Poznan. A huge contingent of away fans was bolstered by the local Polish community, and they were boisterous, colourful and hugely entertaining. They treated us to some bizarre routines, most notably the act of turning their backs on the action, putting their arms round each others' shoulders and bouncing up and down while generating an indecipherable din. It was funny, impressive and weird in equal part, provoking the inevitable and good-natured response of: 'What the fuckin' hell was that?' But a seed had been planted ...

The game itself was also highly entertaining. Adebayor marked a rare start with a superb hat-trick, but the highlight was a spell-binding display from Silva, who set up all three goals and for the first time showed us the full range of his repertoire. Effortless, instant mastery of the ball, great eye for a pass, outrageous sleight of foot and deceptively strong in possession. The pedigree of this guy was becoming clear for everyone to see.

When Arsenal visited four days later, we had a chance to go top. We started like a house on fire, but their first counter-attack saw Fabregas put Chamakh in the clear, only for Boyata to bring him down. Referee Clattenburg produced a red card, provoking anger all around me. Only five minutes had gone, and Clattenburg had 'ruined the game'. Surely he could have given him the benefit of the doubt, and just produced a yellow? Cobblers. It was absolutely the right decision, though past and subsequent evidence suggests he might not have made the same call in the same circumstances at Old Trafford. Keeping Arsenal at bay for eighty-five minutes with ten men is a bit of a challenge, and ultimately proved too much.

When we lost dismally at Wolves the following week, then went down in the return game in Poznan, the press cranked up the pressure on Mancini. The next fixture, at West Brom, was now, ridiculously, being described as make or break. Mancini, and we, would just have to get used to it. When you're the Richest Club In The World, one defeat is newsworthy, two on the trot is a crisis and three …

The trip to the Hawthorns brought a second league start for Balotelli. He'd started at Wolves and shown a few nice touches, but not really made a great impression on the game in a bitterly disappointing team performance. Maybe today he'd show us what he was all about.

We take the game to Albion from the start. After about twenty minutes, Silva releases Tevez with a gorgeous reverse pass, creating our first real opportunity. Tevez fires the ball across the face of goal, and Mario slides in at the far post to glide the ball back past Carson and open his league account. It's a classically Italian goal, a patient build-up followed by a sudden spurt of incisive and accurate passing once the opening presented itself.

Five minutes later, Mario latches onto a lovely floated pass from Silva. Having got the ball under control, he flashes an instant right-footer low past Carson to put us two up, before celebrating in distinctly non-celebratory fashion. He could definitely look like he's enjoying it a bit more, but the away fans more than make up for it, roaring his name in raucous unison.

Into the second half, and West Brom become a bit more feisty. Mario's still in the thick of the action, and starts to take offence at some of the treatment being dished out. He picks up a yellow card for a retaliatory foul, prompting immediate movement on the City bench. Mancini knows his man. The red mist is coming down. Let's get him subbed before he does anything stupid.

Too late. An untidy tangle with Mulumbu has the home fans baying for blood, and sure enough Lee Probert produces an instant red card. It looks harsh at the time, and even harsher on TV re-runs later, but it was a situation that a more disciplined player would never have got involved in. It also gives the headline writers everything they could have dreamt of. The two sides of Mario Balotelli. The indiscipline generates far more column inches than the two brilliant goals, but then who wants to read about a big-money City signing being brilliant? A new bad boy of English football has been born.

It wouldn't be the day's only conception. As City comfortably run the clock down, assisted by Mulumbu's second yellow card for a scything tackle on Tevez, someone has the bright idea of imitating our Polish friends' backs to the action bouncing dance. Soon the whole away end is participating, with an accompanying roar of 'let's all do the Poznan!', much to our mirth and the absolute bemusement of the home supporters. It might just catch on …

Cold Cold Christmas

20 DECEMBER 2010, PREMIER LEAGUE: CITY 1 EVERTON 2

The season's first derby produced one of the dullest encounters in living memory, both teams seemingly content with a point right from the outset. An even more dreary and less defensible goalless draw at home to Birmingham followed, but fears of impotence were quashed the following week, when a superb performance at Craven Cottage dismantled Mark Hughes's Fulham. A special win for Mancini, with the press having been transparently eager to see poor old mistreated Sparky get a measure of revenge for his callous dismissal.

Next up was another Europa League tie, and the sparsely supported FC Salzburg came to town. City were coasting to victory at a snowbound Eastlands when a Salzburg substitution was announced. 'And coming on for Salzburg, replacing number 19 Cziommer, number 27 Alan.' *Alan?* Alan who?

It certainly tickled the fans in the South Stand, who cheered Alan every time he touched the ball and graced him with an array of chants. 'There's only one Alan', 'Alan, Alan, give us a wave', 'Alan is Superman', 'feed Alan and he will score', 'Alan for England!' The poor lad looked completely bewildered, but sent a message of thanks after the game, admitting he'd got no idea why he'd received such a uniquely warm reception from opposition fans. Absurdist humour can't be too prevalent in Brazil.

A trip to Upton Park is always a pleasure, even if the stadium enlargement has stripped it of that intimate and intimidating atmosphere it used to possess. An opportunity to catch up with my old mates Vicky and Paul before the game and, with the Hammers struggling for any kind of form, a great chance for another three points.

A midfield quartet of Barry, Silva, Yaya and de Jong gives us a formidable blend of power, skill and defensive stability; the only question is whether we can turn it into goals without the suspended Tevez. Jo deputises for him, again causing us to reflect that we haven't exactly got strength in depth up front. Adebayor doesn't seem to fit into Mancini's plans and the expectation is that we'll be making a big splash in the January window.

Yaya looks in the mood today, and a surging run sees him power through three opponents before bringing a fine save from Green. A few minutes later he goes one better, getting on the end of a short pass from Barry to lash a first-time twenty-yard left-footer into the roof of the net. It's a screamer, Green barely has time to blink, and those salt-of-the-earth East Enders are treated to their first sight of the Poznan. I'm not sure they totally approve. They certainly don't understand.

In the second half we absolutely batter them. Yaya turns on the afterburners and surges down the wing, before advancing on Green from a narrow angle. He slides the ball past him, and gets lucky as it bounces back from the post onto the keeper's back and into the net. It's a frightening example of the sheer power of the man. He's had a slow start at City, leggy and cumbersome at times, but when freed into a more attacking position to run at defences he looks simply unstoppable. Let him get into his stride and you can wave him goodbye.

We soon move from brutal power to sheer artistry, as Silva picks up a ball centrally, waits for Johnno to make a run inside and, while looking elsewhere, splits the defence with a gorgeous little outside of the foot pass. Johnno effortlessly takes the ball round Green, rolls it into the net, and the points are in the bag. The stand once again bounces to the beat of the Poznan as we celebrate another tremendous away performance. We're joint top, playing some lovely stuff, and everything seems to be coming together very nicely. I'm certainly looking forward to watching this one again when I get home.

The game was indeed very palatable viewing, but the discussion after it somewhat less so. Carlos Tevez had asked for a transfer. Where the hell had this come from? Apparently, he'd cited the breakdown of relationships with the club's senior executives as the reason for wanting away. Sorry? Was he constantly popping into Khaldoon's office for a cup of tea and a chat? I'd seldom heard such a load of bollocks. The story would soon change to one of missing his kids, then about how much he hated Manchester, with its miserable weather and lack of decent restaurants. Hmmm. For a man who hates Manchester to choose to play for not one but two Manchester clubs does seem a tiny bit on the careless side.

Not much doubt as to who was behind this – his agent, adviser, owner and all-round good guy Kia Joorabchian. Agitating for a transfer every couple of years was par for the course, and the timing could hardly be better. City joint top of the table; Tevez our most important and influential player. Losing him would be a hammer blow, with Balotelli yet to settle, Adebayor on his way out and Jo simply helpless.

City robustly refused to accept the transfer request, and acted quickly and pragmatically to get the issue resolved, in the way Joorabchian would have wanted from the outset. By throwing more money at it. The request was miraculously withdrawn, and Mancini fuelled the Tevez ego even more by giving him the captain's armband. After being such a perfect role model, it was the least he deserved …

Tasteless as it was, it was still a huge relief that Tevez was staying. Mancini's strategy seemed clear. Make him feel loved, get the best out of him until the end of the season, then ship him out somewhere a bit nearer his kids.

The next game was at home to Everton, three days before Christmas, and we looked forward to popping into Eastlands en route to the even grimmer north. If Carlos thinks there's not much to do in Manchester, he should try Kirkby Stephen. The land that time forgot. Alas, severe snowfall buggered up this plan , indeed the plans for the whole festive period, so I was left to watch the match unfold on TV. Postponements elsewhere meant that a win would see us top the table at Christmas, albeit having played a couple of games more than most.

Tevez was given a decent enough reception as he took his place in the starting line-up, and despite Everton's mystifying and infuriatingly good record at Eastlands, there was a real air of confidence about the place. We should have known better. A catalogue of errors – an unnecessarily risky throw out from Hart, slack control from Silva, a poor tackling attempt from Zabaleta and a non-existent one from Johnson – led to the ball being crossed in from the right, where our nemesis Tim Cahill stood criminally isolated to nod them in front. This guy scores against us every bloody season. Do you not think it might be a good idea to look out for him if he ventures towards our goal?

Things soon got even worse, as a smart finish from Baines gave us everything to do. But we set about doing it in stirring fashion. Shots rained in from all over the place, only to be blocked by desperate, flailing bodies or an inspired Tim Howard. Eventually, a deflected Yaya shot brought us back in the game with about twenty minutes to go.

Still plenty of time left against a creaking defence but nothing would go for us. Mario dinked the ball over Tim Howard, saw it hit the post, and as he scrambled up to knock the rebound home was barged over by the keeper. The ball broke loose to Tevez, but his shot was smothered and Howard got away with it. Silva's goal-bound shot struck Hibbert's arm but referee Walton's view was masked and again we got nothing.

Games against Everton usually see them stifle the life out of us before sneaking a set-piece goal and nicking the points. This time, we'd created countless opportunities and by any measure other than the scoreline played extremely well. But part of me felt that we'd brought it on ourselves. When half the team choose to turn out in snoods – and MCFC branded snoods at that – did we really deserve anything else? Let this be a lesson to us all.

Half A Boy And Half A Man

17 MARCH 2011, EUROPA LEAGUE ROUND OF 16,
SECOND LEG: CITY 1 DYNAMO KYIV 0

The Everton disappointment was quickly put aside when three straight wins propelled us to the top of the table on New Year's Day. A splendid sight, even if other teams had games in hand. The Boxing Day massacre of Villa featured a Balotelli hat-trick, two of them from penalties dispatched with nonchalant, almost laughable, ease. Then, a great win at Newcastle saw Tevez back to his very best, as if the transfer saga had all been a bad dream.

We got panned after a 0-0 draw at Arsenal, the critics flaying us for an overly defensive display, but Arsenal had started the game so well that we had little choice other than to be pushed back. The enforced absence of Silva didn't help, and emphasised how reliant on him we were for that creative spark. Nevertheless, after the batterings we've had there over the years, I'd take a point at Arsenal any day of the week.

No one could say we'd been overly defensive in the next game, a bizarre 4-3 win over lowly Wolves. New signing Edin Dzeko arrived from Wolfsburg with glowing reports, and physically at least looked an ideal foil for Tevez. The match seemed over at 4-1, with Dzeko's debut containing some nice touches and a lovely assist for Yaya; however, two soft goals, the second from a penalty conceded by Lescott with an act of such staggering stupidity that I'd have gladly seen him banished from the club forevermore, led to a nervous finale. It was nothing like the performance of would-be champions, and when two trips to Birmingham produced but a single point between them, any realistic such aspirations were laid to rest.

Still plenty to play for, though – a Champions League place and two cups. We didn't help ourselves in the FA Cup, requiring replays against both Leicester City and Notts County. It could have been worse; but for Dzeko's first goal for the club – a late equaliser at Meadow Lane – we'd have suffered a humiliating defeat. The need for replays was a source of real angst for Mancini, who constantly bemoaned the fact that we were playing every three days and that the squad wasn't big enough to cope.

Injuries and the number of players out on loan meant that we were genuinely stretched at times, but we'd brought most of the problems on ourselves. I wished Mancini would just button it on this issue – we were hardly going to get the sympathy vote, and if you keep telling players they're too tired, eventually they start to believe you. We certainly didn't need mentally jaded players for the next game – the Old Trafford derby.

Aided by some disgusting refereeing decisions – the failure of the indescribable Philip Walton to award Blackpool a penalty when they were 2-0 up against United a few days previously was gobsmacking, as was the leniency shown towards Gary Neville at West Brom and West Ham – the Reds were making a strong bid for yet another title even though, by their fans' own admission, they'd been in far from vintage form. We went to Old Trafford and played as well as I could remember, Silva missing a great early chance to put us ahead as we knocked the ball about with composure and confidence. A defensive lapse allowed Nani to put them ahead, but we just came on even stronger, equalising with a fluke goal when Dzeko's mishit shot found the net via Silva's back.

It looked like a rare chance of a win at Verminland, but another fluke, if rather more spectacular – Rooney's overhead shinner from Nani's deflected cross flying into the corner of the net – put paid to that. Rooney presented himself to the Stretford End as if the Messiah, his earlier demand for a transfer conveniently forgotten. We'd all welcomed Tevez back after his own aberration, so could hardly mock too much. It was an undeserved defeat, but the performance had shown what we were capable of and – crucially – that we were now confident enough to take the game to United, even on their own patch.

The resumption of the Europa League saw a comfortable win over Aris Salonika, with the away fans again making an impression. This lot were weird. The noise for the full ninety minutes was unrelenting, and bore no relation to what was happening on the pitch. There was none of the cadence you get between lulls in play and goalmouth incidents, just a constant racket accompanied by choreographed dance routines. These guys thought that they, rather than their team, were what people had paid to come and see. I hope it doesn't catch on.

Aston Villa were next in the FA Cup, and Gerard Houllier elected to field almost a reserve team. The fifth round of the FA Cup, a home tie against Reading if you win, and you rest your top players? Villa fans were as disgusted as we were surprised, and an easy 3-0 win was embellished by a beautiful finish from Balotelli, casually clipping a twenty-yarder into the top corner as if it was a two-yard tap-in.

Reading duly arrived for the quarter-final, providing the very real prospect of our first semi-final since 1981. Ours was the last of the sixth round ties to be played, and I'd stopped off in Mary D's for a pre-match pint and to take in the semi-final draw. If we got through, the possible opponents would be Bolton, Stoke or United. We got United. The place went ballistic. I just shook my head. What are this lot on?

Reading had already won at Anfield, were on a tremendous run in the Championship and had nothing to lose. It was a tense game of few chances, but a towering header from Micah Richards was enough to secure our first trip to the new Wembley. Four weeks to wait. I could hardly bear to think about it.

Next in Europe were Dynamo Kyiv, and a 2-0 first leg defeat made Mancini visibly angry and set up a testing second leg. A tea-time kick-off diluted both the attendance and atmosphere, and a predictably meagre contingent of Ukranian fans made little contribution to the experience. Balotelli missed an early sitter at the far post, and was clearly in one of his tetchy moods, his body language deteriorating further as everything he tried failed to come off. When he went in for a high bouncing ball after about half an hour but instead found the thigh of an opponent, the referee instantly put him out of his misery, brandishing a red card which looked certain to end our interest in the tie.

It was a rash, immature episode from Balotelli and, while not malicious, you could certainly see why he'd been dismissed. I wondered if we'd see any more of him this season. There'd been some flashes of real quality, but far more displays of sulky indifference and indiscipline. Yes he was only twenty, yes he'd had an upbringing more difficult and complex than most of us could ever relate to, but there does come a point where you have to say enough's enough. Maybe Mourinho was right. Maybe he is unmanageable. Maybe Mancini's on an ego trip, trying to prove he could succeed where the Special One had given up. Or maybe, just maybe, Mancini genuinely believed that with patience he could bring the balance between brilliance and bedlam to an acceptable level.

City continued to take the game to opponents of zero attacking ambition, and Kolarov got one back just before half-time. We found it difficult to maintain attacking momentum in the second half, but just when it seemed as though the tie was petering out, Kolarov let fly with a low cross-shot. Tevez moved across the line of defenders, in the clear and onside. The faintest touch would divert the ball home, but the ball flashed agonisingly past his foot and wide of the post. The last chance had gone. But there were bigger fish to fry …

There Goes The Fear

16 APRIL 2011, FA CUP SEMI-FINAL:
CITY 1 MANCHESTER UNITED 0

Predictable defeat at Chelsea follows the European exit, but a comprehensive win over Sunderland restores confidence, helps the goal difference and keeps the Champions League quest well on track. Next, six days before the semi-final, we travel to Anfield for a crucial league game. Mancini emphasises the importance he attaches to the Cup by leaving out Silva and de Jong and, from the moment Andy Carroll thunders a twenty-five-yarder past Joe Hart, we're emphatically second best. Tevez does a hamstring after twenty minutes and trudges off disconsolately. He knows, and we know, that hamstrings don't recover in six days. A 3-0 scoreline doesn't flatter Liverpool and the night could hardly have gone worse.

Mancini gets stick after the game from fans and pundits alike. But not from me. Winning the FA Cup or getting into the Champions League? No comparison. It's thirty-five years and counting. I don't want to say 'I was there when we clinched fourth place'. I want to say 'I was there when we won the Cup'. So yes, the performance was abject and the result potentially disastrous, but I still think Mancini has got his priorities right. As long as we win on Sunday.

The closer the day comes, the more daunting the task appears. United players, fans and media are full of how they're on for another treble, and it's a horrible prospect for the rest of us. The Cup in isolation may be their third priority, but keeping City in their place is right at the top of Ferguson's agenda. This won't be like some of their other recent semi-finals – we all know that he'll pick his strongest possible side and that they'll be seriously up for it. And they don't lose semi-finals very often.

For this game, I seem to have corporate hospitality invites coming out of my ears. There is even one from E.ON, the competition's main sponsors, with whom I did some work a few years ago. Kind and much appreciated as they are, I decline the lot. There's only one place you can be on a day like this. At the end of proceedings my emotions will be at one of two absolute extremes, with behaviour to match. Whatever the outcome, it's not right to inflict this on the less committed. They won't understand, and why should they? The only place to be is with hardcore Blues.

We take our places behind the goal with half an hour to spare. *Christ, it's electric!* City's first visit to the 'new' Wembley – though it's taken us so long to get here that it's already getting on a bit – and the fans at least will be putting everything into it. The teams emerge and our tradition of relentless jeering over the announcement of United's side is taken to a new level with a simultaneous elongated demonstration of the Poznan. With 30,000-odd Blues bouncing in unison, structural tests can't come much more rigorous than this. We eventually turn around to face the pitch, and now there's no hiding place. If your stomach's not churning at moments like this, you really shouldn't be here.

The two line-ups are talisman-free, with Rooney suspended and Tevez injured. They go with Berbatov, we go with Balotelli. Mario hasn't done much right of late, and you can get pretty short odds on him seeing red before the day's out. A big call by Mancini.

It's a harrowing start. We can hardly get hold of the ball as United dominate possession, full of the composure that comes with having been here lots of times before. They're not really hurting us, until three quick passes suddenly carve us open, and Berbatov's through on Joe Hart. *Shit!* Hart's out like lightning and makes a crucial, brilliant, block. We breathe again, and hope the escape shocks us into action.

It doesn't. We're caught cold by a short corner and Hernandez plays the ball across the six-yard box, low and inviting. Berbatov slides in unopposed at the far post. Surely no escape this time. At full stretch, he makes clean contact but skies the ball over the bar, and we've got out of jail twice in two minutes. This is horrible. I can hardly bear to watch.

Slowly, painfully slowly, we ease our way into the game, firstly by enjoying some benign possession of our own but then by putting it to more threatening use. Barry's shot on the turn hits the side-netting and seems to instil belief that we can actually hurt these guys. We very nearly do, as Balotelli's effortless thirty-yarder is tipped over, then Lescott blazes a volley just wide. Now, we're well on top, and it's United who are happier to hear the half-time whistle. A half of two halves, with City finishing very much in the ascendancy. Can we keep it up?

We can and we do. United are pressed back, and are lucky when Silva can't quite control van der Sar's mis-cued clearance. What a chance that would have been. United recover possession, and Carrick tries to play his way out of defence. Yaya anticipates his pass, and latches on to the ball, extending his stride as he surges into the area. Vidic makes a trademark grab for his shirt, but it's like putting a child's buggy in the way of a juggernaut. Van der Sar comes out and spreads himself, but Yaya carefully caresses the ball all along the floor and it slides between the keeper's legs. There's only one place this is going, and it hits the net to scenes of unbridled delirium on and off the pitch. What a moment.

We're ahead, and deserve it, but what difference will the goal make to the pattern of play? None at all. We continue on the front foot and create a series of chances in quick succession.

Desperate defence from Ferdinand denies Balotelli; SWP's low cross is almost turned into his own net by van der Sar; Lescott has a free header from Silva's cross but glances it just wide. We're all over them, but I'm far too tense to feel any kind of pleasure. Every time United are in our half I have to look away, and when they get a free kick twenty-five yards out I fear the worst. Nani steps up, clips it over the wall, but Hart awkwardly tips it onto the bar and away to safety. The big screen shows it to be a much better save than it looked; a deflection had changed the pace and direction of the ball, and Hart had to readjust expertly to get it away.

With about twenty minutes to go there's a clash between Zabaleta and Scholes on the halfway line. Zaba goes down and writhes on the turf. This is one South American who only goes down when he's in real pain. Mike Dean immediately shows the red card. Scholes trudges off with not a murmur of dissent, and there's barely a protest from the rest of them. Christ, it must have been bad.

United push desperately forward, but most of the threat comes from our breakaways. Yaya is everywhere, striding through their ranks time and again in an awesome display of power, strength and speed. When you've got a guy like this on your side you must feel invincible. He almost gets on the end of Kolarov's cross but a nudge from Vidic slightly impedes him and van der Sar scrambles the ball to safety. We're still ahead, but it's getting towards the time we fear most. It can't happen again, can it?

Five minutes. Where the hell has that come from? Carrick cuts inside but his hopeful curler is straight down Hart's throat. Overzealous tackles by Rafael give us free kicks and welcome breathing space. We're so close. *Blow that bloody whistle, will you!* At last, referee Dean obliges, prompting scenes of absolute bedlam all around us. As we recover some composure and look up for the first time, the startling sight of half a stadium full of empty red seats greets us. As Adrian

Chiles is noting on ITV's live coverage: 'Say what you like about United fans, but they do know how to empty a stadium.'

On the pitch, the players are as ecstatic as the fans. There's some minor argy-bargy in the centre circle, Mario to the fore, and we'll have to wait until the morning to find what that was all about. At the moment, no one gives a toss, as we all sing along to the inspirationally chosen 'Cum On Feel The Noize'. Noisy neighbours indeed. I wonder what they'd have put on had the Scum won? 'It's the same old song'? 'So you win again'? We'll never know, thank God.

When I get back to see the recording of the game, I hear Clive Tyldesley say 'it's a watershed moment' and he's absolutely spot on. Yes, it's only a semi-final, yes, we've won nowt yet, but it feels like so much more than 'just' reaching a final.

We've had plenty of wins over them in the last ten years or so, but there's always been the sense that the derby means more to us than it does to them, that we're the underdogs raising our game, that they've got bigger fish to fry. And yes, for them the Premier League and Champions League take precedence, but they can't disguise the fact that this defeat really, really hurts. Not just for the result on the day, the end of the treble, the local bragging rights, but for what it portends. A massive game, the biggest stage, and we stood up to the occasion. Not only did they seldom look like getting back into it after we'd scored, but we went at them looking for the killer second. Not 'let's batten down the hatches and keep 'em out', but 'we're better than these, let's finish 'em off'. There's no fear anymore.

It transpires that the post-match contretemps was an adverse reaction from Ferdinand and Vidic to supposed gloating from Mario towards United fans. All three of them left in the stadium, presumably. Of course, they'd have sloped off heads bowed had they won, right? Gary Neville anyone? The most graceless winner in the history of football? The man who runs up to the Kop, taunting Liverpool fans when United score there? Whose mockery and hatred of City is worn like a badge of honour? Rooney, whose all too frequent goals at Eastlands have been celebrated by kissing the badge in front of us in acts of undisguised provocation?

The sorest of sore losers, the vacuous Ferdinand later tweets his justification for his angry reaction, citing a 'lack of respect'. Respect for what, exactly? Mario's given them just the smallest taste of their own medicine, and Ferdinand has reacted as though someone's shot his pet camel.

There has never in history been an individual or institution so willing to give it out and unable to take it as the collective that is Manchester United Football Club. Lose to them and they mock you, gloating about their superiority. Beat them, and they can never, ever, acknowledge that you might have deserved it. Dare to poke fun at them and they come back and belittle you.

Having a laugh at Manchester United's expense is completely off limits. No one takes themselves quite so seriously. It's an integral part of their culture, what they are, and why so many of us utterly detest them. For most of us, key characteristics in our choice of friends are a sense of perspective, a self-awareness, an ability to laugh at themselves. No decent person would choose Manchester United as a friend.

Reflecting on the match on the way back into central London, it's hard to think of a single more influential display than the one given by Yaya today. Awesome doesn't come close. But almost as heartening is Mario's performance, his best for the club so far. He'll get plenty of headlines for the post-match fracas when the blame lies elsewhere, but his influence on the game was immense, his movement, hold up play and willingness to work for the team showing everyone that he can do it when he wants to. And you wonder if he's the kind of player who wants to when the stakes are highest. Unlike most self-styled mavericks, maybe he's one who rises to the big occasion rather than becomes overwhelmed by it.

It's a long night, though not as excessive as might be imagined. The emotional energy expended has left everyone drained, and we're all well aware that the job's not done yet. It'll always be looked back on as a fantastic day, but how bittersweet would it be if we now failed to win the final? For this day to stand proud as one of our very greatest, we need to win one more game, against far less celebrated opposition. The acid test of whether 'typical City' has truly been laid to rest. I think it has, but only time will tell.

Dreams Of Children

14 MAY 2011, FA CUP FINAL: CITY 1 STOKE 0

The thrill of seeing off United in such a high-profile match took a long time to subside, but there were four vital league games to be played before we returned to Wembley. Narrow wins over Blackburn and West Ham were followed by a dispiriting second half capitulation at Goodison Park. A blow to our Champions League hopes, and the manner of Everton's comeback would have been well noted by Tony Pulis and his band of primitives. Two sloppily defended long balls led to headed goals, overturning our well-earned half-time lead.

Spurs come to Eastlands three days before the Cup Final. Last season, their win here guaranteed them fourth place. If we win tonight it'll do the same for us. The symmetry is completed when Peter Crouch hits the same net in which he scored last year's deciding goal, from almost the same spot. This time, though, it's an own goal and enough to see us into the promised land. So, with one of our objectives achieved, we can give our undivided attention to the prospect of Wembley glory.

In 1969 I was 11 years old. I woke up on the morning of 26 April in a state of unprecedented excitement, even more so than on Christmas morning. It was Cup Final day, and City were in it. Washed and dressed, breakfast, then round to my grandparents, where I sat engrossed with my Granddad, taking in every minute of the build-up. I switched between channels to seek out all the bits which featured us rather than Leicester, before settling down for the match itself on BBC, the only proper channel. Neil Young's famous goal secured a 1-0 win. It was the last time we'd won the FA Cup.

Just over forty-two years later, I awoke in a similar state of excitement. The magic of Father Christmas may long since have evaporated as the truth became cruelly apparent but, despite what many would try to have you believe, the magic of the FA Cup was still very much with us. I'd been delighted to reach the Champions League, but nothing like the way I'd feel if we could win this afternoon.

With this year's Champions League Final being played at Wembley, our Final had been rescheduled to a day with a full programme of Premier League matches, kicking off a couple of hours later. Some thought this devalued the impact of the Cup Final, but only those whose teams weren't in it. For us, it still felt like the day's only game, even though United were playing at Blackburn, where just a point would secure them the league title. Usually I'd have been keeping a close eye on proceedings at Ewood Park; today, I couldn't care less. Today was all about us.

We were meeting some friends of Lindsey's for lunch before the match, and got up to London nice and early for a couple of drinks before making our way to the stadium. *Wembley on Cup Final day.* The sense of anticipation and excitement hits you in the face. And the sense of history courses through your mind. All those famous moments I'd witnessed over the years. Charlie George, Porterfield and Montgomery, Bobby Stokes, Alan Sunderland, Ricky Villa, 'and Smith must score', Keith Houchen, 'Yidaho'. Burned on the brain forever. As I walked towards the ground, it felt different from any other game I'd been to. This was an occasion. An occasion where, in my mind, everyone else would be sitting at home in front of the TV, watching the build up, the teams arriving at the stadium, wishing it was their team playing, wishing they were there. But this year, at long long last, it was our turn.

Inside the ground, we grab our programmes and make our way to the restaurant. We see Tony Book and Mike Summerbee, the last City captain to lift the Cup and the creator of the goal that won it, and they kindly pose for photos. It's all very civilised. I enjoy lunch as much as you can when your stomach's knotted and you've got no appetite whatsoever. All I really want to do is get into my seat.

We take our places with over half an hour to go. The stadium is already virtually full, and awash with colour. A sea of sky blue at our end, an equal and opposite sea of red at theirs. Flags are waving everywhere, enormous motifs of past legends are laid out on the pitch, and the noise is unrelenting. No aggression, no abusive chants, no 'who the fuckin' hell are you', just everyone out to play their part in making the day the biggest of occasions and to enjoy it to the full. It's fantastic. The FA Cup dead? You cannot be serious.

The din reaches a crescendo as the teams come out, take their positions, and are introduced to the dignitaries. The obligatory, incongruous 'Abide With Me' is respectfully sung by all and the national anthem by most, and at last we can get underway.

After his brief warm-up outing three days ago, Tevez starts for City and joins Balotelli up front. Stoke have had injury doubts over two of their very few sources of flair and skill, but Etherington and Pennant both start. It's no surprise. They might never get the chance again. We're hot favourites despite not having the best record against Stoke, but the general consensus is that the Wide Open Spaces Of Wembley will act in our favour, giving us more room to play and dampening the effect of Delap's prodigious throw-ins.

We start with real purpose, settling instantly, and Tevez makes an early impact with a cracking shot which Sorensen does well to parry to safety. A few minutes later, the keeper does even better, a fantastic full-stretch save denying Balotelli what would have been a fabulous goal. Shortly afterwards, Mario hits the deck after a collision with Robert Huth – none of us can see what happened and, alas, neither can the referee. We'd later see that it was a blatant, cynical elbow and a certain red card had it been spotted. Mario's on his best behaviour today, though, and seeks retribution only through his footballing skills. He's playing really well, but so is everyone, as we continue to dominate. Stoke can't get anything going at all, but chances come and go, notably for Silva when he hammers a volley into the ground and sees it balloon over a gaping net.

Half-time, no score, and time for a very quick drink. Lindsey's friends say it's just a matter of time before we score, we've been so much the better side. But Wembley Way is lined with rivers of salt from fans of Cup Final teams who've failed to make their period of dominance count. Stoke have been struck by stage fright, and they'll be a different proposition after the break. It's hard to believe that they won't create at least one chance, and if we carry on missing ours you can bet your life they'll take it.

As expected, Stoke emerge in a far more competitive frame of mind and we have twenty minutes of stalemate. Then, the moment we've been dreading arrives. Kenwyne Jones out-muscles Lescott in pursuit of a long ball, and is clean through on goal. Hart comes storming out to meet him, but it looks as though Jones has room to flick the ball past him. Heart in mouth time. Jones manages only to get a toe-end to the ball and Hart makes himself big enough to intercept it. Everyone in the ground knows what they've just seen. The pivotal point of the match. They were always going to have one chance, and that was it.

Almost instantly, we're galvanised, and resume the dominance we'd exerted in the first half. Mario's cute back-heel puts Silva into a dangerous position, and he shows great upper-body strength to hold off Huth and tee Mario up for a shot. It looks goal-bound, but is blocked and rebounds out. Tevez can't latch on to it and it bounces out invitingly, just beyond the penalty spot.

Running in like a steam train is the massive figure of Yaya Toure, who keeps his head down, and summons all his might to produce a hammer blow of a left-footer, the impact causing his standing foot to leave the ground. The ball travels like a shell past Sorensen and crashes into the netting. The explosion of joy is incredible. It's not just that we've scored, it's that we know Stoke have nothing left to give. They've had their chance and they blew it. We're going to win the Cup!

Sure enough, we see out the last fifteen minutes with absolute ease, and what chances there are all come our way. Vieira is allowed a brief cameo appearance to mark what will be the final game of his illustrious career, and Tevez and Balotelli remain energetic and committed up front. They're a troublesome pair and no mistake, but they've both done superbly today. Indeed, it's probably Mario's best game yet for City, earning him the Man Of The Match award, and demonstrating again that his temperament can cope with – indeed, might thrive on – the biggest of occasions. Three minutes of added time pass without incident and the final whistle allows us to get the party started.

At last, we can climb what were once the thirty-nine steps to receive the trophy. It's Tevez's privilege to receive it, but he really lets himself down by discarding a City scarf placed round his neck on his way up the stairs, instead receiving the Cup draped in the Argentinean flag. This annoys the hell out of me, and symbolically seems to confirm that he'll be off in the close season. So what. Thirty-five years of hurt are officially at an end.

As the players return to the pitch, they treat us to their own version of the Poznan, before revealing a banner with the legend '00 YEARS'. There's been much comment about taking that ticker banner at Old Trafford down, and it will now indeed be consigned to history. Funnily enough, it's never bothered me much; I've always thought it was quite amusing. For them.

As the lap of honour proceeds at a snail's pace, the emotions kick in and the tears begin to well up. It's starting to sink in that we've at last won something worth winning. The FA Cup at Wembley. Today's been like a throwback. Two teams whose fans aren't used to Wembley Cup Finals have created a wonderful, celebratory atmosphere throughout. Stoke's fans have all stayed behind to watch the Cup presentation and salute their own disconsolate team, and only begin to file out of the ground as the lap of honour begins. Again, just like it used to be.

I'm just happy to stand there and soak it all in; it's like being in a mellow drunken haze without actually being drunk. Bottle this and you'd make a fortune. Lindsey gets a text from her friends saying they're waiting for us at the bar. She doesn't like to keep people waiting. She gets short shrift: 'I've waited 35 years for this, they can wait another ten minutes.'

As the players at last leave the pitch, we adjourn to the bar, pop the champagne corks, then it's off into town to meet a contingent of Jersey Blues for an evening of proper celebration. By now the news has come through that United have won yet another league title, virtue of an apparently dubious penalty award. No surprises there. Normally this would be the cause for much wailing and gnashing of teeth; today, it hardly registers at all. It's unequivocally our day. Yes, they'll be saying they've kept us in the shade yet again by winning the real big one on the same day that we pick up the little old FA Cup, but they haven't.

We all know the Premier League is more important, but this is a much bigger day for us than it is for them. For them it's just another ill-gotten title. For us, it's a true watershed moment, the end of thirty-five barren years, the proof that we can cope with pressure, that we can win things, that we'll be in the hunt for plenty more trophies. We've learnt a lot about ourselves today; we already know everything there is to know about them. Time for a rare summer of content, then bring it on!

2011/12

FOOTBALL IS REALLY FANTASTIC

The Changingman

28 AUGUST 2011, PREMIER LEAGUE: TOTTENHAM 1 CITY 5

The warm glow of silverware and the promise of a first outing in the Champions League guarantees a relaxing summer, but we all know that further reinforcements will be needed if we're to have a serious tilt at the title. We secure Gael Clichy from Arsenal, and Sergio Aguero from Atletico Madrid, the replacement for the surely on his way but we can't quite seem to get rid of him Tevez. I haven't seen much of Aguero, but everyone who has says he's a real star, a certainty to light up the Premier League. I'm sure some of them said the same thing about Jo.

Pre-season goes extremely well, apart from a mystifying non-performance in the Community Shield. Despite doing nothing to deserve it, we reach half-time 2-0 up, but are even more lethargic in the second half and allow United to come back for a 3-2 win, the winner resulting from a hideous mix-up between Kompany and Clichy. Clichy's capacity for dropping major and costly clangers has always scared me, and this is hardly an auspicious start. Still, as the losers of this fixture always say: 'It's only a friendly.'

We start the season on Monday night, at home to newly promoted Swansea. They play some nice stuff in the first twenty minutes, dominating possession without really threatening a goal. We slowly get to grips, as Silva starts to orchestrate our attacks, and both he and Barry thrash great efforts against the bar. We keep the momentum going in the second half, and when Dzeko turns the ball home from close range a stadium-wide Poznan greets our first goal of the season.

Just under an hour gone, and a limping de Jong comes off to be replaced by the rapturously received Aguero. Within two minutes, Yaya plays the ball towards him on the edge of the box. He lets it roll across him, before turning and unleashing a ferocious left-footer which Vorm claws away. Almost immediately, Aguero links smartly with Dzeko and accelerates past a defender but can't quite get his foot round the ball to finish the job. Just two minutes later Richards' textbook low cross after a flowing move is turned home smoothly and stylishly at the far post. Six minutes for Sergio to open his account.

Two more minutes pass, and yet more gorgeous interplay between Silva and Dzeko sees Aguero surging through. He dinks the ball over the onrushing Vorm, leaps acrobatically to flick it back over his shoulder into the goal-mouth, and the waiting Silva gleefully smashes it home. The guy's been on the pitch for eight minutes, he's scored one, made one and every single touch has been brilliant.

City understandably ease off before, in injury time, Aguero receives the ball thirty yards out, takes a touch, and unleashes a brutal dipping shot that Vorm can only wave into the corner.

Coming out of the ground, there's a buzz the like of which I've seldom heard. It matches a debut the like of which I've seldom seen. 'What the fucking hell was THAT?' It wasn't Jo, that's for sure. There's no doubt we've got something a bit special on our hands. Yes, it's only Swansea, yes it's a tiring defence, but Sergio's verve, skill and sheer quality were unmistakable. This is a seriously class act. Carlos who?

Away at Bolton the following week, we sparkle in attack once more. A couple of poor concessions make the final 3-2 margin look closer than it actually was, but it's another great result, achieved in a style far more expansive than we saw last season.

Having arranged a nice break in Paris, Lindsey was somewhat surprised when I slipped into the conversation that I'd booked the Eurostar back to London for early on Sunday morning. 'Why are we going back on Sunday morning when it's a Bank Holiday weekend?' Fair question. Predictable answer. City have a lunchtime date at White Hart Lane.

We're boosted by the signing of Samir Nasri after a protracted saga, and he's selected to start, To our surprise, it's not at the expense of either of our front two. A front four of Silva, Nasri, Dzeko and Aguero seems almost recklessly adventurous, especially for such a big game, away from home. Mancini is turning into Kevin Keegan.

Spurs have no natural defensive midfielders, and the game is wonderfully open and attractive from the start. City are slick and purposeful, Nasri fitting in as if he's been here for years, and we put together some delightful moves which produce plenty of near misses, most notably for Silva, who is once again sublime. Spurs offer plenty of threat themselves, and it's an absolutely cracking match. Our passing is fantastic, one-touch and penetrating. Such a contrast with this time last year, when we seemed to keep the ball just for the sake of it, with neither the ambition nor capability to make it count for something.

It's from one such move that we eventually take the lead. Nasri and Aguero execute a smart one-two, and Dzeko gets across his defender to stretch out and stud the ball past Friedel for a classic striker's goal. Spurs come within inches of equalising when Crouch's full-length diving header from Bale's unbelievable cross – he may be overhyped but he does some truly spectacular stuff – flashes past the post.

Shortly afterwards, Spurs get a corner on the right. Last year, we'd have had all eleven back. This time, Silva, Aguero and Nasri prowl around the halfway line, forcing more aerially threatening Spurs players to stay back and look after them. Dzeko's in our six-yard box as Kompany clears the ball. Silva picks it up and the break is on. Nasri takes over on the left, dinks the ball over and, after a ninety-yard run, Dzeko arches backwards to float a delicate header past the wrong-footed Friedel. Stunning.

So, a 2-0 half-time lead with two fabulous team goals, both finished by a man who looks every inch the player we thought we were getting last January. And he hasn't finished yet. He completes his hat-trick when Aguero nonchalantly holds the ball up for the overlapping Yaya. The big man squares across goal to give Edin an easy tap in.

The next is even better. Aguero lays off to Nasri, spins away, takes the return in his stride, then shows fantastic upper-body strength to hold off Dawson, wrap his left foot round the ball and flash it past Friedel. Utterly brilliant. We have a sleepy few minutes, in which Kaboul heads home unchallenged from a corner, but coast towards the final whistle.

Into injury-time, and one last treat. Dzeko strolls onto a lovely set up from Barry and bends a glorious first-time twenty-five-yard left-foot curler into Friedel's top corner. It puts the cap on a superb individual and team display. As we slowly make our way out of the ground, the conversations all go along similar lines. 'That's the best I've ever seen City play away from home.' Praise indeed, and as an old lag I want to say 'but what about …?' But I have to admit I'm struggling. We were absolutely fantastic.

This wasn't one of those fluky days when everything you hit goes in – we could have scored lots more, and every one of the five we did get was beautifully constructed, combining great teamwork with individual brilliance. And yet, eye-catching as it is, it won't grab tomorrow's headlines. Three hours later, news of United's 8-2 win over a depleted and hapless Arsenal comes through. But this is no bad thing – the last thing we want is the world and his wife tipping us for the title and piling the pressure on with just three games gone. Let them enjoy their 'anything you can do …' jibes – anyone watching the two games will know which is the more impressive performance. Our first major test has been passed handsomely – a season to remember could be upon us.

Absolute Beginners

14 SEPTEMBER 2011, CHAMPIONS LEAGUE GROUP STAGE:
CITY 1 NAPOLI 1

Dzeko's reward for his heroics at White Hart Lane is to be given a nice rest for the next game, at home to Wigan. With Silva pulling the strings, a hat-trick of surgically precise finishes from Aguero sees them off to make it four straight wins. Perfect preparation for our debut in the Champions League.

The draw hasn't exactly been kind, grouping us with Bayern Munich, Villareal and Napoli. But the way we've left everyone in our wake so far this season means we've no need to fear anyone. Our first opponents, Napoli, are also Champions League debutants. It's a lovely evening, and I decide to walk to the ground from the city centre. I end up close to the heavily escorted phalanx of Italian fans. They're very noisy, their chants at a pitch which I've never heard before; deep-throated, guttural and unmistakeably menacing. Every noise sounds full of violent intent. There's a large police cordon but I keep my distance. I'd love to go over to Naples for the return but this makes my mind up already. Still, hopefully we'll be through by then …

Almost kick-off time. It's a night not many of us thought we'd ever see. The undulating plastic football covering the centre circle, that evocative if somewhat pompous music; it's a real event. City start as strongly as we could have hoped, Nasri almost immediately firing just wide. We look as though we're going to overpower them, but they hold firm and from nowhere almost take the lead. Lavezzi makes Kompany look like a mug, before side-footing a beautiful effort well beyond Hart's dive, flush on to the crossbar. It's a wonderful piece of skill, and a stark warning. These guys are no mugs. They're also far more adventurous than one would expect from Italian sides away from home, although the trademark cynicism is present and correct, three defenders taking yellow cards in turn when the electric Aguero looks sets to cause danger.

Napoli remain comfortable until Aguero lays the ball back for Yaya to crash a thundering shot against the underside of the bar. From my seat, with ever deteriorating eyesight and the all-too-frequent failure to remember my specs, the rippling net makes it look as though it's in, but the ball bounces down and is cleared away. The interval soon follows, no goals but an enthralling half, and clearly the strongest opposition we've met so far this year.

The second half has a totally different feel. They've sussed us out. It may be their Champions League debut, but their tactical nous suggests they've had years of experience. They're squeezing the life out of us when we get to within thirty yards of goal, a task assisted by our lack of penetrative width, and their impressive, electrifyingly quick front three of Lavezzi, Hamsik and Cavani look dangerous every time our attacks break down. Hamsik's volley looks like it's given them the lead as it flashes past Hart, but Kompany makes an astonishing clearance off the line.

We don't heed the warning, continuing to press forward in increasing numbers. There's almost an air of inevitability when they take the lead. The weight of stifling bodies lures Barry into an adventurous and risky flicked pass and Napoli seize possession. Our holding midfielders have been enticed too far forward. In the blink of an eye they've got a two on two, and Maggio slips Cavani through to finish expertly past Hart. A sinister primeval roar emanates from the away fans. We've got our work cut out here, big time.

We're unlucky when a delicate near-post flick from Aguero ricochets off the bar to safety but, a few minutes later, we get a free kick twenty-five yards out. Kolarov manages to get the ball up and down and inside the keeper's near post. There's renewed enthusiasm in the stands as we put them under increasingly unsophisticated pressure but Napoli hold firm and, in the end, both sides seem happy enough to share the spoils.

It could certainly have been worse, but it's immediately clear that there's a wholly different dimension to Champions League games. This is not like playing against Wigan and Bolton. By definition, it's playing against teams who are used to winning football matches, who expect to win them and have the tactical variations in their repertoire to win them. With Bayern away next, there's a very real chance that we'll have only one point from the first two games, and be left with it all to do to get out of the group. But it's been a real occasion and I've enjoyed it enormously, even if it's emphasised the fact that we're not quite ready for world domination just yet. And after all, it's English domination which is the real goal for this season. One step at a time …

I'm Carlos Tevez, I'll Play When I Want

27 SEPTEMBER 2011, CHAMPIONS LEAGUE GROUP STAGE: BAYERN MUNICH 2 CITY 0

Two carelessly tossed-away points at Fulham are followed by a hard-fought win over a typically unloveable Everton, after which it's off to Munich for our first ever Champions League away trip. On the plane, I find myself sitting next to a couple of Blues, up at 3.30 a.m. to get from Manchester to the Heathrow flight. Mike and Daz are top guys, typical Blues, and we natter all the way to Munich, arranging to meet up at the Oktoberfest after checking into our respective hotels.

Bloody great. We can't get served anywhere. For us, it's the beer festival without beer. We chat to a couple of Blues who've clearly sunk our ration as well as their own, and they explain that tables are reserved from 4.30 p.m. onwards. So we stroll out of the festival to seek a conventional alehouse, where we're soon reunited with the guys from the Oktoberfest.

They've had a bit of an adventure. They booked themselves on a 'luxury coach journey' from Manchester Piccadilly to the centre of Munich, twenty hours all told, but boasting super-comfortable seats, lots of leg room, beer and entertainment on board, all for £99 return. Bargain.

'We went upstairs, sat ourselves down, really cramped for space. Asked for beer, were told there was one can per passenger, to last all the way to Munich. We were sat directly above the bog, and straight away this horrible stench started wafting through. No way were we having twenty hours of this. First pick-up point was Manchester Airport, so we told the driver we were getting off and needed our bags. 'Can't you wait till Knutsford?' 'No we fucking can't!' So we got our bags and went to the enquiry desk.'

Enquiries revealed that the best route would be via Zurich. 'Zurich – where the fuck's that? Hadn't got a clue.'

Just the four flights and a night's accommodation to book. The boys had come armed with plenty of euros, but they wouldn't stretch this far.

'A mate of mine's a cabbie, so I gave him a call and he went round our house, got my credit card and brought it to the airport. Told the missus it was an emergency. Then I noticed my suitcase – it was one of hers, bloody flower pattern all over it. Alright being hidden away inside a coach, but I wasn't being seen carting that thing round with me. So I slung it. Bought a new one. Told the missus the wheels had buckled.'

There's a special camaraderie on European nights, borne of respect for real fans, prepared to take such time and trouble to follow their team. And this was no different – the Bayern boys were super-friendly, tremendously helpful and irritatingly fluent in English. They too had spent the afternoon indulging in the local brews, and were in great voice.

Our suitcase slinger got pally with one of the Bayern fans, and they decided to go for a shirt-swap. Not replica shirts, just what they happened to be wearing at the time. So it was that our man traded in his smart designer t-shirt for a hideous red and white checked creation cut straight from a cheap 1970s tablecloth. The legend of 'Gingham Dave' was born.

Approaching the stadium, that giant illuminated tyre, home to one of the most successful teams in European football history, you couldn't help but think that just being here was enough in itself. Anything we got from the game would be a bonus.

Mancini's team selection is ultra-bold, especially after the Napoli game – Aguero, Dzeko, Silva and Nasri all start. Tevez has to make do with a place on the bench. The home fans are pumped up and raucous. So are we. *Come on Blues, let's show them what we've got.* And we do. Less than three minutes gone, and Silva gets the ball on the by-line before executing one of his trademark 180 degree spins. Well, he tries to, but is sent crashing to the deck by a sliding tackle from our old friend Boateng. From 150 yards away it looks a certain penalty. But not from fifteen yards away. The ref gives nothing. TV pictures show that we were right and he was wrong.

Within a minute, Dzeko spurns a great chance; twenty minutes later, Richards' barn-storming run is crudely cut short by Boateng's ill-timed lunge. Again, no penalty. Why not? He cuts across Micah, he doesn't play the ball, it's not shoulder to shoulder. *Jesus, this is like playing at Old Trafford.*

Buoyed by the confidence of knowing there's a twelfth man on their side, Bayern start to take a grip on proceedings and after a couple of near misses take the lead. Hart makes a double save, but is powerless to stop Gomez stabbing home the second rebound. The noise is ear-shattering and we need to get to half-time with no further damage. We make it to forty-five minutes, but the one minute of additional time proves disastrous. Kroos is allowed to get a near-post flick on a free kick, and though Hart saves well, Gomez is there to stab home again. It's a crusher – thirty minutes of being the better side, denied two clear penalties yet two down at half-time. Welcome to the realities of life at the home of Champions League aristocrats.

There's still just a vestige of hope if we can get the next goal, but for the first ten minutes we can hardly even get the ball. Time for a change. Time for Tevez? There's activity on the City bench, but not from Carlos – instead, it's the return of Nigel de Jong, replacing Dzeko. Odd substitution when you're 2-0 down? On the face of it yes, but we need to get more ball, and by pushing Yaya further forward, should still carry plenty of threat.

But we don't. There's no discernible improvement as Bayern look increasingly comfortable and much the more likely scorers. Time for Carlos, surely? The lady next to me stares at her phone and exclaims: 'Tevez has refused to come on!' All around, more and more folk are receiving texts from home, confirming the story. Mancini brings on Milner for

Nasri then Kolarov for Barry. These are not the substitutions of a man chasing the game. With Johnson injured and Balotelli suspended, Tevez is the only outright attacking option. Either he's got injured in the warm-up or the stories are true. We'll find out soon enough.

The match peters out, Hart making a couple of great saves to preserve respectability, but all the talk is of Tevez. We get back into central Munich, and settle into a bar with wall-to-wall TVs. There's no sound but, when Mancini is being interviewed, none is needed. A real life ashen-faced Ron Knee, he's obviously seething, with a demeanour none of us have seen before. Soon enough, the transcripts come through on our smartphones, and it's stunning stuff. Tevez has indeed refused to take the field and, as far as Mancini is concerned, 'is finished'. Carlos has hardly built up a reservoir of goodwill over the last nine months or so, and the immediate reaction of those around us is good riddance.

By the time we reach the airport the next morning, it's front page news. Bloke who gets paid £200,000 a week to play football can't be arsed to play football. Outrage, disgust and contempt spew from the mouths of the usual rent-a-quote merchants.

By now, clearly in receipt of advice from his indispensable braincell activation device Kia Joorabchian, Tevez moves quickly to change his story from the initial 'I didn't feel like it' – poor love – to 'it's all been a terrible misunderstanding'. What he'd actually refused to do was warm up again, as he was already raring to go. Yeah right. Zabaleta's body language on the bench as Tevez tried to explain himself told a very different story.

City are swift to announce an internal investigation, and suspend Tevez for two weeks. Hopes that this is from the rafters with a rope round his neck are dashed when TV pictures show him being refused entry to a local golf club. Media opinion is universal. City and Mancini can't back down now; sack him, let him rot, sell him in January but whatever you do don't ever let him wear the shirt again. I don't think too many fans would argue with that.

While Mancini may be disgusted with the episode, a beneficial side-effect is that it's diverted attention from just how poor City's performance for the last hour had been. After a bright, confident start, we slumped alarmingly, never even suggesting a comeback after the first goal and fortunate not to come away with a more severe beating. Of course, goals change games, and who can say how different things might have been had we scored from one of the penalties we ought to have had? However, the lack of fight is a big worry, and we're already in a perilous position after just two games.

The Shape Of Things To Come

23 OCTOBER 2011, PREMIER LEAGUE:
MANCHESTER UNITED 1 CITY 6

For the next few weeks, all anyone who wasn't a City fan could talk to us about was Tevez. They just didn't get it. We didn't give a toss. We'd expected him to go in the summer anyway, he'd hardly played this season and Aguero had been signed as his replacement and was clearly a significant upgrade. As far as we were concerned, Carlos was history. Can we just concentrate on the players we *have* got, please?

The next game, at Blackburn, was notable for a few 'fuck off Tevez' chants and a couple of stunning goals. Adam Johnson's fabulous curler was the first thing he'd done right all day, but was more than enough to compensate. Then, Balotelli scored a breath-taking second, sprinting thirty yards to reach the near post first before leaping athletically to flick Nasri's waist-high cross inside Robinson's near-post. It was a fabulous instinctive goal, and Mario momentarily forgot himself, rushing towards the delirious fans to take their acclaim rather than adopting his normal too cool for school pose. Lurking beneath that sullen exterior is a guy who loves football.

The next week, his brilliantly improvised overhead kick gave us the lead against Villa, setting up another comfortable win. Mario was turning into Denis Law. No bad thing in any event, and especially timely given our next fixture. The big one. United at Old Trafford.

It's the clash of the top two. We're two points clear but by common and especially Trafford-based consent, we haven't played anyone yet, and this will sort the men out from the boys. 'The biggest derby ever', cry the media. Bollocks. It's game nine of thirty-eight. Bigger than last season's FA Cup semi, the pivotal moment in getting thirty-five years of hurt off our backs? Bigger than Denis Law's back-heel? Bigger than the March 1968 shootout which launched us towards the title? Get real. The eyes of the world will be tuned in, but with twenty-nine games to go afterwards it's hardly going to decide anything. Etihad Stadium, third last game of the season – now that really could be the biggest derby of all time …

The build-up is intense, and plenty of pundits think we'll get something from the game. So do I. Robbed. I play it down to friends, trying to manage my own expectations as much as theirs. I've suffered plenty enough at Verminland and decide not to go. As ever, I just want to get it out of the way. It's a day for watching at home in total isolation, perched nervously on the sofa – and probably behind it.

Mancini surprises many with his inclusion of Balotelli, fresh from newspaper reports about him setting fire to his own house with indoor fireworks (great story, even if it was actually one of his mates) but stunning goals in each of his last two outings make him an obvious choice. Ferguson opts for Welbeck over Hernandez but springs a much bigger surprise by selecting Clattenburg over Webb, who only makes the bench.

The game starts in tentative fashion, United on top but without creating any real chances. Midway through the half, United leave Silva in space from a simple throw in and he plays Milner into the left edge of United's area. His cut-back goes through to Balotelli, on the edge of the box. Mario lets the ball come across him, and calmly side-foots a first-time daisy-cutter six inches inside the post.

Without moving from the scoring position or changing his expression, he celebrates by lifting his shirt over his head to reveal a t-shirt bearing the slogan 'Why Always Me?' Fabulous goal, even better celebration, and well worth taking a yellow card for. At home, my celebration is as calm as Mario's and I just stay seated on the sofa. *No point getting too excited, they'll only come back and get a dodgy pen and an injury time winner, so don't get your hopes up.*

We stay on the front foot, create a couple of promising situations but don't quite manage to get the run of the ball; even so, United scarcely threaten at all. Half-time, and it could hardly have gone better, but the business end of the match is still to come. Time for another beer, and fifteen minutes of trying not to think about what the next fifty might bring.

Just a minute into the second half, Milner heads Ferdinand's clearance to Balotelli. Mario cushions his layoff to Aguero, and spins immediately in anticipation of a return pass. Sergio delivers a delicately weighted through ball, catching Jonny Evans on the wrong side, with Mario's pace and strength taking him through for a one-on-one with de Gea. A desperate Evans makes a grab for Mario, who hits the deck inside the box. I get rather excited. Clattenburg immediately produces a red card that even Ferguson can't dispute, but there's no penalty. I'm livid, until replays show that the foul is clearly just outside the area.

United move to 4-4-1, but we're well on top and attack at will. The outstanding Richards surges inside before Anderson trips him from behind for a blatant spot kick. Not for

Clattenburg though, who indicates graphically his interpretation that this obvious foul had just been a 'coming together'. Clattenburg was perfectly placed, and I can think of only two reasons why he wouldn't have given it. He's either blind or he's bent. And I've yet to see him with a guide dog.

It was, at least, marvellous news for defence lawyers throughout the land.

'The defendant was witnessed kneeing Mr Tapper in the groin, punching him repeatedly in the face before pummelling him with a series of brutal kicks to the head.'

'Indeed, M'Lord, but surely this merely constitutes a coming together between my client and his alleged victim.'

'Absolutely. Case dismissed.'

It's a shocking non-decision, but City shrug off the injustice, moving the ball around fluently and searching patiently for an opening. Once again, Silva's incessant movement provides it, as he spins off Anderson to play Milner in with a cute reverse pass. Milner's instant first-time cross is dispatched unfussily by Balotelli, who remembers to keep his shirt on as he celebrates in more conventional fashion. It's an outstanding team goal, with so many elements to admire.

One more and we can relax, and five minutes later we get it, a slick first-time passing move playing Richards in down the right. Micah's perfect low cross is swept joyously home by the onrushing Aguero for a classic striker's goal. Once again, utterly magical football, and this time I treat the neighbours to a proper celebration. Surely not even United can come back from three down against us, especially as they're down to eleven men …

We're cruising, sub Dzeko firing inches wide with his first touch, but with ten minutes left, Fletcher curls in a twenty-yarder to cut the deficit to 3-1 and trigger the same old commentary: 'They couldn't, could they?' I'm not sitting quite so easily. There's always that vestige of doubt. And fear. Imagine the humiliation – 3-0 up, ten minutes to go, down to ten men and we still couldn't beat them. I'm back to paying too much attention to the top-left corner of the screen, but the reality is that they have nothing to offer.

Almost ninety minutes, and Barry's glancing header from Nasri's corner drifts beyond the far post. Lescott cuts it back for Dzeko to knee in from three yards in classic Goat fashion. All over now for sure, and empty red seats become ever more prominent. The board goes up, showing four minutes of added time, and United surge forward as if they're just the one down. Or maybe they think they can still get it back? They lose possession, the break is on and Dzeko calmly sets Silva through. Into the box, eyes on the advancing de Gea, Silva nonchalantly slides the ball through the biggest available space – between the keeper's legs – and into the net for 5-1. Oh, the memories.

From the restart, Silva is in space yet again, and puts Dzeko clear on goal. Going for power instead of accuracy, Dzeko blazes high and wide and Mancini throws his hands to the heavens in disappointment. Great reaction. He really wants to humiliate them.

United still press forward in search of consolation, but we clear with ease and Ferdinand's weak header finds Silva, well in his own half. A touch to cushion, then a stunning volleyed pass dissects United's central two and allows Dzeko to surge forward without breaking stride. This time going for placement rather than power, he slots past de Gea to send City fans into disbelieving ecstasy and put breakables in our living room in grievous danger.

The final whistle. 6-1. *Six-one.* Did this actually happen? The texts start to pour in, some from folk who think I must have been at the game. Do I wish I had been? Course I do. Am I bothered? Not even slightly. The consolations are plentiful:

1. I am uncontaminated.
2. I have quicker access to champagne.

3. I can rejoice in the sight of Gary Neville.
4. I can spend the rest of my Sunday watching the replays again and again.

First up, even before the champagne, is Gary Neville. Don't listen to what other folk say. A face not even a mother could love? Not a bit of it. Today, Gary Neville's face is a thing of absolute beauty. It exudes agony, misery and pain. I could gaze at it for ever. Dressed presciently in black suit and black tie, he must feel as if he's at the funeral of a loved one. Going through the goals one by one, his discomfort is a joy to behold. It must be excruciating. Come on, Gary, you can't need the money. Why put yourself through it? Be gone from our screens forever. *Please.*

Reflecting on the afternoon, so many thoughts come to mind. First of all, Big Mal. The man for whom humiliating United at Old Trafford meant more than anything. How he'd have rejoiced in this, yet surely even he wouldn't have walked in front of the Stretford End predicting six. Four maybe, but *six*?

Then, Mancini's measured, respectful reaction. Just another three points. Praise for United's mentality in still trying to recover the game when all seemed lost. Acknowledgement that they're still ahead of us, even if the gap is closing. The sending-off helped. The players follow the same line – great result but doesn't suddenly mean we're top dogs. Long long way to go.

Compare and contrast. After the meaningless Charity Shield game, Rooney wasted no time in tweeting his legions of mindless followers that they'd given us a football lesson. After the thrilling Carling Cup semi a couple of years ago, 180 minutes of gripping football decided by an injury time goal, Rooney again dismissed us as totally inferior, while the club, arrogant and loathsome to the core, put out their piss-taking victory song over the PA and locked us in to listen to it. Then Ferguson boasted that they'd absolutely battered us and should have had six or seven. Well, Baconface, here we actually did score six or seven – and it should have been ten – so put that in your graceless, arrogant, bitter, whingeing, whining, repulsive, poisonous gob and smoke on it.

The team were heroes one and all, everyone contributing mightily, but on this biggest of stages there were four real stand-out performers. Richards, Sky's Man of the Match, was a powerhouse both in defence and attack, a player whose renaissance under Mancini has been remarkable. He's back to being the player we thought we'd got when he first broke into the team, and then some. Milner, whose first year was indifferent and uncertain, now looks as though he really belongs, the epitome of a team player but with an ability to hurt teams, evidenced by his vital assists for the first two goals.

Then there's Balotelli. No one can doubt that this is a major talent. This guy could become as loved as all the great mavericks of the past. The affection for Mario – even, amazingly, from a number of United fans I see in the days after the game – suggests he's well on the way to becoming an iconic figure.

Watching the reruns, you can see what a natural striker he is. For his second goal, he makes a run anticipating Silva's cross, steps back when it doesn't come, then makes the same run again as Milner latches onto Silva's little pass. Impeccably timed, well onside, and an easy finish. For Aguero's goal, he sees Sergio make his run and aborts his own, pulling out to an unmarked position on the edge of the box, giving Micah the angle to pick either of them out. This is no muppet. It's a striker with genuine instinct and intelligence for finding space.

Finally, David Silva, week by week climbing the list of my all-time favourite City players. What a performance!

The eye-catcher was his astonishing volleyed pass for the final goal, but the highlight for me was something much less spectacular. His little pass for Milner as he runs behind him to set up the second is something I can watch again and again. How does he know he's there? One of the pundits, Jamie Redknapp I think, describes him as playing as though he's got wing mirrors, and it's a perfect description. Like Ali Bernarbia, he carries a picture in his head of where everyone is and where they're moving to; unlike Ali, we've got him in the prime of his career, rather than the twilight. Younger City fans don't know how lucky they are.

It's a result which will never be forgotten, but it's only three points. Will it have a psychological effect? On United, I doubt it – they've had the odd savage beating before and come back even stronger. On us, I genuinely think so. Mancini talks endlessly about the importance of the players having a strong mentality, and the self-belief which comes from battering your biggest rivals in their own back yard can only help us when we're in the melting pot in future.

Comparing this with the unforgettable 5-1 of 1989 shows just how far we've come. That was an epic day, but only ever a day. None of us expected it to be a springboard to greater things; it was a wonderful one-off where we rammed it up those big-spending bastards. At the final whistle it was the nailed-on highlight of our season, although few of us would have been so pessimistic as to think it would remain the highlight of the next twenty-odd years as well. Today was also fantastic, unforgettable, and will always be enshrined in City folklore, but more than anything it was a statement. *This is how good we really are. This is what the rest of you have got to beat.* Truly a pivotal day.

So, five points clear after nine games. Who'd have thought it? A long long way to go, though. And, after all, we haven't played anyone yet ...

This Is How It Feels To Beat City

12 DECEMBER 2011, PREMIER LEAGUE: CHELSEA 2 CITY 1

No 'after the Lord Mayor's Show' with this City. On the following Wednesday, we batter Wolves in the Carling Cup, before beating them again in the league three days later, the only black mark being Kompany's red card for a professional foul after a rare slip up from Joe.

Kompany is suspended for the trip to QPR, who exploit Savić's inexperience and give us a very uncomfortable time. Eventually, our wealth of attacking flair gets us out of trouble, superb goals from Dzeko, Silva and Yaya securing a 3-2 win in a pulsating game. Next up, a surprisingly unbeaten Newcastle and a comfortable win, the highlight being Mario's preposterously arrogant celebration after opening the scoring from the spot.

Tim Krul had resorted to all kinds of gamesmanship before the kick was taken, claiming the ball wasn't properly on the spot and giving Mario plenty of earache. Mario just ambled up in his familiar stuttering way, eyes on the keeper, and rolled the ball into the corner. He then stood still and imperious, staring straight at Krul, arms folded across his chest. 'Don't fuck with me, boy!' The big-screen replays were lapped up all round the ground.

We've powered on relentlessly since the 6-1, the only disappointment being that we haven't extended our lead at the top. Despite playing as though still shell-shocked, United have eked out three straight wins where their opponents have been the better side but failed to take their chances. Five points isn't that much, and their ability to secure undeserved wins when playing poorly may yet come back to haunt us.

Next is a trip to Anfield, not exactly a happy hunting ground. We get some encouragement the previous day when United are held at home by Newcastle, and the press are full of Ferguson's rage at the decision to award Newcastle a penalty. Even I have to admit that it's a shocking decision, though the equally obvious error in awarding United a free kick from which they score their own goal receives rather less attention.

With Kompany reinstated, our first half performance at Anfield is controlled and accomplished. Vinny's 'header' gives us a fully deserved lead, but Liverpool soon level when Lescott's deflection of Adam's wayward shot wrong-foots an overcommitted Hart. The second half is much more even, and when Mario is harshly sent off near the end, we're hanging on. Hart makes an absolutely stunning save to deny Carroll at the death, following up with a great block as Suarez attempts to net the rebound. Just how vital might Hart's heroics prove to be when the points are totted up at the end of the season?

Meanwhile, our Champions League adventure is nearing an end. We secure two victories over Villareal, the first at home with an injury-time winner which sees Mancini's emotions on the touchline fully unleashed, then in much more comfortable style at El Madrigal. Everything rests on our trip to Napoli and, like most City fans, I'm just not brave enough to travel. We concede soft goals early in each half and miss a host of late chances to get the equaliser which would put us back in control of our destiny. It's a frustrating, bitterly disappointing evening, and though I try to console myself with the thought that the season's real target is the Premier League, I still slope off to bed feeling really gutted.

Norwich are next up, and they're well in the game until we pull away towards the end, in what is becoming trademark fashion. This game brings a first – the first City goal I've ever witnessed to which I've reacted by bursting out laughing. Who else but Mario? Clever play from Johnno sets him up just six yards out, and his first attempt hits Ruddy and balloons into the air. Mario follows it in and, as the ball descends just beneath the crossbar, nonchalantly turns it into the net with a flick of his shoulder. It's an extravagant piece of showmanship which brings the house down when it's replayed on the big screen. And inevitably brings cries of 'disrespecting the opposition' from the likes of Crooks et al. Get over yourselves, you pious knobheads. In the next breath you'll be bemoaning the fact that there aren't entertainers in the game anymore.

Our final Champions League group match brings Bayern to the Etihad, and a reunion with Mike and Daz. We reminisce about our fantastic trip to Munich while enjoying a traditional Brazilian dining concept in Bem Brasil. Basically you just sit there for as long as you like, while waiters relentlessly proffer various cuts of meat and slice off as much as you want. Not many doctors would encourage eating half your own body weight of meat in a single sitting. And it doesn't half bugger up your digestive system for the next couple of days. Unreservedly recommended nonetheless.

We need to win, and hope that whipping boys Villareal can somehow stifle Napoli. Smart goals from Silva and Yaya see us comfortably home, but Napoli ease past their opponents to consign us to the Europa League. One big consolation is that we'll be joined there by United, whose shock defeat in Basel knocks them out of the easiest group of the eight. They really aren't that good, and tonight is much more of a blow to them than it is to us.

But now it's crunch time. Chelsea away, then Arsenal at home. Get through these unscathed and we'll be in great shape. The Chelsea game is a Monday nighter. I've got a spare ticket and I am joined by my Gooner mate the Pollster. He's taken me to a few big Arsenal games over recent years, and it's been very much how the other half live. They've been the team in the running for honours, playing the best football, and I've enjoyed being able to watch important games largely free from emotional attachment. Now the boot's on the other foot. We're the hottest ticket in town, the team that everyone wants to see in the flesh.

Chelsea's form under the spectacularly unengaging Andre Villas-Boas has been pretty indifferent, and if they lose to us tonight they'll be thirteen points adrift. We start majestically, with Aguero's superb spin and pass putting Balotelli clean through. He side-steps Cech with typical nonchalance before rolling the ball into the net and celebrating in that 'just doing my job' kind of way. Less than two minutes in, and it's party time already. Pollster sustains a cut to the forehead, unprepared for my overzealous enthusiasm. These southerners just don't celebrate goals like we do.

For the next twenty minutes we play our best football of the season, which really is saying something. Balotelli is utterly imperious, his movement, speed and supreme close control making him stand out even in this exalted company. Aguero carves himself a great chance after a flowing move, but drags the ball wide. Shortly afterwards, some more slick play frees Silva in the area. He tries to cut across Bosingwa, only to be brought down for what looks like the most obvious of penalties. Clattenburg, for it is he, is ten yards away with a clear view, and implores Silva to get up. City players are visibly bewildered. When I see the replays later, I'm incensed. It's such a clear-cut decision that you can't see how a visually competent, honest man wouldn't have given it.

We remain in the ascendancy, but Chelsea start to come more into it and, with their first attack of any note, they equalise. Sturridge easily gets past Clichy and his cutback is volleyed home by the unattended Meireles. We hear from the home fans for the first time tonight.

The rest of the game is well balanced until a stupid foul from Clichy earns him a second yellow. It's not been Clichy's best evening, and this could be a very costly transgression.

We've got more than half an hour to survive, but are coping well enough as we enter the final ten minutes. Then, a Chelsea corner is cleared and Sturridge's shot is blocked at point-blank range by Lescott. Chelsea players and fans appeal in unison for handball, and Clattenburg points immediately to the spot with theatrical relish. Harsh, but you've seen them given, though seldom with such undisguised enthusiasm. Lampard ignores Hart's attempts to psych him out, and dispatches the kick with aplomb.

We're not coming back from this, and the final whistle confirms our first league defeat. 'One Step Beyond' booms from the PA as Chelsea fans celebrate as though they've won the Premier League, FA Cup, Champions League, World Cup, Grand National and Superbowl simultaneously. *This is how it feels to beat City.*

I go home muttering about the non-penalty, and am almost speechless when I see the incident again. A 2-0 lead against a team short on confidence would have been bloody tough to claw back, even with such a long time to play. Our lead is down to just two points, and we've got a resurgent Arsenal to face at the weekend. It's a bit early in the season for squeaky bum time, but it feels like it's upon us already.

All Is Quiet On New Year's Day

1 JANUARY 2012, PREMIER LEAGUE: SUNDERLAND 1 CITY 0

The Arsenal game is huge, and not just for us. They've recovered well from their dismal, injury-strewn start to the season and are now the in-form team, with seven wins in their last eight. It promises to be a cracker, and it is. There's only one goal, a scrappy tap-in from Silva, but this belies the quality of both teams' football and the plethora of near misses at both ends.

Balotelli produces a jaw-dropping piece of skill to bring down a high ball in a crowded box, but Szceszny saves brilliantly. He and Hart bring off a series of other great saves, Zabaleta thunders one against their post and van Persie's late strike is ruled out on a hairsbreadth offside decision which could easily have gone against us. The general consensus is that we just deserved it and also that, despite the various eye-catching scorelines over the past three months, it's the game of the season so far. It's certainly an emphatic way for us to show the world that the Chelsea defeat was an unlucky one-off, and that we're ready to embark on another long unbeaten run.

Stoke are next, and put up minimal resistance as we dispatch them 3-0, ensuring that we're the Christmas Number One. The usual stat is trotted out – no team top of the Premier League at Christmas has ever failed to go on and win the title. I can't imagine any City fan taking a blind bit of notice. There's a first time for everything.

The next two games look highly winnable, away at West Brom and Sunderland. The Baggies play like an away side, parking the bus from the start, but their fans don't seem to mind. We're out of sorts, and lucky to survive when Albion hit the post, but slowly assert ourselves. Mario thumps a twenty-five-yarder against the bar, and in the second half his spectacular, if mishit, effort finds the net, only to be wrongly disallowed for offside. Aguero misses a great chance late on and we come away with just a point. Albion fans party like its 1999. Just stopping us winning is cause for major celebration. We're going to have to get used to this sort of thing.

Sunderland on New Year's Day. I've got tickets and Plan A had been to spend New Year's Eve in Manchester and then drive to the match. Instead, we decide to go out with some friends of Lindsey's in Brighton. Brighton to Sunderland with a raging hangover and limited transport options is not a feasible proposition. I'll have to write off the tickets and watch it on telly.

On our way to the coast, I'm following United's game at home to Blackburn, which produces the staggering bonus of a 3-2 defeat. I'll certainly be in party mood tonight. Lindsey warns me that one of the chaps we're meeting is a United fan, and not to wind him up. It transpires that he didn't even know they'd played today, let alone lost. When they boast about having countless millions of fans, presumably this is what they mean. I bring him up to date with events in a typically understated way.

We return home in time to watch our game on TV, and it's an ideal opportunity to take advantage of United's cock-up. Sunderland have just appointed Martin O'Neill, and we're first in line to suffer from the inevitable upsurge in form that follows a change in leadership. However, their injury list is so long that even the most elastic New Manager Bounce seems unlikely to lift them high enough to get a result. With a ridiculous fixture schedule requiring us to take on Liverpool at home just forty-eight hours later, Mancini puts Silva and Aguero on the bench. No one seriously imagines that we'll need them.

O'Neill sets his team up in a similar formation to that employed by Roy Hodgson a few days earlier. Offer him a draw at kick-off and he'll bite your hand off. City dominate possession but, without Silva's creative spark, there aren't many real chances. Half-time arrives without us having troubled the scorers, but I'm still reasonably relaxed. The big guns will be coming on soon.

The second half continues in similar vein, though we're now showing rather more urgency. It's just a matter of time. Silva joins the fray after an hour and immediately makes a difference, but still no breakthrough. The clock ticks on. Aguero gets the call. I'm getting more concerned. Silva's shot is parried by Mignolet, and the marauding Richards pounces on the rebound. He hits the ball into the ground, it bounces up past the keeper and comes back off the bar. Sunderland hack it clear. I beat the floor in frustration. I'm getting seriously wound up now. Surely we can't fail to beat this lot?

As we move into added time, it looks as though we'll be shut out again. We create one final opening. Aguero's shot is well struck but hammers flush into the body of a Sunderland defender. The ball rebounds to one of their players and they move it upfield. Looks like that's that. But suddenly, for the first time, they throw men forward. They move the ball through to Sessegnon on the edge of the area, and his reverse ball plays in Ji, with just Hart to beat. I can scarcely believe my eyes. Ji stays calm, rounds Hart, and rolls the ball home. Martin Tyler screeches in ecstasy. Lindsey utters 'oh my God!' I can't speak at all.

The final whistle blows. We weren't great, but still did enough to have won comfortably. They've had one chance all game, which replays are now showing to have been offside, and they've scored from it. One point from two games where everyone expected six. We've worked so hard, played so brilliantly, to establish a lead at the top and it's been frittered away in the space of just five days. I'm absolutely at boiling point. Normally I just get depressed when we lose, but this time the red mist descends. I need to take it out on something. We don't have a cat, so the kitchen bin gets it instead. Really gets it. An unscheduled trip to Homebase beckons.

I calm down soon enough, slipping into the more familiar state of resignation. I can't remember the last time I'd felt so ridiculously angry. Probably 1987, after the filthy cheating Palace scum brutalised our youngsters at Maine Road. I've never forgiven that club and still wish them nothing but ill. I don't feel remotely that way towards Sunderland, they played the way anyone would have done against us in the circumstances and just got lucky. Very lucky. When professional in-love-with-himself attention-seeking witless pillock Robbie Savage later claims that they deserved to win, it confirms everything you need to know about him.

I'm not pleased about losing my temper, and reflect on why it happened. Partly the circumstances, a travesty of a result secured by a last-minute offside goal. Partly Martin Tyler's joy at seeing the goal go in, and the sense that he was delighted we'd been done over. But it's his job to generate excitement, and it was such an unimaginable denouement that you can hardly blame him. Partly the hangover, which put me in an even more grouchy mood than normal. But more than anything, it's the fact that I'd assumed – presumed – that we were going to win. This is not like me at all. It's not like City fans at all. We never take anything for granted. That's what *they* do, that's part of why everyone hates them. That's why they're such appallingly graceless losers, that arrogant, blithe assumption that they'll always win making their defeats so much harder to stomach.

It's a lesson well learned. This sort of thing has to be nipped in the bud. From now on, I'll be back to the traditional City mentality of thinking that something's bound to go wrong. If it does, then I won't be quite so disappointed, and certainly not angry; if it doesn't, the delight will be intensified. For one fleeting moment I'd experienced what it's like to be a United fan, and I can tell you it's truly, truly, horrible. It makes you really not a very nice person. It won't be happening again.

Mind-Blowing Decision

8 JANUARY 2012, FA CUP THIRD ROUND:
CITY 2 MANCHESTER UNITED 3

The day after we hammer Norwich, I'm doing a bit of Christmas shopping in Manchester when I remember it's third round draw day. My mind flashes back to that wonderful afternoon at Wembley. I wouldn't mind another one of those. I scroll onto the BBC Sport page on my Blackberry, fully expecting to see the usual tie against a lower league team. Instead, second tie out of the hat, it says Manchester City v Manchester United. I think for a moment that I must be on the wrong page, that it's rerunning some of the pivotal games from last season's competition. But it isn't.

Bloody hell, this is all we need. We've already got Liverpool, Everton and Spurs to play in January. Now we've also got two Carling Cup semi-final ties against Liverpool as well as a cup-tie derby. It's an horrendous schedule, coming at a time when we lose the Toures to the African Cup of Nations. I don't expect any sympathy. Neither should we get any. It's what United have had to put up with for decades. Mancini will have to manage his resources very skilfully. But while I'd love us to win another cup, there's only one thing that really matters. The Premier League. I'd give up the cup games now – yes, even one against United – if it guaranteed we'd win the title.

The build-up, certainly in Manchester, has been way over the top. Yet another biggest derby of all time. Give over. Truth be told, I reckon neither camp would be too upset to go out. Laughably, but predictably, the United press contingent position the match as a season's derby decider, balancing our 6-1 demolition job in the league with their win in the Community Shield.

I arrive at the ground in the least anxious state I've ever been for a derby game. Of course I want us to win, but I'm so preoccupied with the league that this game almost feels like a nuisance. If we get through to the later stages then I'm sure I'll feel differently. I half expect Mancini to leave out a few key players, but he springs a surprise by resting only Joe Hart to give Costel Pantilimon – who looks about seven feet tall – some big match experience. United are at full strength, and we enjoy serenading their contingent of fans with repeated renditions of 'you lucky bastards, it should have been ten'.

The game kicks off and straight away we're camped in their half, probing for openings. A couple of half-chances come to nothing, and United eventually get some respite, with Rooney picking the ball up just in our half. Behind me, Oscar greets him with a lusty cry of 'fuck off, Rooney, you fat granny-shagger!' Rooney plays the ball out wide to Valencia and sprints towards the area. As Valencia's cross comes in, Rooney contorts himself to power a header against the underside of the bar, whence it rebounds over the line.

Stuffy bastards! First time they've been anywhere near our goal and they've bloody well scored. Pantilimon's first touch is to pick the ball out of the net. But there's plenty of time left, and no need to get too concerned just yet.

A couple of minutes later, Nani has the ball in midfield but is dispossessed by an exquisite Kompany tackle, taking the ball cleanly on the slide before playing the ball out to start another City attack. Rooney's straight into referee Chris Foy's ear. The referee hadn't remotely looked like blowing his whistle but suddenly does so, before immediately brandishing a red card at Kompany. *What the hell is that about?* There's disbelief all around.

Mr Angry in front of me turns round and asks: 'Did I fucking miss something there?' I just shake my head. It looked a perfectly good – indeed quite superb – tackle to me, but TV replays so often show something very different from what you thought you saw at the time. You have to assume that this is one of those. Kompany's reaction suggests otherwise. He trudges off, clearly in a state of complete shock.

We respond well, urged on by an aggrieved crowd now far more passionate than at the start of the match. But United are set up to counter-attack, and against ten men can do so even more effectively. Welbeck scores when de Jong is slow to close him down, then Valencia is brought down by the hapless Kolarov for a clear penalty. Rooney's shot is saved by Pantilimon but the rebound comes straight back to him, and he nods it home before kissing his badge provocatively in front of the City fans. I've always acknowledged Rooney as a fantastic footballer, but my God he's a revolting piece of work.

Half-time, 3-0 down and down to ten men. It's not ideal. They could get six here. Or seven. Our period of extravagant celebration of the 6-1 could be much shorter than we ever imagined. I'd settle for a 3-0 defeat right now – just put it down as one of those days and concentrate on winning the big one.

In the second half, United don't show too much appetite for rubbing our noses in it, despite the exhortations of the moronic hordes. Instead, when City get a free kick twenty-five yards out, Kolarov bends the ball over the wall and past Lindegaard to at least bring about a shred of respectability. United bring on Paul Scholes, news of whose return to the fray prior to the match had been greeted with derision by Blues everywhere. Who next, Eric Cantona? Bryan Robson? Bobby Charlton?

We're trying to make a real go of this, but look set to be put completely out of it when a clumsy challenge from Kolarov upends Valencia for an obvious penalty. Chris Foy waves play on. Riddled with guilt? Afraid of causing a riot? Or just totally incompetent?

A few minutes later, Scholes makes his first meaningful contribution with a misplaced pass which puts Milner in space. His low cross is swept towards goal by Aguero, and Lindegaard can only parry it back out. Sergio slams the loose ball home and, with half-an-hour left, it's 3-2 and definitely game on. As the rain lashes down, the prospect of an embarrassing massacre has given way to the very real possibility of an extraordinary comeback.

The force is with us. United are under constant pressure and have a lucky escape when Kolarov's cross is handled by Phil Jones. Urged on by a frenzied crowd, we just don't get the run of the ball in United's area as ricochets and deflections fall agonisingly out of reach. A late free kick from Kolarov brings one final chance, and the rational part of my brain thinks 'the last thing we need is a bloody replay'. But as Tina Turner never said, what's rational thinking got to do with it? Everyone's out of their seats as Kolarov lashes the ball goalwards. Lindegaard can only parry it out, and Lescott looks set to bury the rebound. Excruciatingly, the ball somehow evades him and is hacked to safety.

Seconds later, the final whistle blows and the response of the two sets of fans is extraordinary. United's muted celebrations reflect relief rather than ecstasy, while City are given a rousing ovation. It's very strange. I've never been less distraught immediately after losing a derby. The talk is all about City's 'moral victory'. And the consolation prize of at least being able to concentrate on the league for once has a material value. Had we won, it transpires that we'd have been away at Liverpool, three days after playing there in the Carling Cup semi. We needed that like a hole in the head.

It's only as we make the long journey home that I start to feel like a man whose team has lost a derby ought to feel. Moral victories don't count for much once the emotions have died down. We're out of the Cup at the first hurdle, to our bitterest rivals. The fact that folks on the radio are saying Kompany's dismissal was absolutely ridiculous doesn't help. We're still out.

Back home, there's only one thing to do. Take a look at that red card. I fast forward to the incident and am utterly gobsmacked. It's the worst decision I've seen in over forty-five years of watching football. The ball is taken cleanly and fairly.

Two-footed, arguably – what sliding tackle isn't – but nowhere in the laws is 'two-footed tackle' referred to as punishable. The criteria are recklessness, danger to the opponent, excessive force, being out of control. The tackle is not reckless. It's not dangerous. Vinny is not out of control. He doesn't use excessive force. There's nothing wrong with it at all.

Inevitably, despite the overwhelming evidence and opinion to the contrary, Ferguson is adamant that the tackle was a bad one: 'Nani could have been seriously hurt had he not jumped out of the way.' This is not a compelling argument. Nani would leap out of the way if approached by a four-year-old girl brandishing a soft-scoop vanilla ice cream garnished with extra-menacing hundreds and thousands. As always, Ferguson's motives are transparent – try to make sure that the FA uphold the sending off in the wake of the inevitable appeal. The outcome is as inevitable as the appeal itself, with the authorities choosing to back the referee as they always do unless he himself admits to a mistake. And how often do these guys do that?

Only after the appeal is denied does Vinny make his point. He posts a measured entry on his Facebook page, asking that interpretations of 'dangerous' tackles are made clear, and pleading that his own dismissal shouldn't be seen as a benchmark for future decisions. No bleating, just trying to make sure that other games aren't ruined by any similarly absurd interpretations. Now that's class. Something *they* would never understand. But then nice guys never win, do they? Or do they?

Beauty And The Beast

22 JANUARY 2012, PREMIER LEAGUE: CITY 3 TOTTENHAM 2

After a narrow, nervy win at Wigan, we're just about keeping United at bay. But according to the media – albeit primarily the southern element – they're not the only ones we should be worried about. Spurs have put together a tremendous run of form, and are just a couple of points behind United. Apparently, they're playing the best football of any team in the league – indeed the way some of the press go on, you'd think it was the best in the history of the game, making the Barca of recent years, Brazil's 1970 team and the Real Madrid of Puskas and di Stefano look like plodding cart-horses by comparison.

I've a good few mates who are Spurs fans, all top blokes but all afflicted by that hereditary condition common to Tottenham supporters – they think their team is better than it is. Always have done. Always will do. They can't help themselves, any more than City fans can stop ourselves fearing the worst, thinking that we'll find a way to pluck defeat from certain victory, that we're not safe even if we're three goals up and well into added time. It's in our respective DNAs.

The game gets a big build-up, with everyone expecting an end-to-end thriller, but the first half is anything but. Spurs' main priority is containment and City aren't moving the ball quickly enough to engineer clear openings. Silva, as ever, is at the heart of our best moments but the half-chances we do create don't seriously trouble Friedel. Tottenham don't cause Hart any concern whatsoever.

The second half is very different, and we start to pin Spurs back. We finally open them up when Silva makes one of his delightful reverse passes and Nasri latches on to it with a run reminiscent of his Arsenal days. Without breaking stride, he puts his foot through the ball, lashing it high past Friedel to give us a well-deserved lead. It's a glorious goal, fitting the occasion, and demands Spurs to come out and show us what all the fuss has been about. But before they even get the chance to do so they're two down, with a goal as scruffy as the first one was magnificent. Nasri's corner is flicked on by Dzeko and bundled home at the far post by Lescott.

We just need to consolidate, be sensible for a few minutes, and let them get used to the idea of being out of the game. Instead, a routine hoof downfield brings about a hideous misjudgement from Savić. He gets too far under the ball and his misdirected header sets Defoe away towards the corner of the box. Hart makes his job easier by storming out to meet him. Defoe calmly sidesteps the keeper and rolls the ball home. From nowhere, Spurs are back in the game.

Within three minutes, they're level. This time there's nothing anybody could have done as Gareth Bale clips a superb, curling twenty-yard side-footer across and beyond Hart and into the net. It's a terrific goal, the Spurs fans understandably go ballistic and the rest of us can't believe it. Just four minutes ago we were two up and set to wallop them – now, they have all the momentum and are favourites to win.

Mancini reacts to the shock turn of events by bringing on Balotelli for Dzeko. Spurs are defending for all they're worth, and shut the door on a couple of half-openings, the second seeing Scott Parker get in a brave block from Balotelli which leads to a minor kerfuffle before play continues.

As we move towards added time, both teams continue to look for a winner, and at least the second half has provided the spectacle that Sky were promising their viewers. Suddenly, another blunder from Savić allows Spurs to play in Bale down the left, and we're in real danger. We can see Defoe peeling off towards the far post, in acres of space. Bale looks up, and slides a low ball across the face of goal. It looks perfect. Hart has been taken out of the game and it's just a question of whether Defoe can get a foot to the ball to slide it home. He does get a foot to the ball. *What a fucking nightmare. 2-0 and we fucked it up.* I can scarcely look as I wait to see the net bulge but, incredibly, it doesn't. Defoe hasn't quite been able to get enough on the ball, and has steered it just wide. It's an unbelievable escape, Gazza against the Germans at Euro '96 revisited. A couple of minutes ago, I'd have been really disappointed with a point, but now it doesn't feel so bad.

We're well into added time. Clichy lumps a hopeful ball forward and, somehow, Mario finds himself bearing down on goal, trying to tame the bouncing ball. As he looks to get a shot away, a clumsy, lunging scissor tackle by Ledley King drags him to the ground. Howard Webb duly points to the spot and there's little protest from the Spurs defenders.

It'll be pretty much the last kick of the game. It's worth two points which could ultimately define our season. Pressure doesn't come any more intense than this. But Mario has never missed a penalty for us. Apparently, he's never missed a penalty for anyone. His technique of watching the keeper while shaping to strike the ball, then directing his shot accordingly, looks foolproof. I wouldn't say I'm serene, but I'm certainly pretty relaxed, even though Friedel should know what to expect. Last year, with Villa, he was on the receiving end of two Mario penalties, being made to look stupid both times.

Mario's preferred approach is to roll the ball to the keeper's left. When he pauses during his run-up, Friedel takes a big step to his left, narrowing the gap on that side. Mario watches what's going on and calmly side-foots the ball into the opposite corner. Friedel dives across at full stretch but can't get anywhere near it. Mario raises his arms to the horizontal and takes the acclaim. He knew he'd score. Everyone knew he'd score. It's a priceless three points which, when the ball flashed across to Defoe just two minutes earlier, looked like it would have been no points at all. It makes our celebrations all the more ecstatic, the dismay for Spurs and their fans all the more extreme.

It's a jubilant jog back to the car for a nice drive home. It'll be even better if Arsenal can beat United while we're on the road. I'm full of that warm glow you get with a last-minute winner in a huge game. Then I switch on the radio. Outrage is pouring out of the speakers. Balotelli the antichrist stamped on Parker's head and should be thrown out of the game. Lescott brutally elbowed a couple of Spurs players and should have been sent off. Our darling, daring, dashing Tottenham have been denied their rightful spoils in an appalling travesty of justice. All that money and still grubby, classless, northern Manchester City have to resort to savage brutality to quell the finest purest purveyors of the beautiful game this country has ever seen.

I listen to this stuff in stunned silence. Were they at the same game as me? Sure, we got lucky with Defoe's miss but no-one can argue that over the game as a whole we were worthy winners. But for Savić's ghastly error, Spurs were on for a real caning. I don't remember any great protests about these alleged incidents of extreme violence. It completely spoils the journey, as does the news of a scarcely merited win for United at the Emirates. I arrive back home in a pretty grouchy mood, ridiculous given the thrilling victory I'd witnessed just three hours earlier. I head straight for the Sky+.

The incident everyone is talking about is replayed again and again. In real time, there's nothing to it. In super-slow motion it looks appalling. Parker charges down Mario's shot and, as they tangle in the aftermath, Mario takes what looks to be a deliberate step backwards and stamps very close to the prone Parker's head. The pundits are disgusted, most notably Graeme Souness, whose status as one of the most ruthless thugs ever to set foot on a football field seems to have been conveniently airbrushed from history. An indignant 'Arry delves into the deepest depths of his extensive vocabulary to exclaim:"'E's stamped on 'is 'ead.'

In my view, there's a compelling case for Stamping On Scott Parker's Head being classified as an Olympic sport. Or a demonstration event at the very least. So I'm struggling to see what the fuss is about. And as I watch it time and time again, I genuinely can't decide whether it's deliberate. At no time does Mario even glance anywhere near the player. The only person who really knows what, if any, intent there was is Mario himself. By the time we reach Monday afternoon, most impartial observers, including former referees, reckon that Mario won't – and shouldn't – be charged by the FA.

Mario gets a four-match ban. No surprises there then. At least there's no action taken against Lescott, who can certainly count himself lucky as, for no apparent reason, he seemed to barge his way through a couple of Spurs players elbows first. Even so, it's hard not to feel victimised. We may have all the loot but we certainly don't have the influence with the authorities. Not yet, anyway …

Too Blind To See It

25 JANUARY 2012, CARLING CUP SEMI-FINAL SECOND LEG: LIVERPOOL 2 CITY 2

It may be the fourth priority, but it's clear that Mancini is taking the Carling Cup pretty seriously. One trophy in thirty-six years hasn't exactly sated our hunger for silverware, and this should be the easiest one to win.

We started off with a comfortable win over unlikely holders Birmingham, a match notable mainly for a terrific goal from the recently acquired Owen Hargreaves. It would have been sweet indeed if he could have made a major contribution to the season, but sadly this was as good as it got. Next came a 5-2 win at Wolves, with City clearly the better of two understrength sides and still riding the crest of the 6-1 wave.

The quarter-final draw sentenced us to a trip to the Emirates. This would be a severe test. Wenger traditionally plays his youngsters in the Carling Cup, but wouldn't he want to put one over on a club he openly despises, the club that represents everything he thinks is wrong with football? The club that's lured away Adebayor, Toure, Clichy and Nasri, by paying salaries which his idealistic philosophy makes untenable for the paupers of North London?

Arsène is nothing if not a man of principle, and Arsenal's team is the usual Carling Cup selection; Mancini's is a bit more experienced with some star names on the bench. It's a 60,000 full house and, reserve team or not, a chance to get our first win at Arsenal since 1975 is not to be sniffed at.

It's not the greatest game, with Arsenal's youngsters holding their own and Oxlade-Chamberlain looking impressive. With twenty minutes left and the scoresheet blank, Mancini sends for reinforcements. Aguero comes off the bench and within minutes makes the vital contribution. From an Arsenal corner, Dzeko intercepts and, with a deceptive turn of pace, gets free of a couple of Arsenal players before surging down the touch-line. He looks up and plays a superb pass into Johnson's stride. Johnno takes a touch, half-spins and plays a lovely little ball into the onrushing Sergio's path. He's clean through, one on one, and side-foots the ball firmly past Fabianski.

City fans go berserk. Yes it's only the Carling Cup, yes it's against a second-string team, but very, very few of us can ever have seen us win at Arsenal. And very, very few of us have ever seen City score such a stunning counter-attack goal from an opposition corner. Mancini's policy of leaving a couple of players upfield when defending corners has paid off again. We're through to the semis with a goal fit to grace an occasion far more significant than this one.

We've gone twenty-nine years without a cup semi-final, and now it's three in a row. The minimum we should expect given our financial clout, but it still feels great. We must never take it for granted. Our potential opponents are Liverpool, Cardiff and Palace; we're pulled out of the hat with Liverpool, with a second leg trip to face one of those Anfield nights they're always going on about.

Playing the first leg three days after the United Cup tie is not ideal. Liverpool are completely dominant early on, pouring forward and forcing Hart into three outstanding saves. He can't well the dam forever, though, and Liverpool make the breakthrough when Savić, in for the suspended Kompany, makes a clumsy challenge on Agger to gift them a penalty. Gerrard ignores Hart's chit-chat to slam the spot-kick home. The crowd has been subdued from the start, and it stays that way for the rest of the half. City make a better fist of it in the second half and create a few chances, but Liverpool hold out to take a lead into the second leg.

We need an outright win at Anfield to get through to Wembley. It's a big ask. Mancini selects a strong team, albeit not completely first choice. Liverpool are at full strength, reflecting the priority of silverware in the light of their mediocre league form. I make the journey more in hope than expectation.

It looks like we're trying to hold on and nick something on the break. Suddenly, de Jong receives a short square pass and strikes for goal, over twenty-five yards out. He slips as he's about to hit it, but this just makes the contact all the sweeter. The unintended angle of approach imparts a lovely swerve onto the ball, and it arcs in gracefully from a couple of yards outside the post, leaving Reina helpless as it sails into the top corner.

Next objective – hold on until half-time. Liverpool press and Agger has a half chance on the edge of the box. Richards dives across to make a superbly timed block, but there's a huge appeal from players and crowd alike. Phil Dowd points to the spot. He's immediately surrounded by protesting City players, and their intensity of feeling makes you think something's not right.

Dowd deals with the protests by repeatedly gesturing with his arms outstretched, indicating that Richards had 'saved' the shot. It didn't look that way from behind the goal, but Dowd was very close to the incident and had an unimpeded view. Once again, Hart gives Gerrard a ton of verbals; once again Gerrard buries the pen with aplomb. Time to bin this particular tactic, Joe – it makes you look a bit of a prat and patently doesn't work.

Liverpool open the second half storming towards the Kop end, trying to kill the tie off. Hart carries on where he left off in the league game, with some blinding saves to repel Kuyt, Skrtel and Downing. He's all that's standing between us and a battering. Savić is having an absolute nightmare, being mocked by the home crowd as he barely puts a foot right. It looks only a matter of time before we're put out of our misery, but on a rare excursion upfield we stun the hosts. Kolarov surges down the left wing and whips in a magnificent low cross, which Dzeko anticipates superbly and buries at the far post. A classic sucker punch, and all square on aggregate again.

Not for long. A slick move on the right gives Craig Bellamy a clear sight of goal. We know only too well what an accomplished finisher he is, and even as he shapes to strike the ball, I expect the worst. Sure enough, he slots the ball unerringly past Hart to send the Kop wild. It's hard to deny him his moment – he was a terrific player for us and there've been plenty of matches since where we really could have done with him.

We don't come close to forcing extra time, and I make a swift exit as their fans and players get the party started. Over the two legs, no one can dispute that the better side won. Our reliance on Vinny and Yaya has been exposed, and Savić's lack of confidence cruelly exploited. He'll do well to come back from this. I head back to Manchester disappointed but with no real sense of grievance. How this changes when I see the penalty incident on TV.

Phil Dowd has made himself look a right twat. He was ten yards away from the incident with an unobstructed view.

He indicated insistently that Micah had 'saved' the shot with outstretched arms. What actually happened was nothing like that at all. Richards' slide across to block with his legs was perfectly timed. The ball ricocheted vertically upwards from his shin to strike his arm, right in front of his body. It didn't prevent a possible goal and his arm wasn't outstretched. We later learn that Dowd went into the City dressing room after the game to apologise to Micah and City. Nice gesture, but no consolation.

I'm even more antagonised when I see Kenny Dalglish's interview. He's becoming more like Ferguson with every passing year. His disgraceful behaviour in light of the Suarez/Evra dispute has already damaged his stock – and it would soon get much worse – but his arrogant, grace-less, smart-arse attitude in every interview is rapidly making him one of the most disliked figures in football. Really sad for someone who was such a wonderfully talented player. Asked about the 'handball' decision, his response is: 'You said it – handball.' How difficult is it to say 'yes, we got a bit lucky there, but over the two legs I thought we were worthy winners'. No one would have argued with that. Kenny, in order to be a smart-arse, you firstly need to be smart. These days, you're just an arse.

I go to bed a bloody sight angrier than I was when I left the ground. Out of two cups in the space of three weeks, and stitched up both times. We've always said that the main objective is the Premier League, and we did have some luck against Spurs last week. Would I rather have lost that game and won this one? No. If we're going to be stitched up by refs, better in the cups than in the league. But better still if we weren't stitched up at all …

Give Me Just A Little More Time

15 MARCH 2012, EUROPA LEAGUE LAST 16:
CITY 3 SPORTING LISBON 2

When we bowed out of the Champions League with the consolation prize of a Europa League place – a ridiculous concept in itself – no one realistically thought we'd take it seriously. Then, the draw gave us the toughest possible assignment – Porto, the holders and fellow Champions League evacuees.

It was also the most attractive possible assignment, a truly beautiful city with the prospect of some February sunshine. With its array of picturesque riverside bars and historic old port-houses there was plenty to keep us entertained, and it was a very mellow bunch of Blues that increasingly took the area over as Thursday progressed. We bumped into Dave and Sue from *King of the Kippax* – a fanzine still thriving after almost twenty-five years, now that's what I call devotion to the cause – and sat down for a few beers with a couple of guys they knew from previous trips, Steve and Mad Ian. The beers quickly gave way to white ports – well, when in Rome – with inevitable consequences.

Dave had just released his *Us and Them* book – an extraordinarily thorough account of our record against every opposition team we've encountered in our history. Mad Ian was taking Dave to task for one of two errors he'd spotted, inevitable in a book of such detailed nature. We all leapt to Dave's defence, and Ian backtracked, saying: 'Don't get me wrong, it's 99 per cent accurate.' Dave did the sums. The book's got about 300 pages. 'So what you're saying is that there are three pages' worth of absolute crap, is it?'

The afternoon became increasingly fuzzy as the port and banter flowed, and by now the whole area was a sea of blue and white, interspersed with the odd local. A hugely enjoyable, good-natured trip with fantastic camaraderie among the Blues. If having all this money is meant to be changing us, there's no sign of it yet.

Despite Lindsey's protestations of being too hammered to watch the football, we hop on the tube to the stadium and take our place among a full away quota. It's a smart modern stadium, a full house, a lovely evening, and it feels much more like a Champions League game than a mere Europa League tie.

City start well enough, but fall behind to a slick Porto counter-attack. These guys look a class act, but we defend well and there aren't too many scares. Half-time, 1-0 down. Could be worse.

In the second half, we show more attacking intent. Yaya pushes further forward and we deservedly equalise when Clichy's long ball sees Mario put his marker under such pressure that he can only chest the ball back towards his own goal. The keeper's gone walkabout, and the ball finds its way into the back of the net. Time to Poznan in Porto.

We're now completely on top, and the introduction of Aguero emphasises Mancini's determination to make it count. Just a few minutes remain when Yaya surges forward and squares the ball across the six-yard box to give Sergio a simple tap-in. The final whistle confirms a tremendous result, and we're in a perfect position to put the holders and favourites out. A taxi back to the hotel, and time for a celebratory nightcap with other jubilant blues. Away trips don't come much better than this.

The next day's papers are full of accusations of supposed racist taunts aimed at Mario by the Porto fans. I didn't hear anything, but Porto officials don't help themselves by suggesting that the noises were actually City fans chanting 'Kun! Kun! Kun!' A chant we've never entertained, not just on the evening, but ever.

The second leg's a week later, at the rather daft midweek kick-off time of 5 p.m. Despite this, a decent crowd turns out and those who get into the stadium on time are rewarded with an Aguero goal after twenty-five seconds, as he steers Yaya's precise pass into the far corner. It's a long way back for Porto now, even though they monopolise possession in that traditional Iberian short-passing style. Much-vaunted striker Hulk fails to impress, with his Drogba-esque tendency to hit the deck if anyone so much as breathes on him provoking mockery all round. When he falls over his own feet, he's serenaded with a lusty rendition of: 'You're not Incredible.'

The introduction of recent loan signing David Pizarro provides a more incisive edge, and three late goals give us an emphatic, if slightly flattering, 4-0 win and a resounding 6-1 aggregate victory. An even bigger smile arrives the next day when Porto officials say that they're considering making an official complaint to UEFA over the mockery of Hulk. So, the splendid British wit of 'you're not Incredible' is on a par with racist taunting? Strange people.

Our reward is another trip to Portugal, to face Sporting Lisbon. The away leg coincides with a conference in Edinburgh to which I'm already committed. With the utmost reluctance, I'm forced to forego the Lisbon trip – receiving frequent texts from Mad Ian telling me what a great time they're having – instead watching on TV as we fall to a narrow and slightly unlucky 1-0 defeat.

The next week sees the return leg, and all at the club are adamant that despite the increasing tension at the top of the league, we'll be putting everything into it. Our first-half performance suggests otherwise. It's much the worst we've played all season, and Sporting go in at the interval 2-0 up. We need to score four second-half goals without reply to go through.

It's a long shot, but when Aguero plants home a smart finish after about an hour, the game changes. Three more in thirty minutes is still a tall order, but suddenly there's belief.

Sergio is brought down for a penalty ten minutes later, and Mario rolls it home in customary fashion. Two in twenty minutes. Another ten minutes, another smart Aguero finish, another goal. *Bloody hell!* Sporting are all over the shop, and we need just one more goal to do it.

In that time honoured tradition of bloody foreigners, Sporting respond by indulging in the most ridiculous display of time-wasting. Keeper Rui Patricio's antics are a sight to behold, writhing in mock agony, getting up after treatment only to find himself incapable of walking and plunging to the turf once again. It's so over the top that you almost want to laugh. We have to trust the referee to give us a fair chunk of added time, but the four minutes allocated are almost as laughable as the antics themselves. We've had three second half goals, five substitutions and several minutes' worth of treatment for non-existent injuries.

The four minutes are almost up as we earn what looks certain to be the last chance. It's a corner, and Joe Hart hurtles upfield to join the fray. The ball is eventually played across to the far post, clearing the defence, and Joe rises to meet it. He plants a textbook header back across the keeper. I'm right behind the line of it. It's going in. Rui Patricio flicks out an arm and his finger-tips divert the ball slightly but crucially. It passes agonisingly into the gap between the far post and the onrushing Dzeko and goes out of play for a corner. A corner which will never be taken, as the referee blows immediately for full time.

Hart slumps to his haunches and there's exasperation everywhere. It's been a fantastic last half-hour, we should have had at least another three or four minutes to get the extra goal, and it's been a real thriller. But we're still out, and our eggs are now all in one basket. Yes, it's the biggest basket of all, but there are no consolation prizes left. It's the Premier League or nothing.

I Can't Stand Up For Falling Down

21 MARCH 2012, PREMIER LEAGUE: CITY 2 CHELSEA 1

After predictable defeat at Everton, three straight wins kept our noses in front. A narrow win in a dour game at Villa Park was secured by a Lescott goal and a brilliant late save from Hart to deny Darren Bent an equaliser from point blank range. Hart had had next to nothing to do for the whole game, making his ability to produce such crucial saves all the more impressive.

Home games against Blackburn and Bolton delivered routine wins, with Balotelli's cute finish opening the door against Blackburn and a deflected hopeful Clichy shot breaking Bolton's stubborn resistance. Next up, a trip to Swansea and a first visit to the Liberty Stadium. It's a smart, compact ground, and the first thing you notice is the noise. These guys just never shut up. I normally enjoy this sort of thing, but as City struggle to get to grips with an impressive Swansea team, it really starts to get on my nerves. You can hardly hear yourself think.

The absence of both Kompany and Lescott is a major blow, and a central defensive pairing of an undercooked Kolo Toure and walking cock-up machine Savić is hardly confidence-inspiring. Swansea get an early penalty but Hart reads Scott Sinclair's intentions and saves comfortably. We fail to capitalise on the let-off, and a passive first half display ends scoreless.

We look more threatening after the interval, but we're hardly throwing the kitchen sink at them. *Come on City, we need to win this!* The crowd noise is relentless and, as our frustration increases, ever more irritating. *Will you lot shut the fuck up!* With less than five minutes to go, another blunder from Savić gives Swansea a man over on the right. We still have time to get ourselves organised, but Routledge's far post cross is headed home by the unattended Luke Moore. Noise deafening, pain excruciating.

Now it really is kitchen sink time, and a diagonal ball is powered home by Richards at the far post. Richards goes berserk, as do the rest of us – at least a point will keep us top of the league – but a glance to our left shows the linesman with flag raised. Well, lineswoman, actually – it's Sian Massey, who inadvertently achieved notoriety after being the subject of comments by Messrs Gray and Keys that ended their *Sky Sports* careers. And who could, therefore, be said to be largely responsible for the disturbing ever-presence of Gary Neville on our TV screens.

I'm surprised to see the flag, but later TV viewings show that the decision, albeit marginal, was absolutely right. Ms Massey received the usual patronising plaudits from the pundits – that was a really good decision (unspoken – for a woman) as if it's truly astonishing that a mere female could possess the eyesight, knowledge of the laws of the game and ability to stand in the right place to be competent in a man's world.

The full time whistle blows, and our reign at the top is over. United lead by a point. We still have the insurance of their visit to the Etihad to come, but the shift in momentum is unmistakeable. The next game is an absolute must-win – a completely revitalised Chelsea.

Bloody typical – United play them when they're in total disarray under the hapless AVB; we play them when they're on a crest of a wave under di Matteo, four straight wins and even Torres has started to score.

It is a big test, and interest in an already compelling fixture is intensified with the expectation that Carlos Tevez will be on the bench. We would all have preferred it if he'd never darkened our doorways again, but the word on everyone's lips is pragmatism. With Dzeko out of touch and Mario infuriatingly unreliable, we could certainly do with freshening up in attack. And Tevez should certainly be fresh, after a few months allegedly spent primarily improving his golf swing. It's reached that stage where we'd have welcomed Adolf Hitler into the fold if we thought he could do a job for us; to listen to some of the pundits, you'd think that Tevez had perpetuated a few heinous war crimes of his own.

We start superbly. Yaya plays a terrific through ball to Nasri, who clips it sweetly over Cech, only to watch in agony as the ball rebounds flush off the crossbar. Then, Mario intercepts a wayward pass from Lampard, bears down on goal, but allows Cech to get a touch on an unconvincing finish. Roars of frustration all round. We shouldn't be getting desperate so early on, but we can't stop ourselves. We absolutely have to win this one. We stay well on top up to the interval but have nothing to show for it.

Mancini takes swift action, removing the ineffective Balotelli and bringing on Barry, thereby freeing Yaya to move further forward. But, suddenly, out of nowhere, Chelsea take the lead, as Cahill's mishit shot from a corner takes a horrible deflection and loops past the stranded Hart. Everything's going wrong. Desperate times call for desperate measures, and Tevez is summoned from the bench. If he can help turn this one around, he'll have taken a big step towards redemption.

Despite looking significantly bulkier than when we last saw him, Tevez gets stuck straight into the action. But we still can't get the breakthrough, and Dzeko is brought on with just fifteen minutes to go. Aguero, Tevez and Dzeko up front together. We're really going for it now. We don't have a choice.

Within two minutes we get a stroke of luck. Zabaleta's powerful shot is heading over the bar, but strikes Essien's outstretched arm. Mike Dean is well placed, and seldom averse to pointing to the spot. He doesn't disappoint. There are no protests from Chelsea – it's unlucky, but a definite spot-kick. Super-cool Mario has long since left the action, so the responsibility passes to Aguero. He doesn't flinch, calmly sending Cech the wrong way to bring us level.

Everyone recognises the importance of the next few minutes. Just four remain when Nasri feeds the ball into Tevez, on the edge of the box. Nasri continues his run, and Tevez plays a lovely little reverse pass into his stride. It's a crowded area, but Nasri has a couple of yards of space as Cech comes out, sprawling at his feet. There's only time for one touch, but it's enough. Nasri scoops the ball delicately over Cech's body and it trundles towards the net, taking what seems like half a lifetime before crawling just inside the post and nestling in the rigging.

There's an explosion of joy and relief. I'm in such a state of abandon that I lose my footing, overbalance and tumble over the seats in front, crashing into the fans before ending up a dishevelled heap on the ground. I believe the technical term for this manoeuvre is Arse Over Tit. There's much mirth as I'm helped to my feet and restored to my proper place. It's not a particularly dignified way for a fifty-something to behave, but I'm far too ecstatic to even think about being embarrassed. I wonder if the pre-match vat of wine had anything to do with it.

We see out the last few minutes comfortably to secure an absolutely critical three points. We've bounced back like true champions, deservedly beating the most difficult of opponents in a must-win game. Tevez will get all the headlines tomorrow, and we can't deny that his cameo appearance made a difference. But it's Nasri who's been the real star, with undoubtedly his best performance for City so far. This is the player we thought we were getting all along. What we need to do now is sort out the away form.

It's All Over Now

8 APRIL 2012, PREMIER LEAGUE: ARSENAL 1 CITY 0

Buoyed by the Chelsea win, it's with an unusual sense of optimism that I arrive at the Britannia Stadium for an appointment with the kings of anti-football. 'Never an easy place to go' is the well-worn cliché, but since the Cup Final, we've twice rolled them over with ease. They've been so meek that it seems we've got a psychological hold over them, but this time we also have to deal with their fans. We'll have faced the two noisiest home crowds in successive away games. We need to make a better fist of it than we did in Wales.

We have an early escape when a clumsy challenge from Barry goes unpunished, but generally look the better side. The home side are route one all the way, and their usual uncompromising and occasionally brutal selves. Their fans are passionate and hostile. As ever, we wonder how they can turn up week after week to watch fare like this.

Midway through the half there's an ugly challenge by Dean Whitehead on Silva, looking like a deliberate elbow to the head. Webb doesn't even produce a card. It takes some time for Silva to be patched up, and he ends up with thirteen stitches in a head wound, returning to the fray heavily bandaged. His every subsequent touch is greeted by raucous jeers from the neanderthal home crowd. When you start to boo people for the crime of having their heads cut open by a flailing elbow, perhaps you should try and find something else to do with your leisure time.

Half-time comes and, not for the first time, I vow never to return to this ground. It's been an ugly match and my optimism has evaporated in the face of Wimbledon-esque thuggery and unbridled hostility. But if we can tough it out and somehow scrape a little one–niller, it'll still be a great day.

Just on the hour mark, a long clearance from Begovic is flicked on to Crouch, who cushions the ball some twenty-five yards out, beyond the corner of the area. He pivots, and shapes to strike the ball on the volley. As soon as he hits it, I know it's in. It's an unbelievable goal, giving Hart no chance whatsoever, an instant Goal of the Season. But why does it have to be against us?

For the second time in three days, we're a goal down in a game we have to win. Every tackle, every misplaced pass is roared on by an almost psychopathic crowd. Tevez is brought on as Mancini once again goes for a three-up-front throw of the dice, but this time he makes little impact. Instead, Yaya Toure smashes a thirty-yarder which clips off Shawcross and finds its way through Begovic's fingers into the net. That'll shut the bastards up.

It does for a while, and we press urgently for a winner, getting close when another Yaya piledriver flies inches over the top. But the full-time whistle signals two more dropped points, with Stoke's essentially irrelevant point celebrated by the home crowd as though it's a vital victory.

With United not playing until Monday night, the point at least puts us back on top, but their game at home to Fulham doesn't look too demanding. I'm travelling through Paris on the evening of the match and, against my better judgment, I decide to watch the second half, installing myself in the nearest Irish bar. It's 1-0 to United when I arrive, get myself a Guinness, and settle down to watch the silent big screen. To be honest, I'd settle for 1-0 – it won't eat much into our goal difference advantage and it's hardly a match I expect them to slip up in. However, Fulham keep them out with increasing comfort, and as we get to the last ten minutes, start to pose a bit of a threat themselves.

Just a minute or so remains when Danny Murphy bursts into the United area only to be upended by Evans. I can't believe it. *Penalty! And Murphy doesn't miss many!*

I'm steeling myself for the tension of the spot-kick when the horrible truth dawns. Fulham players are surrounding the referee. They look incredulous. *He hasn't fucking given it! The fucking cheating bastard!* I hammer my fist into the bar in fury and frustration.

The locals look round. None of them have been watching the game. There's no point trying to explain. The final whistle goes shortly afterwards, and their ill-gotten win puts United three points clear. I'm so angry I hardly know what to do with myself. Yes, we've not exactly helped ourselves these last few weeks, but the whole thing seems utterly pointless. We're not even going to be allowed to have a chance to win it.

City's mindset seems similarly negative at the start of the next game, at home to Sunderland. Still no Aguero, supposedly missing due to an allergic reaction to a pain-healing spray. We're getting back into 'cups for cock-ups' territory. A sloppy start sees the visitors take the lead, and we look totally out of sorts. We get a break when Dzeko wins a soft penalty which Mario rolls in with typical insouciance, and home and away fans alike expect us to go on and win comfortably. Instead, some slipshod defending allows Sessegnon oceans of space to find Bendtner, whose far-post header soars across Hart to give Sunderland the interval lead. When Larsson scores from a breakaway early in the second half, it looks like curtains – and not just for today.

It's a pretty morose atmosphere. Then, out of nowhere, Balotelli conjures a screamer and just sixty seconds later, Kolarov buries a low twenty-five-yarder past the unsighted Mignolet to bring us level. Frowning silence gives way to pandemonium, but we can't find another and have to settle for a point. A miserable, inadequate point. But maybe someone, somewhere, is uttering that immortal cliché: 'You never know just how important that point might turn out to be.'

When United grab a late win at Blackburn, their lead extends to five. For the first time all season, the title is no longer in our hands. What's more, the 'insurance' of the home derby now has a very different perspective – it could be the game where United win the title. That really would be the bitterest pill. I might be giving the derby a miss.

Our game at the Emirates now looks like the last-chance saloon. That's if the last chance hasn't already left town. We already need United to slip up and their fixtures don't exactly look brutal. If we don't win today, we can forget it altogether. The pressure's on, and there are few sets of fans – other than United's – who'd love to finish us off more than Arsenal's. We're the crass, vulgar lottery winners who've lured away their top players one by one.

I meet up with Pollster and his lad before the game and can sense that even they are revelling in our fall from grace. My mood isn't improved when I catch sight of the TV while ordering a pint – United take the lead against QPR when a disgusting dive from the offside Ashley Young results in a penalty, together with a red card for the alleged offender. Three travesties of justice in a single decision must be some sort of record. Just give 'em the fucking trophy now and get it over with.

We kick off eight points down, but don't exactly show the urgency you'd expect from a team desperate for a win. Our away form has fallen off the cliff. Arsenal are on top, and we're lucky when van Persie's goalbound header hits Vermaelen and flies to safety. There's a real heated moment when the crowd goes berserk after a challenge from Mario on Alex Song, but the ref is close by and gives nothing but a free kick.

We reach half-time unbreached but unimpressive. There's a brief improvement at the start of the second half but Arsenal soon start to turn the screw. Van Persie's header smashes against the foot of the post; shortly afterwards he finds the net only to be ruled offside. Hart tips Walcott's shot against the post, and Lescott somehow denies Vermaelen from the rebound.

Just when it looks as though we might get away with a fortunate point – a good result in isolation albeit inadequate in the context of the bigger picture – Pizarro's poor control from a senselessly risky pass from Barry sets Arteta free. His twenty-five-yarder squeezes past Hart to give Arsenal a wholly merited lead. The only meaningful action in the time remaining is for Mario to get himself sent off for a second bookable offence. He's been tetchy all afternoon, but to my eyes and those of the fans around me, it's at least looked as though he's put a shift in. He won't be getting the opportunity to put in many more – if any more – this season.

The final whistle blows to an ecstatic mocking roar. They're more delighted about what it means for us than what it means for them. Jesus, another team to add to my list of hates. It'll soon be a full house. It's us against the world. Walking back to the tube, the chants of 'we fucked your title up' ring out loud and clear. It feels much more like we've fucked it up ourselves. Ten points dropped in the last five games. Nowhere near good enough.

By the time I'm back into central London, I'm remarkably calm. Lindsey and her mum were fearing the worst. Instead, I'm philosophical; indeed there's almost a sense of relief. Week after week, the pressure has been building, each game seemingly more important than the last, United never letting go, refereeing abominations adding to the agony. Now, there's time to reflect and relax. The first half of the season proved that we're plenty good enough to win the title; recent weeks have shown what else we need to finish the job. Despite the perceived size of our squad, the fact is that we're still short on quality cover in some key areas, and over-dependent on the likes of Kompany, Yaya, Aguero and Silva.

We'll still get a good few points more than last year, maybe even more than United got in winning the thing. And painful, disappointing and anti-climactic as it is, to fall away like this is far, far less agonising than losing it on the last day of the season. Just imagine that. United get an injury time winner at Sunderland to snatch the title from under our noses. Now that really would be too much to bear.

So, let's be grateful for small mercies, put it down to experience, enjoy the last few games of the season now the pressure's off and look forward to a glorious Olympic summer. Then we can start to put ourselves through the wringer all over again.

Boys Keep Swinging

14 APRIL 2012, PREMIER LEAGUE: NORWICH 1 CITY 6

The way the media react, you'd think Mario was single-handedly responsible for our defeat, indeed for our general decline in form, not to mention the recession, the banking crisis, the price of petrol, the collapse of the euro and the deplorable reduction in the size of Uncle Joe's Mint Balls. However, watching the highlights, it's no wonder his tackle on Song had the natives up in arms. It's a shocker, a definite red card had Martin Atkinson seen it. No one, not even Mancini, knows what goes through this guy's head at times. His critics consistently fail to credit him for the immense talent he possesses, but you just can't keep on behaving like this. Eventually, Mancini's patience will run out – maybe it already has?

Three days after the Emirates debacle, we're at home to West Brom. It's nice to go to a game without feeling quite so tense. Mario's enforced absence means a first start for Tevez and almost immediately we see encouraging signs of intuitive link up play between him and Aguero. When Sergio puts us ahead early on with a searing twenty-yarder, everyone can see that the tension has fallen away from the players as well. It's our most fluent performance for weeks, a sure indication that the pressure at the top had been getting

to us. A 1-0 half-time lead is scant reward for our dominance, but early in the second half a smart move sees Nasri
put Aguero through for an unerring finish.

For once United are playing simultaneously, but it's away
at Wigan, who've failed to take a single point off them in
967 league meetings. Little wonder that no one's paying
much attention to what's happening there; conclusions
don't come much more foregone. Even when news filters
through that Wigan have scored, no one gets too excited.
United were probably taking it a bit easy and the goal will
just galvanise them into action.

We carry on in our own sweet way, with an oblique
cut back by Aguero allowing Tevez to get himself on the
scoresheet, before Sergio plays in a revitalised Silva to clip a
delicious chip over Carson. The opposition hasn't been up
to much, but this is definitely the City of autumn.

Meanwhile, there's been pretty much no news from Wigan,
until the score rings out at our final whistle. They've only
gone and beaten them. Astonishing. We'd heard *ad nauseam*
that United had all the experience, how they're so strong
in the run in, how they'll never let it slip from here, that it
seems a far bigger shock than it actually is. Wigan had played
superbly at Chelsea just four days earlier, outplaying the home
side only to be kippered by two abominable decisions from
the linesman. They had to get a big scalp sooner or later.

Still a bit too late for us though. The gap's down to five
points with five games left, but where else – apart from at
the Etihad – might United drop points? We've long since
learnt their remaining fixtures off by heart – as they have
ours – and they don't look at all demanding. Perhaps a bit of
complacency had set in, but there's no chance of it happening again. After all, they're *so* experienced.

Mancini tries to quell expectations by stating categori-
cally that we've still got no chance whatsoever. Part of me
wants to believe him – it's much less painful that way – but

I can't stop myself feeling that there's just a little bit of hope. Bugger it. We all know it's the hope that kills you.

What's for sure is that we absolutely have to win every single remaining game. The next one's at Norwich, one of my favourite trips and a ground where we've had some decent results down the years. I wonder if Delia will be as gloriously lashed up as she was on our last visit.

It's a beautiful day, and there's a definite air of optimism among us, instead of the increasing sense of tension which had preceded the last few away games. From the start, the game is wonderfully open and entertaining, with Norwich giving as good as they get. No intention of parking the bus here. It's a pleasant change, and the main cause for concern is the identity of the referee – the dreaded Chris Foy. It's his first City game since the FA Cup derby. Norwich almost score when Hart is blatantly baulked from a corner, then when Tevez goes down in the area Foy is quick to react – not to point to the spot, but to book the prodigal for diving. TV pictures show an obvious foul, with Foy in close attendance. What is it with this guy?

Undeterred, we take the lead when a Tevez shot from the corner of the area somehow finds its way past Ruddy. A few minutes later comes a goal of sheer beauty. Aguero plays Tevez into the channel down the left and keeps moving in anticipation of the return. Tevez back-heels the ball inside and, adjusting his stride slightly in order to hit it first-time, Aguero smashes a screaming twenty-yard half-volley into the top corner at the near post. It's a brilliant goal, as good as any we've hit in a season so rich in brilliant goals, and fleetingly puts me in mind of the Bernarbia/Goater classic at Gillingham back in Keegan's promotion season. In itself, a little reminder of just how much things have changed.

Norwich pull one back just after half-time, but a few minutes later it's game over. Yaya's shot is knocked into the air by Ruddy for Tevez to nod in the rebound, then Aguero scores a fabulous individual goal, running at and inside the Norwich defence before bending a beauty into the corner. A dreadful back-pass soon gives Tevez the chance to advance unopposed on Ruddy, round him with ease and roll the ball home to complete his hat-trick. He's had plenty of stick from the Norwich fans about his golfing holiday, and comes over to celebrate by executing a huge golf swing. It's very funny, though I'm not sure exactly why.

It's one-way traffic as Aguero and Johnno both see superb efforts come back off the woodwork before we set the seal on a great day with a magnificent sixth. Aguero plays a fantastic fifty-yard diagonal ball, which the onrushing Clichy meets deep in the left side of the Norwich area. His instant cross is met first-time by Johnno, who side-foots home from around the penalty spot. It's sensational football, and brings up our second 6-1 away win of the season.

It's such a joy to see us play like this again. The pressure released by apparently falling out of the race has so obviously been the major factor in our sudden return to form, but a far more appealing story for the media has been the return of Tevez. The line being peddled is that we'd have had the title sewn up if it hadn't been for his prolonged absence. Would we really? At the time of the Munich episode, he wasn't playing well enough – nor anywhere near fit enough – to get close to a starting position, and was fourth out of four strikers in the pecking order. And for the three months that followed, most of us had forgotten he even existed.

Afterwards, well yes, it would have helped to have another striking option, with Dzeko out of sorts, Balotelli inconsistent and Aguero sometimes running on empty. But Tevez's form would have had to have improved beyond recognition for him to have made any sort of difference. As ever, conjecture is futile. No one can say what would have happened. We're just glad we're playing to our potential again. Probably too late, but still better late than never.

A lovely sunlit stroll back to the station and time for a quick beer before catching the train back to London. The only tinge of disappointment is that Liverpool have won the Merseyside derby FA Cup semi-final. Apart from bringing the possibility of another trophy for Dalglish, it's a potentially demoralising blow to Everton, whose next opponents are you know who …

Just Running Scared

30 APRIL 2012, PREMIER LEAGUE:
CITY 1 MANCHESTER UNITED 0

I'm in the car on the way to Molineux. United are just kicking off at home to Everton. We need them to drop two points somewhere; Sunderland away looks the best bet, but it's their final game and that would be cutting it a bit fine. Some think that today is where they'll slip up, but Moyes's boys are a very different side when they go to Old Trafford from the one that turns up at the Etihad. Against us, they're feisty, aggressive and sweat blood to get a result; against them, they're pathetic compliant patsies. I'm not filled with optimism as I tune into the commentary.

Everton start well, and to my amazement take the lead after about half an hour. The commentators excitedly remind us that United haven't won all season in games where they've fallen behind. But they soon equalise, and just after half-time take the lead. That's that then. I change channels and listen to the Grand Prix, where they soon bring a scoreflash from Old Trafford − 3-1. Soon comes news of another goal − one back for Everton. A few minutes later, the two-goal margin is restored. Same old same old. Just blow the whistle now. Sunderland, it's down to you.

But the scoreflashes don't stop. Another one back for Everton, 4-3. What the hell's going on? *Just one more score-*

flash, please! It comes with about five minutes left. I'm approaching the ring road around Wolverhampton, concentrating on getting into the right lane. An incredulous reporter tells us that Everton have equalised. The lights turn green. I'm all over the shop. I just go straight on without even looking at the signs.

I need to stop driving. I take the next exit and park up. *Please, please, keep them out!* Five extra minutes. That'll be seven in reality. I count them down one by one. They pass without any real scares. Truly incredible. Mr Moyes, please accept my heartfelt apologies. You're still a miserable, grouchy, archetypal Glaswegian whinger but maybe not the scheming political roll-over merchant I thought you were.

I'm stunned. Just two weeks after giving it up, almost relieved that the tension was over for a few months, it's back in our hands. Win four games and it's ours. Just four games.

Wolves are virtually down already, and this should be the easiest of the four. Gradually we take control, missing a few great chances before Aguero latches on to a superb Clichy pass to slide us ahead. Nasri makes the game safe in the second half but, despite Mancini visibly urging us on to get more goals, we can't add to our lead. The win's what really matters though – three points behind, six goals better off and the mother of all derbies in eight days' time.

Sky Sports are very good at hype. This match doesn't need it. Still gets it in spades, but doesn't need it. 'Unmissable' is the tag line. The biggest Manchester derby of all time. They've said it a few times over the last couple of years, but this time it really is.

Bizarrely, the game is set for a Monday 8pm kick off. Maximum time for the two sets of fans to get bevvied up. But also maximum time for the build-up to grip the nation. Day by day, the anticipation intensifies. A vital question is who'll be refereeing. Please not Webb, please not Clattenburg and please, please, please not Foy. The Premier League reveal that it's Andre Marriner. I don't have strong feelings one way or the other. Mike Dean would have been my preference, but then I'd want him to do every single one of our games. That would never do. People would talk.

I'm up in Manchester from the previous Thursday in order to take in a New Order gig. It's New Order without Hooky, and it's more like a Stock Aitken Waterman convention. Absolute bobbins. But as long as it's the only anti-climax of my visit, I'll live with it. The build-up to the game is fabulous and all-encompassing. Papers, TV, radio, pubs, billboards, video screens – there's no escape. If you're a Mancunian not into football, just go away for a long weekend. In fact, just go away.

United only need a draw. I'm utterly convinced that Ferguson will go for a containing, defensive formation, but he sounds affronted when this is suggested to him. Manchester United always go for the win. They don't know any other way. Meanwhile, Mancini remains super-cool, at least on the surface. United are still strong favourites. Even if we win, we've got two extremely tough games to go, whereas they've got two doddles against teams whose material interest in the season has long gone.

The pundits, seemingly to a man, still favour United. Fair enough. A draw or better at the Etihad and it's all over. Those who are ex-United players are dismissive; it's all about experience, and this is where the years will tell. Just like they did against Wigan and Everton then …

Dion Dublin, United legend, is so condescendingly contemptuous of our prospects that you wonder if we should even bother to turn up. Even if United lose the derby, they'll still win the league. But there's no way they'll lose the derby. Smug no-mark. The desire to ram it down the throats of obnoxious arrogant tossers like this gives the game an even greater edge. You wouldn't have thought it possible.

The day comes and it's going to be a very long one. Watching *Sky Sports News*, listening to the radio, walking around outside, you'd think that there's nothing happening at all in the rest of the world. Manchester is the centre of the universe. The arrangements have long been in place. A long lunch in the lucky Bem Brasil restaurant. A pint or two at the sports bar at the Etihad. Then it's game time.

At the restaurant, we try to keep each other calm. We're a better side than them. Our home record is fantastic. The momentum is with us. If we don't get stitched up à la Foy, we should do it. We're pretty restrained on the booze – this could be a night we'll want to remember for a long time. Into a cab to the sports bar, where the team news flashes up on the screens. United never play for a draw? They've brought in Park Ji-Sung, are putting Rooney on his own up front, and Giggs and Scholes both start. They've gone for experience and caution in the extreme. It's the definitive line-up of fear. No Valencia, no Welbeck, no Hernandez, no Young. Their fans take pride in wearing yellow and green. Tonight, just yellow would do. The shape of the match has already been determined.

Inside the stadium, there's already an atmosphere bristling with expectation and tension. It's not actually that noisy yet, it's as if everyone's too fraught to let themselves go. At one time, we hoped that this would be the game where we won the title. More recently, we feared it would be the game where United won it. Now, it's absolutely critical for both of us. *Unmissable.* A raucous Poznan greets the announcement of their team. I politely ask Oscar not to call Rooney a fat granny-shagger – when he did it in the cup tie, Rooney scored ten seconds later.

Off we go. United win an early corner and City defend sloppily. There's a half-chance for Carrick, but his poked shot is chested away by Kompany. Rooney implores the referee to give a penalty. It's the shape of things to come. After his success in getting Kompany sent off, Rooney decides –

or has been instructed – to man mark the referee. He's perpetually in Marriner's ear, chirping away, protesting, never giving him a minute's peace. It's like David Connor on Alan Ball in the '69 Cup semi-final. We need Marriner to remain strong under this intense provocation, but when Rooney remains on the turf following an innocuous challenge from Kompany – in which Rooney actually kicked Vinny rather than the other way round – the referee produces a yellow card. Rooney immediately springs to his feet and bounds off, openly flaunting his influence over officialdom.

City boss possession, probing away, with United set up to stifle, producing nothing going forward. It's like playing against Everton or Blackburn or Stoke. This is what they've been reduced to. We just need to stay patient and chances will come. Aguero blazes a volley over – not easy, but within his compass – and we win a few corners, from which de Gea betrays some insecurities. From a nice move down the right, we force another one, just as the board for two minutes of additional time goes up. Silva whips in an inswinger, Vinny loses Chris Smalling, leaps prodigiously and, with an awesome twitch of his neck muscles, powers in a header which is past the keeper before he can move. Payback time.

Half-time, and we're all buzzing. We know United will look to attack more at some stage, but that'll suit us. Initially, nothing changes at all, we're completely comfortable and Joe remains a spectator. After an hour, we make the first tactical switch – de Jong on for Tevez. Ostensibly a defensive move – and still seen as such by so many ignorant pundits and journalists so eager to jump on Mancini's 'Italian mentality' – it's actually a switch to Plan B, releasing Yaya to play a more advanced role, with license to storm at the United defence. It gives them a new problem to deal with without compromising our defensive security.

Ferguson responds by bringing on Welbeck, and the two substitutes soon tangle, as de Jong goes sliding in and catches the United striker. It's certainly a foul, and Marriner sees fit to issue a yellow card. As we await the free kick, there's a great roar from the other side of the ground, and we look across to see Ferguson and Mancini gesticulating furiously at each other, the fourth official struggling to keep them apart.

Mancini refuses to back down, coming back to give Ferguson more stick, with David Platt trying manfully to calm him down. Some people doubtless find this unedifying; I think it's bloody brilliant. At last there's someone prepared to stand up to the sour-faced tyrant, and let him know that his intimidation and bullying won't wash with us.

United have to press for an equaliser, but they're getting nowhere. In contrast, we're now much more of a threat, with Yaya at the heart of everything, a beast unleashed. Twice he drives at the United defence to power shots narrowly wide, then an incredible crossfield sprint sees him keep the ball in, storm to the by-line and cut the ball back for Nasri. Still unable to shake off his Arsenal upbringing, Nasri tries to beat one man too many instead of shooting, and the chance is lost. Clichy and Aguero also come close and United are being over-run as seldom before.

Despite the belated introduction of Young and Valencia, they still scarcely cause our hearts to flutter. When Rooney yet again gives the referee the benefit of his wisdom, an unfamiliar voice behind me bellows: 'Fuck off Rooney, you fat granny-shagger!' I turn round. Oscar shrugs his shoulders, opens his palms and says: 'It wasn't me!' We both smile. Bad omen or not, there's no way that this evening's Rooney will be causing us any problems. From the start, he's been so obsessed with haranguing the referee at every turn that he's rendered himself impotent. The grannies of Beswick can sleep safely in their beds tonight.

Four minutes of Fergie time pass almost without incident and the final whistle blows to a cacophonous roar. No one's left early to beat the traffic tonight. Players and crowd are united in jubilation as 'Hey Jude' blasts out from the PA, and the original lyrics don't get a look in. We're back on top with just two games to go.

It's been even more one-sided than the 6-1. United haven't managed a single shot on target. Not one single shot. The United that never sets out to play for a draw, that will never in Ferguson's lifetime be second-best to City, that always brings its experience to bear in the run-in, has performed abysmally, been comprehensively beaten and has now surrendered an eight-point lead. We've won a seismic encounter and put ourselves in pole position. Just two more battles to be won.

Everybody's Happy Nowadays

6 MAY 2012, PREMIER LEAGUE: NEWCASTLE 0 CITY 2

The derby win reverberates around the world, front page news in all the next day's papers. Even Ferguson concedes that we carried the greater threat – hardly difficult when they themselves carried none at all – and that we're now favourites. Mancini's having none of it. We still have two really tough games left – at Newcastle, fighting for a Champions League place, then at home to QPR, battling against relegation. I keep telling myself that it shouldn't matter, we're a better side than either of them and back in the groove. But I'd certainly prefer United's fixtures.

Two days after the derby, Newcastle go to Chelsea for a game crucial to their Champions League hopes. If they lose, they'll have less to play for against us. Instead, they pull off a tremendous 2-0 victory, with Papiss Cisse scoring two spectacular goals. Bloody typical. We'll be facing them on top form, full of confidence, and with a huge incentive to win.

Getting from Maidenhead to Newcastle for a Sunday lunchtime kick-off when you've been out on Saturday night is not ideal. I opt for the train route, arriving at Kings Cross well in time for the first departure. Plenty of Blues and plenty of Geordies. I'm way too tired and tense for any banter, and just want a nice quiet trip.

It doesn't start well, the astonishing incapacity of the Great British travelling public to sit in their designated seats causing at least half-an-hour's kerfuffle before everyone settles down. Mike's going to board the train at York. I get a bit of kip before he arrives, and we enjoy a couple of looseners. Big day ahead.

Sports Direct Arena? You're having a laugh. It'll never catch on. It's just not right. St James's Park is a truly evocative name, host to countless great footballing memories down the years, especially for City fans. It's where we won the title in '68. And where we could win it today, if we win and United lose at home to Swansea. Fat chance of that though.

We take in a couple of pit stops on the stroll up to the ground, each full of City and Newcastle fans mixing happily. They hope we win the league, we hope they get into the Champions League. We all know they can't both happen. Today's winner will destroy the other's ambitions. A draw, and we're both dead. Nonetheless, we all wish each other well.

We arrive at the ground with time to spare, a good job given the traipse required to get to our seats up in the gods. It's my first visit here for some seven years, and what a delight it is to find that they've made a material improvement. They now sell balti pies.

This is the acid test. The sort of game champions win. We're good enough. We can't fail to be up for it. *Come on City!* As we take the field, the roar of encouragement matches anything I've heard from travelling Blues at an away game. I'm not surprised. I haven't been to a more important one.

We start in a composed, controlled way, as ever. No one's scored against us in the first twenty-five minutes of any league game all season. What an incredible stat that is. Slowly, we start to make inroads. Silva has a decent chance on the left, but fires across the far post. Cisse and Ba are being kept completely in check by Vinny and Joleon, but we've seen enough to know that they're well capable of feeding on scraps. From a rare home corner, the ball is deflected out to Ben Arfa, whose ten-yard snapshot is expertly kept out by Hart at his near post. It's a warning.

Just before half-time comes our first big chance. A slick move down the left ends up with Barry in space inside the area. His first shot is blocked, but the rebound falls invitingly back to him. Going for placement rather than putting his foot through it, his second attempt is cleared off the line. *Just bloody leather it!*

Half-time, no score. We've controlled the game, had a couple of chances, shown the home crowd who's boss. Any other game this season and we'd have been happy enough. But this isn't any other game. Nothing but a win will do.

Second half, and City are kicking towards us. Lots of possession, but no clear chances. With an hour gone, Mancini makes his move. Time for Plan B. De Jong replaces Nasri, freeing Yaya to do what he does best. We've never needed him to do it as much as we do today.

Just fifteen minutes left. Yaya picks the ball up forty yards out, and plays it into Aguero on the edge of the area. Usually, he'd try to roll his man and get a shot in. This time, he takes a touch and lays the ball back into Yaya's path. From twenty-five yards out Yaya strikes a firm side-footer in that languid way of his. His timing and placement are perfect. I'm right in the line of the shot. I can see it's going in. He's arced it in from outside the post and Krul doesn't get near it. It's a majestic goal, and a fantastic moment. Mancini's Plan B has borne its biggest harvest of fruit. There's no way we'll let this one slip.

Instead of sitting back, we look to put the game to bed. Aguero is played in by Silva's delightful chip; his first touch is impeccable but his attempted slide-rule finish shaves the outside of the post. Then, fabulous play from Aguero puts

Yaya clean through. He elects to go round the keeper, but slips in the act of doing so and the chance is lost.

Finally, a passage of controlled possession football sets up Clichy, on the left. He slots it through a defender's legs into Yaya, eight yards out. A touch to control, then a left-foot side-footer past Krul. Game over, and party time. For the first time all season, we sing the words I never thought I'd hear again. 'So now you're gonna believe us, we're gonna win the league.' The last time I recall singing them is forty years ago. And we didn't …

There's time for Hart to make a tremendous save from Ameobi's snapshot, but that's the only slight scare. The final whistle blows, and 'we're gonna win the league' reverberates around the stadium, down the multiple flights of stairs, into the concourse below, outside the ground and all the way back to the station. It's not won yet, but after two such accomplished, authoritative performances in the toughest games we could have faced, surely we've laid the curse of 'typical City' to bed. Only QPR lie between us and the title, they of the worst away record in the whole league.

Having been going to City away games for over forty years, I've got to know all sorts of folk. People I've travelled to games with, shared pints with, been at supporters' club meetings with, happened to sit next to at games and so on. Sometimes I don't see anyone I know. Other times one or two.

Today, it's as if my whole City-supporting life is flashing before me. Everywhere I turn, there are familiar faces, reminders of City of old. It feels symbolic. Before the game, in the concourse, I bump into Tony, with whom I travelled to pretty well every game in the mid-1970s. We tell each other that we haven't changed. But City certainly have. I see Steve from the Porto trip at half-time and what seems like a cast of thousands on the way out of the ground, every single one beaming broadly. Sue from *King of the Kippax* gets a giant bearhug. I hope she recovers in time for next week. 'We're gonna win the league ...'

There's no time for celebratory beers, as Mike and I have our respective trains to catch. We get some cans to sustain us on the way home and say cheerio until next week. I settle into my seat, match programme and beer for company, and start to relax. Only briefly. *Shit, what if United score six?*

Their game with Swansea is just kicking off. If they lose, we're champions, but that's hardly a realistic prospect. All we ask is for Swansea to keep the margin of defeat down. We're ten goals better off. Offer me 4-0 now and I'd take it. Then they'd need to get at least six at Sunderland, and that ain't gonna happen. I decide on my strategy. Whatever's happening, I'll only look at the BBC Sport update every ten minutes.

The text commentary talks of a deflated, downbeat, depressed atmosphere at Old Trafford. Ten minutes, 0-0. Twenty minutes, 0-0. This'll do nicely. The next update reveals that Scholes has scored, but there's no talk of them racing to get the ball back for the kick off. They get another before half-time, and I know they could easily get four or five more in the second half. I'm not resting easy just yet. However, each further update tells of Swansea keeping the ball well, the odd missed chance, the general sense of United being resigned to their fate. Full-time, 2-0. That'll do. They aren't going to score eight at Sunderland. Win next week and it's ours.

Let England Shake

13 MAY 2012, PREMIER LEAGUE: CITY 3 QPR 2

The day finally arrives. The previous two games have been seismic, intense and agonisingly slow to arrive. Crucial wins, but neither of them definitive. This one will be. No last chances after this. The eyes of the world are watching.

Even as I wake up, it feels like my heart's beating in my throat. I try not to think about what it would feel like to win. The minutes pass slowly. It's going to be the longest day.

We arrange to meet Mike and Daz for a full English before taking in a couple of al fresco pints. On the way we pass a Ladbrokes shop – its sample bet display shows 'Man City to beat QPR 3-2 – 28/1'. As if anyone would be daft enough to have a punt on that …

Daz and Mike are much more confident than I am. Mike thinks we're fated to win – it's his lad Max's eleventh birthday. He's City mad, a season-ticket holder and surely City wouldn't dare to spoil a youngster's big day? We tell him he doesn't know how lucky he is – we've had to endure decades of suffering before reaching this point, whereas it must just feel like a breeze to him. It almost seems unfair – he hasn't earned it – but then I'm reminded of our last title win, back in 1968. I was ten, and it was my very first season. I hadn't earned it then either, but I haven't half paid for it since.

Lindsey's also confident, and everyone seems convinced that QPR are so bad that we'll just have to turn up to win. I wish I could be so relaxed. They'll be fighting for their lives, and nobody should underestimate the curse of Mark Hughes.

We arrive at the stadium a fair bit earlier than normal, make our provisional arrangements for after the game, and hit the concourse. Today, of all days, balti pies are obligatory. 'I've just had a huge breakfast!' protests Lindsey, to no avail whatsoever. Nothing can be left to chance.

We take our seats, and it's clear right away that everyone is on edge. Lurking within each and every one of us is that fear that something will go wrong, that the 'typical City' we're daring to hope has been put to bed will re-emerge, and the hideous consequences should it do so. We'd win this game nineteen times out of twenty. But what if this turns out to be the one?

The teams come out to the most deafening roar, and I just hope we can all get behind them and not transmit our nerves.

An early goal wouldn't half help, but we don't score too many of those, and today's no different. Despite ostensibly setting up with two front men, QPR drop everyone behind the ball and a familiar pattern of play emerges. We create a couple of half-chances, but they hold firm and no doubt take encouragement on hearing a huge roar from their supporters after about ten minutes. If Bolton don't win at Stoke, QPR are safe no matter what, and Stoke have just scored.

We carry on with our patient build-ups, but continue to meet stern resistance. How could anyone have expected anything else? A voice of frustration behind me bellows 'come on City, you're playing as if it's a normal game!' *Jesus!* Playing it like a normal game is exactly what we *should* be doing, exactly what's brought us twenty-two wins and a draw from the last twenty-three home games, exactly what Mancini would want. The art of winning games which aren't normal is to be able to treat them as if they are. Way too early to start panicking yet, even though news has come through that United are leading at Sunderland. I'm honestly not bothered. Win, and it doesn't matter what they do.

Yaya looks like he's struggling, but then he so often does, before setting off on an electric fifty-yard burst and leaving half the opposition in his wake. This time, though, there's real concern and signs of movement on the bench. It looks as though Plan B may no longer be an option. But we haven't finished with Plan A yet ...

Zaba plays the ball infield yet again to Nasri, but this time makes a run into the box instead of staying wide. Nasri feeds Yaya, who prods a perfectly timed three-yard pass straight into Zaba's path. It's our first clear sight of goal. Zaba thumps it goalwards, no finesse but plenty of power, straight at Paddy Kenny.

The keeper gets a good hand to it but the ball loops over him towards the far post and there's an agonising wait to see where it lands. It hits the inside of the post, and Kenny's despairing lunge backwards only results in him claw-ing the ball into the side netting. The breakthrough has arrived from an unlikely but so deserving source. The stands explode with jubilation and relief as Zaba surges in ecstasy towards the touchline, his teammates in frenzied pursuit.

Well, all but one of his teammates. Yaya's down again, and his afternoon and season are over. His final contribution, that lovely little pass, was such a telling one, and he receives the warmest of ovations as he limps off to be replaced by de Jong. In the thrall of having taken the lead, it doesn't seem that important, but what if they somehow get back in the game? For now, though, all they seem bothered about is not conceding another. Half-time, and halfway way there.

The scores from elsewhere confirm United's interval lead, but more worryingly show that Bolton have turned things around and lead at Stoke. If things stay the same, QPR are down. They've got to throw everything at us in the second half. And if they equalise, there's no Yaya to save us.

From the restart, Aguero's smart near-post flick almost delivers that killer second. Rangers survive the corner, and clear upfield for Shaun Wright-Phillips to knock a hopeful ball forward in the general direction of Cisse. It should be meat and drink to Lescott, but he gets too far under it and misdirects his header straight into Cisse's path. *Fuck!* He's clean through. In my mind's eye, it's Michel Vonk against the Scum in '93, gifting them the foothold to come back from 2-0 down. I feel sick even before Cisse hits the ball. I just know he's going to score. And he does, drilling the ball emphatically beneath the helpless Hart.

It's a stunner. Lescott's been rock-solid all season, an inte-gral part of the meanest defence in the league. It's the first real clanger he's dropped all year. How sick must he feel? How can he possibly get it out of his mind for the rest of the game? *The chance to erase forty-four years of pain lost because of me. The greatest day in the lives of all these people destroyed because of me. Just because of me.* I can't imagine what he must feel like. It has to be even worse than I'm feeling, and that doesn't seem possible.

The goal's come out of nowhere, and there's a sense of disbelief all around. Rangers can now drop back into their shell, having equalised after hardly coming out of it. But we've got the best part of forty-five minutes left, and we score most of our goals in the second half. No need for desperation yet.

We quickly reassert our grip on the game. Then, as QPR clear another attack, we notice Tevez prone in the area, with the linesman in front of us flagging furiously. He continues to signal until Mike Dean extricates himself from the inevitable melee and comes across to discover exactly what the linesman saw. Meanwhile, accusations and gesticulations continue, and it's clear that the player at the centre of the incident is the great Sir Joseph Barton himself. *Quelle surprise.*

After a brief chat, Dean walks back towards the crime scene and brandishes a red card to our less than favourite son. Barton protests his innocence for a while and then loses the plot completely, smashing his knee brutally into the back of Aguero before trying to nut Kompany. He's a bar-room brawler ready to take on the world, but eventually his old teammate Micah Richards calms him down and escorts him towards the tunnel. Mario comes off the bench looking worryingly as though he fancies a piece of the action, but Joe Hart intercepts him, denying us a spectacular sideshow.

The dismissal restores belief and volume to the crowd. The players respond and Rangers are creaking. Kenny makes great saves from Tevez and Nasri, and then a ball ricochets around the six-yard box, clearly striking Onuoha's arm. As the other City players appeal, the ball falls to Aguero, five yards out, but his snapshot is miraculously saved by Kenny, who parries it before clutching it on the line. In the blur of action, the appeals for a penalty are forgotten. To a dispassionate neutral, it must seem only a matter of time before we score again, but where would you find one of those?

Suddenly, QPR release Traore down the left. Vinny comes across to intercept, but Traore pushes the ball past him and sprints forwards into acres of space. Vinny had the chance to take him out, take a yellow for the team, but chose not to do so. QPR have a man over, surging towards the far post, but it'll be a hell of a cross to find him from right on the touchline.

It *is* a hell of a cross. The ball arcs over the City defenders and the unopposed Mackie meets it with a downward header which flashes past Hart, bounces up from the turf, and evades Lescott's spread-eagled attempt to clear it off the line. The ball hits the roof of the net, the QPR fans cavort in a mass of disbelieving euphoria and a cloak of silence envelops the rest of the ground. I can't speak or move. They've been in our area twice in the whole game, and scored two goals. How the hell could this have happened?

My brain is scrambled. No one in the ground, of whatever persuasion, could possibly have expected this. Sullen, shell-shocked faces are all around, and mine's one of them. The sick-making image of a jubilant Ferguson keeps flashing through my mind. It's a full five minutes before I can focus properly on the game again. And think rationally again. We've got more than twenty minutes to score twice against ten men. It's more than achievable. We score so many in the last twenty. If we get one, we'll get another. That's what I say to Lindsey – who looks as stunned and disbelieving as anyone – trying to give us both grounds for hope. But after starting the day as overwhelming favourites, we're now outsiders, ever more so with every minute that ticks by.

QPR now have margin for error, and drop even more deeply into their own half. They have absolutely no attacking ambition, not that they had much to start with. It's not a Premier League decider; it's attack and defence. We can have the ball thirty yards out, we can have it on the wings, but the density of bodies within the penalty area make it impossible to get any further.

If we can't get through them, maybe we can get over them, and Mancini brings on Dzeko for Barry. Not much need for holding midfielders here. Barry's been superb this season, and would normally have exited to a sustained standing ovation. Here it's more 'get off the bloody pitch so we can get another striker on'. Another five minutes and it's Mario time – on for Tevez. It's Mario's first appearance since the Arsenal debacle and he doesn't half owe us one.

The minutes roll by one by one – blocked shots, weak headers, comfortable saves. Clichy and, especially, Zabaleta see loads of the ball, and in space, but they're not men to beat a defender or two and make inroads. Instead it's just a succession of hopeful but fruitless crosses, invariably intercepted to produce hopeful but fruitless corners.

QPR have adopted a 4-1-4 formation – four across the six-yard line, four on the eighteen-yard line and a holding player on the penalty spot. Even with 90 per cent of possession, we look impotent. We've run out of ideas. Or, as Paul Merson is telling *Sky Sports* viewers, out of complete and utter ideas. That sounds much more serious.

Less than five minutes of normal time to go. It's desperate. Lindsey says she feels sick, that she wants to go outside because they never win when she's here. 'Course we do,' I say. 'If we get one, we'll get another.' The one almost comes when Dzeko tries to slide the ball in at the near post, but it clips Kenny's heel and hits the side netting. For a fleeting, agonising moment, I thought it was in.

I've kept up the 'get one, and we'll get another' mantra for almost twenty minutes now, but as normal time draws to a close I can't kid myself any longer. It's not going to happen. The announcement of five extra minutes would normally bring a desperate roar of encouragement, but we're all too numb to respond.

Five minutes – the iconic Gillingham number. Many cite it as the catalyst for what followed that day, but let's not forget that we'd just pulled a goal back before the board went up. This time, we still need two and five minutes is a real disappoint-ment – it took almost that long to get Barton sent off, so surely we should be looking at seven or eight? The way things are going, it could be seventy or eighty and we still wouldn't score.

The corner count was already sixteen as the added time board went up. Corner seventeen sees Balotelli's close-range header batted out by Kenny, hit Taiwo two yards out and rebound inches wide of the post. How much more of this can anyone be expected to take? Corner eighteen comes to nothing. Zabaleta's attempted cross goes out for corner nineteen. Silva swings it in, Kenny elects to stay at home and Dzeko moves nimbly then climbs well to bury a five-yard header. We're all out of our seats, screaming at everyone to get back in position more than celebrating the goal. There's got to be at least three minutes left. It seems to take almost that long to get QPR to kick off again.

The goal gives us just a chance, but as we wait for Rangers to restart I suddenly feel even worse than before. Isn't this bloody typical? – we're going to get as close as we possibly can to pull-ing it round without actually doing so. Absolutely maximise the agony. Give us one final straw to clutch at and then drag it away. There'll be one last chance, we'll hit the post or miss a sitter and the full-time whistle will blow. Heroic failure has been a feature this season – almost turning around the cup derby with ten men from 3-0 down; getting three of the four needed against Sporting Lisbon and then seeing Joe Hart's last-second header touched around the post. Failing to beat a crap team down to ten men could hardly be described as heroic, but if we fail by a hairsbreadth it'll be the most unbearable, unfor-gettable, desperate failure of all time. *Typical City.*

QPR kick off rugby style, a diagonal punt into the corner, getting the ball as far away from their goal as possible. No one chases after it, they just park themselves thirty yards from goal, trusting themselves to resist for the last couple of minutes. Almost instantly, their bench is a scene of wild celebration. The news must have come through that Bolton haven't won. Rangers are safe even if they lose.

We get the ball forward in double quick time, but QPR intercept and Wright-Phillips brings it clear, well into the City half. *For God's sake Shaun, you're meant to be a Blue!* Zabaleta slides in, gets a touch, but the retreating Nasri lets the ball go out for a throw, mistakenly thinking it's ours. It isn't. QPR don't exactly rush to take it. It feels like another minute has gone by. Despair and desperation everywhere. If we're really, really lucky we'll have just one more chance.

Lescott wins his header from the throw, and de Jong picks up the loose ball, bringing it forward, unopposed as usual. Aguero drops off and finds space to receive the pass, thirty yards out. He turns and looks to play that familiar little round the corner ball into Mario, back to goal, on the edge of the box. *Do something Mario!* He tries to turn Ferdinand, slips under the challenge, but at least holds the ball up. As he falls, he manages to prod it into the surging Aguero's path. Can Sergio get a shot in before Taiwo's sliding challenge intercepts? He doesn't even try, electing instead to nick the ball past the defender and into space. His touch has been perfect. He's ten yards out with one shot to win the title. The roar of anticipation rises to a crescendo. He smashes the ball on the half-turn and it flashes past Kenny at his near post before crashing into the rigging.

It's the closest I've ever been to an out of body experience. All around me everyone is hugging and kissing each other, there are tears, and it's a scene the like of which I've never witnessed. I want to join in but I can't. This is just about me and City. Despite the extraordinary din, I can hear myself screaming 'YES!! YES!! YES!' at the top of my voice, in an impossibly high pitch. I can see and feel myself leaping up and down as though possessed by Zebedee. I've lost control of my body. I just keep on and on and on until exhaustion forces me to stop.

It's not just a goal celebration, it's a catharsis. An exorcism. Jamie Pollock's own-goal, Alan Ball Football Genius, playing keep-ball to ensure relegation, Shrewsbury, Halifax, Bury, Sunderland, Gordon Banks, Ricky Villa, Gary Crosby, David Pleat's motorised white shoes, Swales out, Lee out, every fucker out, Alf Grey, Alan Wilkie, Norman Burtenshaw, George Courtney, twenty years of gloating scum, three Baconface-time derby defeats in one season, Lee Bradbury, Eddie McGoldrick, Robert Hopkins, Eike Immel, Fowler, Sinclair and McManaman, battered at Stockport, drubbed at Lincoln, are you watching Macclesfield, endless hours of motorway traffic jams, will we make it in time for kick-off, why the fuck did we bother ... all gone.

All gone, and I know they're not coming back. I'm cured. There's no pain anymore. My over-riding image of City from now on will be this moment, this moment of unbridled, unprecedented, unrepeatable ecstasy rather than the misery, underachievement and disappointment which has been the core of our being for so long. This single moment has changed forever the very essence of Manchester City.

QPR again kick off by punting the ball down towards the corner flag, and once more nobody follows it up. Hart collects the ball, takes his time, and still no QPR player ventures within forty yards. They're safe, we're champions, let's just get on and celebrate. Mike Dean knows the score in every sense and blows his whistle to get the party started. CHAMPIONS!!

There's never been a moment in football like it. Not just two goals in injury time to win a match, not even two goals in injury time to win a championship, not even two goals in injury time to win a championship for the first time in forty-four years. The crucial extra ingredients were who'd have won it if we hadn't, and what we'd have been subjected to. Instead, we've silenced their moronic tweeting players, their bitter graceless manager, their smug phalanx of vacuous pundits and journos, all transparently desperate for us to fail. It's a unique set of circumstances, fully befitting a unique level of celebration. And it doesn't half get it.

There's a huge pitch invasion, as what seems like almost all of the lower tier supporters pour on to the pitch. It's not a very sensible option for those of us in the third tier, so it's hugs and kisses all round. Even Mr Angry in front of me, whose moronic, vitriolic criticism of everything we do which doesn't lead to a goal has driven us all mad this season, gets a hug. Pete, a fellow southern Blue, comes across for a quick chat. I've seen him at most of our games this season, usually when we've both been in a state of high anxiety. At last we can relax. Ed, a guy I went to games with in the 1980s, seeks me out. It's great to see him. He's symbolic of the dross we had to put up with in those dark days, and how far we've come since.

Eventually the pitch invaders return to their seats and the components of the presentation podium are brought out and assembled. *I've seen this happen in other people's lives, now it's happening in mine.* The backroom staff come out, followed by most of those who remain from the heroes of '68. And two of them, Tony Book and Mike Summerbee, have the honour of bringing the Premier League trophy to the podium. It's so typical of the club, never forgetting the history which those from the outskirts of the city so like to pretend we don't have. Football didn't start in 1992.

At last, Mancini and the players emerge from the tunnel, one by one making their way to receive their medals, each received by a raucous, ecstatic cheer. Vinny is last up, and the roar of expectancy escalates as he pauses for effect before grasping the trophy and raising it aloft. Flares, ticker-tape, streamers, blue and white smoke – it's a scene, and a feeling, of the most incredible joy. Even most of the Rangers fans, with plenty to celebrate themselves, have remained in the ground to join in the fun. YouTube video will later show them urging us on to get the winner once they knew they were safe – what more definitive statement of contempt for Manchester United can there be?

The lap of honour begins, and no one's in much of a hurry. We all just stand there, soaking it in, still not really sure how it happened. We were two minutes from being condemned to a summer of hibernation, to a level of ridicule and suffering which even City fans have never experienced before. Now, we're the team whose name is on everyone's lips, the winners of the most extraordinary match of all time, a game to be replayed and revered for decades to come.

Slowly, the stands start to empty and with some reluctance we leave the ground. Lindsey has a train to catch and, after a ten-minute walk, she gets a cab to the station. Now I need to find my way to the other side of the ground, where Daz and Mike are waiting. I'm going against the flow, but what an experience it is. Every single face is characterised by an idiotic, slightly dazed grin. I wish I'd had the wit to take some photos and videos. Instead, I just give them all an idiotic, slightly dazed grin back.

Eventually, I'm reunited with Mike and Daz and we set off to begin the business of serious celebration. We start at their local supporters' club and I can honestly say I've never seen so much happiness in a single room. *Sky Sports News* shows endless repeats of the reactions to those dramatic few moments, each one greeted by a resounding cheer and another trip to the bar.

Pictures alternate between misery then ecstasy at the Etihad and the reverse emotions at the Stadium of Light. The sight of Ferguson, Rooney, Phil Jones, and what even by their own lofty standards seem a stunningly dimwitted selection of their supporters, generates roars as raucous as those reserved for the sight of Vinny raising the prize. The emotions are equal and opposite – unbelievable joy for us, utter devastation for them. It's truly beautiful.

Last year's FA Cup win, that first pot for thirty-five years, was a fantastic, emotional, special day, a day many of us thought we'd never see. This is absolutely off the scale. It emphasises what players and managers always say – the league is the number one target, what they want to win above everything else, even the Champions League. The only competition that gives you the right to say you're the best. People are already talking about this being a changing of the guard, the beginning of a new dynasty. At the moment, I couldn't care less. Let's enjoy this one first. We can worry about the future later.

Nicely loosened up, we jump in a cab to get to Daz and Mike's local, Normally a mix of Red and Blue, tonight it's a Red-free zone. A few more pints, then on to the obligatory Champagne. Then, that moment when you really know you've had way too much to drink – a look at the wine list and the sense of absolute obligation to buy the most expensive bottle. As if we'd have the slightest chance of appreciating it. Fortunately for us, the limited demand for high end wines in downtown Delph means that the wallet doesn't take the battering our drunken idiocy deserves. We toast anyone and everyone before deciding there's only one thing left to do – back home to watch the match all over again.

I pour myself a glass of wine, slump onto the sofa and sit back to tuck into a televisual feast. First *Match of the Day*, then the whole game on Sky. It's still unbelievable – if anything, even more so than it was at the time. The commentaries, the cutting back and forth between our game and theirs, the despair and frustration on our fans' faces, Mancini's increasingly desperate and animated antics on the touchline. It looks inevitable that the day will end in disaster. Martin Tyler's commentary manages to do justice to a moment I thought beyond effective description, his primal 'AGUEROOOOOOOOO!!!' followed, after a brief pause for breath and consideration, by: 'I swear you'll never see anything like this ever again!' Back in the studio, the pundits agree – no one's ever seen anything like it, anywhere. Gary Neville tries to put a brave face on it, but his hurt almost bursts through the screen. Graeme Souness can scarcely conceal how much he's enjoying Neville's discomfort.

I doze off while watching the post-match interviews, waking up around 5.30 a.m. Maybe it's time to go to bed. The glass of wine poured over four hours ago remains completely untouched.

The following day brings the victory parade, but firstly a bloody great hangover needs to be dealt with. Round the corner for a full English, accompanied by every single morning paper. How different those headlines might have been. How close we came to being branded the ultimate chokers. Now, everyone's saying how much we deserve it, how the champions always deserve it, how they're always the best team over the season. So, but for that single moment, would United have deserved it? Would anyone honestly say that they were the best team this season? Even their own fans?

The parade is superbly organised and central Manchester is a sea of sky blue. It's a glorious, sunny afternoon, another massive celebration, another severely late night extended by the irrepressible urge to watch the match again when I get in. And another bloody great hangover. You wouldn't call it a textbook lifestyle. That can wait until I come back down to earth. If I ever do.

So many aspects of the day bear repeated viewing, but the images laying bare the raw emotions of the fans are utterly compelling. Such a dramatic transformation within two minutes – the human body wasn't built to cope with this. After every extraordinary sporting event, you normally get some killjoy to come out and say, well, yes, it's amazing, but not as incredible as that time in …. But on this occasion nobody does. No one can think of anything that compares. Quite something when you think about it.

There's a gleeful sadistic joy in seeing the reactions of the United fans at Sunderland, as they move from jubilation to bewilderment and despair in a second. It absolutely illustrates the difference between us and them. They were armed with phones and radios, all aware that our game had a couple of minutes to go, all aware that we'd got back to 2-2. Why were some of them – most notably the stupendously gormless 'Lady In Red' centre screen, an obvious contender for the first known case of a human being with a negative IQ – chanting in jubilation? Any normal fans would have been anxiously waiting for news, not daring to celebrate until it was all over. But this is the club where fans buy their champions t-shirts long before they've won it, where their celebrity bookie pays out even though it's nowhere near all over. *Look at me, I'm so minted I can afford to pay out on losing bets.* Shame it only cost him half a million. They so richly deserve every moment of their pain.

A man who deserves pain in abundance is Joey Barton. What a knobhead. Would anyone want to see this deluded thug on a football pitch ever again? After the game, he claimed to have been acting on a teammate's suggestion to try to get a City player to retaliate and be red-carded as well – hardly the smartest thing to say in the first place and patently complete bollocks. As he smashed into the back of Aguero, Barton's face was a frightening picture, contorted with hate, rage and a lust for violence. This was no pre-meditated assault – rather the red mist action of a pathetic, petulant yob incapable of self-control.

Barton can't help himself after the game, showing no remorse and attacking his critics. What a piece of work. It makes you feel dirty to think he ever even played for us, though it occurs to me that his most memorable contribution in a City shirt was also to get sent off – reducing us to ten men at Spurs in the 2004 FA Cup game and making the subsequent comeback from 3-0 down even more incredible. So, thanks for the memories, Joey – now just do one.

It's more than a week before I spend an evening not watching a rerun of the game. Every time I hear the commentaries talk about the crushing disappointment which seems so inevitable, and see the absolute desolation and despair on our fans' faces, I feel myself welling up. The devastation would have lasted for months, years – maybe forever. It was so close to being the worst day ever. Instead, it's the best. Next season can wait and wait. Nothing could be better than this.

2012/13

THE MAN WHO
FELL TO EARTH

It Doesn't Matter Anymore

19 AUGUST 2012, PREMIER LEAGUE: CITY 3 SOUTHAMPTON 2

Summer would have been fulfilling enough spent simply replaying the QPR game over and over until the Sky Plus Box collapsed with repetitive strain injury, but there was so much more to enjoy. A magnificent Wimbledon final brought the perfect outcome – Federer glory and Murray misery – and this was supplemented by a Euro 2012 filled with unusually adventurous football, at least from everyone but England. Mario played a starring role for the impressive Italians, bringing the promise of spectacular things to come in the season ahead. And then, of course, came the Olympics.

London 2012 proved to be more successful than anyone could have imagined. The shameless repositioning of the cynics and naysayers, who'd spent the previous seven years smugly forecasting a financial and logistical disaster, was remarkable. As it became apparent that the event was destined to become an overwhelming triumphant success, the millions of moaners who'd whinged *ad nauseam* about disruption, cost and hype were quick to realign themselves as passionate supporters of Team GB.

For those of us who'd maintained a child-like excitement ever since the day London was awarded the Games, it was one of the very few occasions where we experienced a collective pride in being British – well, English, and British when it suited us. The events, transport and spectator facilities were all superbly organised, with the 'Games Makers' justifiably lauded for their enthusiasm, helpfulness and humour – not things one expects to experience in London. Indeed, the place was utterly transformed, the usual surly haven't-got-the-time behaviour being replaced with a warmth and friendliness completely alien to the city. Travelling to and attending an Olympic event was like being on holiday in a place that wasn't London. We all knew it'd never last, making it even more important to enjoy it while it did. 'Don't know, don't care and I gotta go, mate' would be back soon enough.

As, of course, would football, even if I'd happily have spent an extra month or two basking in the warm afterglow without having to worry about what sort of fist we'd make of defending our title. *Our title.* It still sounded unreal, and one of the most heartening things about it was how well received it had been by fans of other clubs. Understandable enough amongst the huge, and ever-burgeoning, Anyone But United brigade, but there was also a sense of people being genuinely pleased for City, and for us, the fans, in particular.

This reaction was completely at odds with what so many predicted when the money came in, the expectation being that jealousy and contempt for a club hell-bent on 'ruining football' would soon have us up there with Chelsea as the team they all wanted to see fall flat on their faces. But, other than Arsenal fans, their bitterness fuelled as much by their own club's repeated failure to land any silverware and stubborn reluctance to speculate to accumulate, there seemed to be an overwhelming feeling of delight across the nation. Why?

There were lots of factors, I suspect; a sense of justice that the best team over the season had won, the utterly thrilling denouement and the feeling that our loyalty throughout so many barren decades, so many heartaches, so many cock-ups, and so much misery, had finally been rewarded in the most spectacular way. But such positive reaction could only have been achieved because of the way the club, and all within it, had behaved since winning the lottery. Other than the flow of embarrassing gaffes from the now-departed Garry Cook, no one was ever heard shouting the odds, boasting about what we were going to do, or implying that we were better just because we'd got money. The owners had behaved as owners should behave – staying completely out of the public eye – whilst players and management had consistently resisted the temptation to get ahead of themselves, constantly playing down our prospects even after the most spectacular victories.

The club's culture still feels the same as it ever was. As a fan, contrary to the well-publicised views of certain individuals who've elected to stay away from the 'new City' – and thus have no right to express any opinion on the way things have changed – I feel more engaged with the club than ever before. It's much easier to keep supporters informed these days, but the efforts made to provide insights from behind the scenes, to improve all aspects of the match day experience, to involve and embrace the local community and to provide information and guidance for travelling fans, goes far beyond what anyone could reasonably have expected. There's also a real wit and verve about the way in which the club connects with its fans; lovable but hapless has been smoothly transformed into highly professional, but without sacrificing personality. And it's all underpinned by an acute understanding that the best way to engender loyalty from this, and future, generations is to make us feel valued.

Surveys would show that, in our Championship season, City offered the second cheapest season tickets in the Premier League. Impressive enough in itself, but it would have been easy for the club to ratchet up prices on the back of the Championship win, knowing that there'd be plenty of Johnny-come-latelies from far-flung fields to take up the slack from those priced out of the market. Instead, increases were modest, and easily justifiable not just by the quality of players on display but also by the consistent improvements in facilities and services made available to fans.

And what about the fans? Have *we* changed? Have we gone all Chelsea? Well, we walk a bit taller but that's about it. We just can't believe our good fortune. For years, we've been the Albert King of football – Born under a bad sign. *If it wasn't for bad luck, we wouldn't have no luck at all.* As those opposing fans who almost ironically ask 'where were you when you were shit?' know only too well, we were playing to full houses long before the money came in, so there's not much room to accommodate glory hunters. The core support remains those who've suffered for decades, who've remained defiantly loyal through the years of disappointment and humiliation and who've relied on self-deprecation and gallows humour as defence mechanisms to keep spirits high. We're a long way from having the sense of entitlement which so defines United, Chelsea and Arsenal fans. Win a few more pots and it might start to come, but I doubt it. From self-flagellating masochists to brazen glory hunters is a major transition, and you don't get there in the space of a couple of trophies.

With the nation enthralled by, and obsessed with, the Olympics, no one was in any hurry for football to start again. We were all happy to luxuriate in the memories of last May's grand finale, and rejoice in the suffering of our neighbours.

But the new season waits for no man, and it seemed almost crass to schedule the Community Shield curtain raiser for the final weekend of the Games; big, bullying football couldn't bear to let the Games have the full limelight. Yet, if anything, the scheduling made the Shield seem even less significant than usual, its venue relegated to Villa Park with Wembley having just been used for the Olympic Finals. No one, other than City and Chelsea fans, seemed remotely interested, and even then neither set of fans could muster sufficient enthusiasm to sell out their allocations.

The game proved rather better than might have been anticipated, City easing to a deserved 3-2 win, albeit against opponents reduced to ten men just before half-time. Whilst never a fixture to provide serious indications of what might lie ahead, there was a definite plus in the form and physical condition of Tevez, who'd evidently shed some serious tonnage over the summer. His twenty-yard screamer was the pick of an impressive trio of goals, and everything in the garden seemed rosy as Vinny raised the Shield in what we all hoped was a rehearsal for more meaningful ceremonies in the months ahead.

The only cloud was the lack of transfer activity, despite everyone imploring the club to strengthen while we were on top. There'd been lots of rumours but precious little action, and in particular the sale of Robin van Persie to United from the evidently declining Arsenal, now reduced to a selling club with a transparent lack of ambition, had the potential to be seriously damaging. A move to City had previously been described as a done deal, so how and why had he slipped through our fingers? Mancini made little attempt to hide his frustration and disappointment, making it abundantly clear that shackles imposed behind the scenes had been responsible.

The looming, if still somewhat vague, threat of Financial Fair Play – which no one seemed to fully understand and less still be capable of articulating – was generally reckoned to have been accountable, but why? If we'd have signed van Persie, surely we'd have offloaded a similarly paid striker, so where was the problem? Harsh, maybe, but strengthening at the right time requires the balls to replace players who've brought you success with ones who are capable of bringing even more. If van Persie stayed fit, we all knew what a difference he could make.

So, as the season began, United were significantly stronger than last year and we were just the same. Mentally fortified by the title win, sure, and starting from a position of superiority more substantial than the final league table had suggested, but the fact remained that we'd won the title on goal difference with seconds of the season to spare. The slightest shift in relative strength of personnel could be decisive, and signing the nailed-on favourite to be the Premier League's top scorer represented more than the slightest shift. City fans may no longer be burdened with a permanent expectation of impending doom, but we're still realistic; United were clear favourites for the title even without a ball having been kicked.

Still, as we took the field for our opener against newly promoted Southampton, it was no time to be worrying about *them*. A carnival atmosphere greeted the teams' entrance, and we were invited to welcome onto the pitch 'THE CHAMPIONS!!'; not something you'd tire of hearing in a hurry. City predictably dominated but squandered a number of chances, most notably when Silva's feeble penalty was easily saved. However, much more worrying was the sight of Aguero being stretchered off after collapsing to the ground with no one near him. Whenever this happens, fans are conditioned to think 'cruciate', and a hushed concern enveloped the ground as we contemplated the potential consequences.

A smart finish from the impressive, lean and hungry Tevez gave us the lead and we sat back and waited for the second half procession we'd seen so many times last year. Instead, Southampton really went at us, exploiting an unexpectedly soft underbelly. Two quick goals saw them take the lead with about twenty minutes to go, putting everyone in mind of our previous, rather more important, home game. Yet there was no sense of panic in the stands, nor on the pitch. After what we witnessed on that famous day in May, recovering from this seemed an almost trivial task. Dzeko and Nasri duly obliged, securing yet another 3-2 victory.

We'd been pretty average, but no one had been remotely surprised when we came back to win. A horrible thought occurred to me. We were turning into United. 'We're playing crap but don't worry, we'll nick a couple of goals near the end.' But more than anything, I left the ground feeling almost flat. First match of the season, Champions, yet it was as if the match hardly mattered at all. After last season's finale, it'll take a while before games feel important again. I suppose it's inevitable. In the meantime, let's pick up as many points as we can and wait for the real excitement to return.

Spanish Stroll

18 SEPTEMBER 2012, CHAMPIONS LEAGUE GROUP STAGE:
REAL MADRID 3 CITY 2

A lucky draw at Anfield, an unconvincing win against QPR and a could've been better point at Stoke amounted to a solid, unbeaten but unspectacular start to our title defence. There was also good news in that Aguero's injury was nowhere near as bad as we'd feared. However, the transfer window had closed with an undignified, nay desperate, flurry of last day activity, astonishing for a club standing at the pinnacle of the English game. The worryingly injury-prone Jack Rodwell was joined by Javi Garcia, Maicon, Scott Sinclair and Matija Nastasic. Game changers? Hardly. Improvements on what we already had? Doubt it. Ones for the future? Maybe. More depth in the squad? With de Jong and Johnno having departed, not by much. Would our best team, the team we'd put out in the games that really matter, be improved? For a £54m outlay, you'd have rather hoped so.

By now, we'd endured the bloated, shameless extravaganza of self-importance known as the Champions League draw. The press had been salivating at the prospect of us ending up in another 'group of death', and we didn't half get it; Real Madrid, Borussia Dortmund and Ajax. It couldn't possibly have been tougher, and there were plenty who revelled in what they saw as our misfortune. They just didn't get it. To see City play at the most famous and iconic grounds in Europe was exactly what most of us had wanted.

Most pundits still expected us to get through to the knockout stages and, if we did, well, anything could happen. Look at Chelsea the previous year, outplayed in the quarter-final, semi-final *and* final, yet somehow still coming away with the trophy; a strong reminder that this is still a cup competition and that luck plays a massive part. Indeed, the three greatest travesties of justice I've ever seen in football have all come in this very competition, with Chelsea's triumph rivalling those of Liverpool in 2005 and United in 1999 as bordering on the criminal. You don't get unworthy league champions; undeserving Champions League winners are ten a penny. That's why our title really is the biggest prize.

Our first game was away at Real Madrid. City at the Bernabeu. Unbelievable. Mike is well up for the trip, and comes down south the night before the match. We know that the Spanish lifestyle and our natural instincts will lead to an horrendously late night after the game, so it's best to get an early one before the flight. Not a chance. We're a pair of over-excited overgrown schoolboys, nattering feverishly about the prospects for the day ahead whilst enjoying the sounds of classic vinyl washed down with a wide range of beverages. We eventually decide to call it a night at 4 a.m., but only after seriously debating whether it's worth going to bed at all. It's times like this where you realise that you're never, ever, going to grow up. And that you'll never, ever regret it.

We lurch into Heathrow the following morning, boarding a flight with a healthy sprinkling of other Blues, and managing a couple of hours' kip. Duly revitalised, we check in to our hotel and head to Plaza Major to meet up with friends old and new. Dave and Sue, Steve and Mad Ian, Pete and a cast of thousands. It's a gloriously sunny afternoon, everyone's in great spirits, the marked-up-for-the-day pints are flowing as fast as the bar staff can pour them and the banter is fantastic. It's as if every single one of us has to keep pinching ourselves. City at the Bernabeu!

We leave ourselves plenty of time to get to the stadium, and it's truly magnificent. Spectacular and awe-inspiring from the outside; simply gobsmacking from the inside. The banking is so steep that there's a crash barrier in between every single row of seats. It's simply majestic, without doubt the most breathtaking stadium I've had the privilege to be inside. And to be in it to watch City, well …

I don't think many of us expect to get anything from the game. Madrid have had a difficult start to the season, and there are rumours of unrest behind the scenes. Twas ever thus with Mourinho. But love him or loathe him, the guy certainly knows how to win in Europe.

There's no sense of a fractured spirit amongst the home team, and we're under the cosh from the start. Ronaldo cuts inside Maicon at will, and only brilliance and bravery from Hart keeps him and Benzema at bay. The noise is incredible. We scarcely mount an attack of note at the other end. *We're the champions of England, for God's sake, we shouldn't be getting outplayed quite so badly!* Despite this, with every minute that passes, I'm enjoying it more and more. We somehow reach half-time unbreached, and still very much with a foothold in the game. We've had a half to get used to these new, most rarefied of surroundings – can we start to impose ourselves a bit more after the break?

Second half and still second best, but not by such a margin. Yaya makes a surging run which comes to nothing, but at least offers a threat. Mancini then brings Dzeko on for Silva, suggesting a more direct approach. David gets a fabulous reception from the home fans, appreciative of his role in the national team's raft of recent successes. Don't think it would happen over here, though chance would be a fine thing. We're well in the game now and, when Madrid lose possession, the counter-attack is on. Yaya's off on his turbo-powered travels again, and he smoothly puts Dzeko through on Casillas. The keeper falls limply to his left as Edin strokes the ball to his right and, incredibly, we're ahead. There's bedlam all around as the crash barriers get put to serious test.

Twenty minutes to go. Yaya misses a great chance to give us an improbable two-goal lead, and I'm muttering to myself that we can't afford to miss chances like that. *Get a hold of yourself, man! You're watching City at the Bernabeu, and we're winning!* Alas, not for long, as Marcelo's shot takes a deflection and loops past Hart.

Up in the Gods, we'd take a draw here and now, but on the pitch there's an evident belief that we can stand with them toe to toe. It's thrilling and nerve-shredding in equal measure. A terrific move down the right sees Zaba fail to connect with an absolute sitter, and when we get a free kick forty yards out, with five minutes left, Kolarov looks seriously interested. Mike says 'score here and you'll be a hero forever'. Kolarov whips in an inswinger towards the far post, and the delivery is perfect. City players strive to get a touch, and Casillas can't commit until he sees whether any of them do. The ball skids past everyone, the keeper just can't adjust in time, and it sneaks in at the far post. A hero forever?

Only if we can hold out for the last five minutes. We're not exactly trying to batten down the hatches, and when

Benzema turns Nastasic on the edge of the box, he creates just enough space to get a shot in. There's only one place he can put the ball, and I'm expecting Joe to get across and save it, but the ball squeezes past him, passing inches inside the post.

It's such a soft goal to give away, but we need to forget it and make sure we hold on to what we've got. Instead, we're still way too open and Real go for the jugular. Ronaldo cuts inside Zaba to fire at goal, Vinny seems to duck out of the way and Joe is deceived, allowing the ball past even though it's right by him. It bounces up into the roof of the net and it's time for The One Show, as Special and Precious exult in separate knee sliding celebrations.

It's horrible. Five minutes ago we were ahead. How can we give up two terrible goals like that? I can't believe it. We're kept behind for twenty minutes, our initial silence broken only when the sight of Roy Keane on the touchline provokes predictable indignation. We were so close to the mother of all parties, but now it's a gloomy traipse back into the centre of Madrid, where Steve's hospitality host has arranged access to an exclusive bar.

It's so exclusive that we're the only ones in it, and we're not exactly the life and soul of the party. A couple of quadruple gin and tonics soon get us more animated and philosophical. It's been a fantastic trip, an epic match, and we could hardly deny that Real deserved it. It's also our toughest match out of the way first. Things could be worse.

A few more folk gradually filter into the bar, including a couple of young ladies with model looks and dresses which would have looked a bit on the short side even in the swinging sixties. A couple more quadruples and one of our gang asks if they'd mind posing in City shirts. They're happy to oblige as their chaperones look on in mild amusement. They certainly look better in sky-blue than the shirts' owners, and are so swamped that it looks as though the shirts are all they're wearing. Still, never let the facts get in the way of a good picture, doubtless destined to be the source of a few 'it's not what it looks like' discussions in the fullness of time.

We're left with some great memories of a fabulous trip, but it's impossible to shake off that nagging feeling that we might pay very dearly for passing up such a wonderful opportunity to announce ourselves on the European stage. Time would tell …

Old Amsterdam, it's become much too much …

24 OCTOBER 2012, CHAMPIONS LEAGUE GROUP STAGE: AJAX 3 CITY 1

A disappointing home draw with Arsenal – which in itself means we've now dropped as many home points as during the whole of last season – is followed by a limp Capital One Cup exit at home to Villa. I'm really disappointed. The season's lowest priority maybe, but we're not yet so awash with silverware that we can just toss these competitions aside. Why sign so many squad players if not to ensure that we can have a decent tilt at all four trophies?

Next is Fulham away, and Daz comes down south for a trip to this most genteel of grounds. It's so civilised that it almost seems out of place in the Premier League, though at least they still cater for our palates by offering a range of pies. However, here we're not looking at meat and potato and chicken balti; it's lamb, mint and rosemary all the way. Outstandingly good they are too, though I'm not sure they'd sell too many at the Etihad. A late goal from substitute Dzeko gets us the three points, which look even better when news of a Spurs win at United comes through.

Next up, home to Dortmund and the consequences of defeat in Madrid now look rather more stark. All well and good having got the hardest game out of the way first, but if we lose tonight, and Real win in Amsterdam, we'll be six points adrift of qualification with just four games to go. The pressure's on. It's another cracking game, but the ease with which Dortmund create chances is frightening. Joe makes a series of great saves to keep them out, and Weidenfeller matches him as we create plenty of chances of our own.

Somehow, a thrilling half ends up goalless, but after the interval it's one-way traffic. Dortmund rip through us time and again in a fashion not seen since Arsenal used to turn up at Maine Road, score four in twenty minutes and then declare. Joe is fantastic, continuing to produce breathtaking saves, but even he can't well the dam forever. A bad mistake from Rodwell – his second costly error in a difficult start to his City career – ends up with them having a man over, and Reus powers home. It's the least they deserve, and they continue to storm forward, forcing Joe into ever more spectacular action.

We look well beaten, but get an unlikely last-minute lifeline from a harsh penalty. Mario's on as sub, and the keeper's in his face as he prepares to spot the ball up. Forty-odd thousand City fans' minds are as one; 'you're wasting your time, son'. It's a last-minute penalty upon which any realistic hope of qualification depends, but the concept of pressure is totally alien to Balotelli. He ambles up, pauses while Weidenfeller commits himself, then gently rolls the ball home. No one is in raptures for too long though – we've been absolutely battered by a really classy and incisive team, and, but for one of the greatest displays of goalkeeping this side of Billy The Fish, would have been on the end of total humiliation. Even so, we're already at serious risk of another group stage exit, and desperately need good results in our back-to-back games with Ajax, generally regarded as the group's weakest link.

The first one is away, bringing a much-anticipated jaunt to Amsterdam. Our league form has improved by then, a convincing win over Sunderland being followed by a terrific performance at the Hawthorns, where we overcome Milner's early red card and a breakaway Albion goal to secure a richly deserved win. It looks like our season is properly taking off, and we arrive in Amsterdam full of optimism.

I'm expecting another day of fun and banter, but as soon as we hit the city centre you can tell it's going to be entirely different. It's a reminder of Britain in the 70s and 80s, a city filled with a hooligan culture, and there's an unpleasant, edgy vibe throughout. Mad Ian and I head off the beaten track to an old favourite restaurant of his and, although it's really good, I was hardly expecting it to be the highlight of the trip. But that's what it proves to be.

Arriving at the stadium forty-five minutes before kick off, we queue with increasing exasperation to get through the elaborate security checks and one of the two turnstiles, only doing so a few minutes after the game has started. The fences, gates and excessive policing en route to our seats make it feel more like being in a prison, and I'm astonished that such an austere, soulless, poorly thought-out ground could actually have hosted a Champions League final.

There's a strangely muted atmosphere amongst the Blues, a far cry from the celebratory can't-believe-we're-here mood we've seen at the other European away games. Still, without impressing particularly, we take the lead when Milner releases Nasri to put away a clean finish. We look comfortable enough but, just seconds from the interval, a low cross from the right is finished crisply by de Jong.

It's a bad blow, and as I leave my seat in search of a half-time cuppa, the reason for the subdued atmosphere becomes apparent. Everywhere I look, there are comatose City fans, spark out in their seats. A trip to Amsterdam brings with it the expectation of a certain sort of behaviour, and plenty of folk have clearly come here specifically to get absolutely bladdered rather than having a few beers as a natural prelude to the game. There's a lot of Blues here who might as well have stayed in town and not come to the stadium at all.

I wish I'd been one of them. In the second half, we're absolutely hopeless, giving up two terrible goals as we capitulate to an embarrassing, and thoroughly deserved, defeat. A simple near-post header from a corner and a deflected goal resulting from a failure to routinely close down a shot are both inexcusable. Mancini goes into tactical meltdown, switching to and from three at the back and ending the game with Tevez, Aguero, Dzeko and Balotelli all on the pitch. It's a school playground formation, where the big blokes at the back just lump it up for the goal hangers to run onto. Doesn't work too well at Champions League level. Full-time, a fully merited 3-1 defeat, and we need a miracle to get through the group.

We're kept in the ground for a full forty-five minutes afterwards, meaning that even those of us who've managed to stay awake have spent more time waiting to get in and out of this abominable place than we have watching the football. It's been utterly miserable, and I'll be giving it a miss if we're drawn here again.

Back in the city, I meet up for a drink with Steve and his mates, but no one's in much of a mood to party. In the end, I'm just glad to get back to the hotel and get some kip. It's alright for those who got forty winks during the game, but the rest of us are knackered. And depressed. Our other Champions League defeats have at least been really enjoyable trips; this was anything but. Amsterdam may have its attractions, but it's no place for watching football.

Mancini gets some stick for his chopping and changing during the game, but no formation can cope with failing to pick up people at corners or not closing down players as they prepare to shoot from the edge of the box. However, the four strikers at the end was definitely the action of a man whose brain had become completely scrambled. He'd said after the Dortmund game that he knew what had been going wrong. He's got a funny way of proving it.

If it happens again, I'm leaving

28 NOVEMBER 2012, PREMIER LEAGUE: WIGAN 0 CITY 2

It's not just the fans who suffer a hangover from their European adventures. The team labours to a narrow and fortunate win over Swansea, then can't break down West Ham's stubborn resistance at Upton Park. There's little fluency or attacking threat in either game. Nevertheless, the pundits still expect us to turn Ajax over in the return leg, to keep alive our faint hopes of qualification.

Within twenty minutes we're two down, yet more sloppy defending from set pieces suggesting that nothing at all has been learned from the debacle in Amsterdam. If that game was embarrassing, this one looks set to deliver full-blown humiliation. At least we respond with spirit, and Yaya pulls back a crucial goal before half-time. When Sergio drills home an equaliser midway through the second half, we're odds on for the win we need. We pile on the pressure, apparently rewarded when Sergio slots home from Kolarov's superb low cross, but the linesman's flag is raised. The players' reaction suggests he might have got it wrong.

Mario, still to make any kind of impact this season, is brought on and deep into added time is clearly hauled back by the shirt as he contests a lofted ball in the six-yard box. It's on the linesman's side and just five yards away from the chocolate teapot on the byline. Everyone in the ground can see it, but no flags are raised, no whistles blown. The one whistle we don't want to hear comes a few seconds later, greeted with howls of derision and frustration. We probably deserved better, but a draw is just not good enough. We still have a mathematical chance of qualifying, but no one's holding their breath. Not even Garth Crooks.

Mancini is furious with the officials, as TV replays have shown that Sergio's goal should have stood and that Mario was obviously fouled. If the first was a very close decision rather than an obvious howler, the second is much harder to understand. But, despite the rough justice at the end, there's little sympathy for Mancini. Defend like that and you deserve what you get.

It's desperately disappointing, even if for most of us the Premier League remains the main target. Despite the generous pricing, the Ajax game attracted a crowd more than 5,000 shy of capacity. Yes, times are tough, but it's clear that the Champions League hasn't captured the imagination of City fans in the way you might have expected. Though it might help if we were a bit better at it.

Real Madrid are next at the Etihad, but the tie's glamour is much diminished by the state of the group. Our exit and their qualification are both almost foregone conclusions, and they're easily the better side for most of the game. We equalise with another harsh penalty which also sees Madrid reduced to ten men, but aren't good enough to take advantage. The game peters out to a draw, and the only remaining question is whether we can still finish third in order to secure a Europa League place. Most of us fervently hope not.

At least we come back to life in the league, with home wins over Spurs and Villa seeing us top the table for the first time all season. Despite not having hit last year's heights, we're right in there and can surely only improve as the season goes on. Next up is a trip to Stamford Bridge, where Chelsea unveil their new manager, Rafa Benitez, to a reception quite possibly unique in the history of football. At first, I presume the jeering and abuse is coming from City fans, but there are only 2,000 of us and even we're not that loud. It's soon apparent that the hostility is emanating from the home crowd, and very heartfelt it is too. Surprising really. Such an unlovable club, such an unlovable man – surely a perfect match?

With the home crowd unsure whether to back their team or not, it's a great chance for us to capitalise, but we're not able to create much and the goalless draw feels like a missed opportunity. We're off the top after just one week, and need to win at Wigan to avoid slipping further behind you know who. Mike and I recover from the shock of them having run out of pies to take our place amongst the 6,000 Blues behind the goal.

From the start, the guys behind and alongside us are laying into the team; 'Come on, you should be hammering these. Bloody pathetic. Haven't paid this money to watch us struggle against rubbish like this!' There have always been plenty of moaners, but the root of the sentiment here is a bit different. We just have to turn up to win. Just turn up to win an away game in the Premier League. Get real. Every player gets a slating, but especially Balotelli, the 'lazy bastard', who gets more stick than Wayne Rooney at the Etihad. With friends like these …

We get more and more exasperated, and eventually I turn round: 'Are we fuckin' champions or what? Hey? Are we? And all you lot can do is fuckin' moan! Have you forgotten where we've come from? Why don't you just fuck off and watch United?'

Midway through the second half, Balotelli puts away a smart finish, and there are the usual scenes of delirium, notably from the bloke next to me who has been giving him dog's abuse ever since the game started. I've got really pissed off with this guy, and it's a chance to release some serious pent-up frustration. I turn to him with clenched fist, and reprise his evening's output with exaggerated aggression. 'Fuck off Balotelli, you fucking wanker, you're fucking useless, you fucking lazy bastard!' He looks affronted, and totally bemused. Just doesn't get it at all. Last year Mario scored the only City goal that has made me burst out laughing; now he's got the only one that's sent me into a rage. Even when he's just doing his job, he can't help but be memorable.

Jimmy Milner hits a screamer to seal the win, and it's a vital three points. I'm delighted with the result, after a decent if hardly outstanding performance, but utterly dismayed by the knobheads we've been surrounded by this evening. A sign of things to come? Since the Premier League began, reasons for any rational person to turn away from football have escalated year by year, but those of us afflicted by the bug have stuck with it. The one thing that would make me seriously think of jacking it all in is if we become like *them*, feeble-minded glory hunters who just turn up and think they have a divine right to win every game. Throughout the long trophy-less decades, it was the ethos of the club, the attitude, loyalty and humour of the fans, that most made me proud to be Blue. It's fantastic to have silverware to celebrate, and to be in the running for plenty more, but it must never change us. If it does, we'll no longer be City. And I'll be able to do something a bit more worthwhile with my spare time …

Keeping the Dream Alive

13 JANUARY 2013, PREMIER LEAGUE: ARSENAL 0 CITY 2

The arrival of our nemesis, Everton, sees us drop another two points and we go into the season's first derby three points behind United. Memories of last year's two commanding victories are fresh in the mind, but we're not playing anywhere near as well now as we were then. So much of our play has been too narrow, too slow, and lacking a cutting edge. If Ferguson sets United up to get at us with quick counterattacks – rather than adopting last year's cowardly defensive approach – then I really fear the worst. When I hear the teams – Valencia and Young start, supplementing Rooney and van Persie – I don't just fear the worst, I know it's coming.

And it does. The first half begins with City dominating possession but creating little. United soak up the pressure with few alarms, then counter-attack at speed, cutting us apart down the left and creating a chance for Rooney. His shot is miserably mishit, but passes between Barry's legs and crawls into the corner of the net as the static, wrong-footed Hart fails to react. Yet another stuffy goal, but the manner of its creation is utterly predictable. A second follows before half-time, a swift break down the right setting up Rooney again, and we're two down at the interval. Those around me are bemoaning that we've dominated possession, that United have hardly been in our half, but to my eyes we've been totally outmanoeuvred. We're so painfully ponderous, reverting back to the style of play we saw when Mancini first arrived. I'm not looking forward to the second half.

It looks like getting worse, as van Persie hits the woodwork and Welbeck nets the rebound, only to be ruled offside. Wrongly, as it turns out. We take heart from the reprieve, and when Yaya pulls a goal back, the game changes completely. We batter them, suddenly finding the pace and urgency so lacking in the first half. Silva is desperately unlucky when some magical skill ends with a shot which deflects off the unwitting de Gea and smashes against the bar but, when a corner is only partially cleared, Zaba drills the ball low and emphatically into the corner. Just four minutes, plus Fergie time, to go, and there's only one winner here.

United are hanging on grimly, and they're grateful to get some relief by hoofing the ball long. Instead of clearing, Clichy tries to be too clever, gets dispossessed, and the retreating Tevez brushes against Rafael to concede a free kick, well into Fergie time. It's in prime van Persie territory, by the right-hand corner of the box. Joe lines his wall up, and we hold our breath as van Persie shoots. The ball deflects off the end of the wall, squeezes past Hart's dive, clips the inside of the post, and bounces into the net. Their players go berserk, Zaba slumps on the post in despair, and I can hardly bear to look. I'm livid with Clichy, who's reverted to his Arsenal days and perpetrated a crucial, careless, match-losing blunder.

That's until I see the replay of the goal. The shot is well hit, but directed straight at the man on the end of the wall. Alas, that man is Samir Nasri, timidly cowering behind Dzeko. His only contribution to defending our goal is to proffer a limp leg, in the style of Brian Luckhurst hanging his bat out to dry against the Aussies back in the 70s, and the ball takes a crucial deflection to travel on its fateful course. Everybody makes mistakes, but this is more than a mistake. It's an act of irresponsible pathetic cowardice, so reprehensible that you couldn't blame Mancini if he told Nasri 'you'll never play for this club again'. Clichy's aberration now looks minor by comparison.

United's celebrations are hideous to behold and provocative in the extreme. They result in Ferdinand apparently being struck by a coin, after which a lone City fan runs onto the pitch towards him and is restrained by a furious Joe Hart. Not good at all. Full-time, and we slink off home. Unlucky in the end, maybe, but the defeat is utterly self-inflicted. It's a massive shift in United's favour and we've got to get it out of our system immediately.

Travelling to Newcastle, we do exactly that by putting in our best performance of the season so far to register a 3-1 win. The day starts at 7 a.m. with a tram journey into Oldham to be picked up by Mike and Daz, and ends some twenty hours later in some trendy Manc bar, having taken in a hearty Novocastrian full English washed down with Guinness, a tremendous City display, a couple of pints in Delph, some top Italian scoff and wines, a few more beers at a raucous Hives gig and God knows how many nightcaps. A gruelling schedule, but you just have to get through it. If Nasri had shown half our steel and commitment last week, we'd never have lost that derby ...

There's huge relief that City have shown no sense of a hangover. And so typically, the man of the match is Nasri himself, almost provocatively selected by Mancini, but who put in a classy accomplished performance of the sort we wished we'd seen more often. It'll take a lot more than this to earn forgiveness, but at least it's a start.

A comfortable win over Stoke is marred by an injury to the outstanding Aguero, now out for a few games just when he was hitting top form. Then, off to Sunderland where, just like last year, we fall to a 1-0 defeat, despite almost totally dominating. Inevitably, the goal came from Adam Johnson; depressingly, it arrived via a Joe Hart clanger, one of several mainstays whose form has dipped alarmingly from last season. Johnno's replacement, Scott Sinclair, was by now doing a highly credible impression of the Invisible Man and must certainly have wished he wasn't really here.

The pain of defeat was exacerbated by the news from Old Trafford, where United had trailed Newcastle for most of the afternoon, only to snatch a Fergie time winner. Ferguson had really excelled himself in this one, escorting referee Mike Dean off the pitch at half-time and giving him a very public haranguing, having previously laid into a linesman and the fourth official. Still, the end justified the means and, much to the disgust of most observers, he even managed to escape FA punishment. One rule for Baconface ...

With United racking up win after win, a plethora of late goals glossing over unconvincing displays, we could barely afford any more slip-ups. Our trip to Carrow Road produced another seven-goal extravaganza; this time we only got four of them, but it was just enough to take the points. The next game was crucial, season defining, and every other cliché under the sun – Arsenal away. We kicked off ten points behind United with this game in hand. We hadn't won in the league at Arsenal since 1975. We had no choice other than to do so this time.

We met Pollster for a very civilised pre-match meal, and made our way to our much-publicised £62 seats. Living down south has made me a bit blasé about seat prices – the cost of getting to a City game usually dwarfs the cost of getting into it – but this really did seem excessive. That stadium's got to be paid for somehow, I suppose. At least we only have to pay it once a season – for them, it must be pretty galling to pay top dollar prices for year after year of trophy-less football. No wonder they've become so bitter.

A confident start brought its reward when Dzeko was hauled to the deck by Vermaelen as he looked set to put us ahead. Mike Dean was in the limelight again and had the balls to make the right call, dismissing the defender and awarding a penalty, provoking outrage and derision from the home fans. Nice to hear them make a noise for a change. Bizarrely, Dzeko was selected to take the spot-kick, and tamely slotted it into the arms of Szczesny.

Arsenal's reprieve was short-lived, as City took advantage of the extra man in exemplary fashion, with delightful goals from Milner and Dzeko putting us two up at the break. We remained comfortable until Kompany went into a slide tackle on Wilshere at a fair old pace. Even though he seemed to take the ball cleanly, I feared the worst straight away, and wasn't surprised to see the red card. Arsenal still had about twenty minutes to mount a comeback, but we saw time out with relative ease and celebrated the landmark long and hard. A league win at Arsenal. Hallelujah.

It really felt like the most significant of results. Having to win here or face a ten-point deficit was pressure of the most intense kind. To respond so positively – and we'd looked really good even before the sending off – was a massive boost. Every Blue leaving the ground would have felt the same thing. '*We can still reel 'em in!*'

As ever, with so many column inches and programme time to fill, media comment abounded on the two dismissals.

There was widespread praise for Dean's dismissal of Vermaelen, since these type of offences so often go unpunished. The only dissenters were the old pros, still bemoaning the fact that the game's not what it was in their day and putting forward the tiresome argument that if you penalised every one of these incidents you'd have ten penalties a game. No you wouldn't, because people would just stop doing it. Sadly, the moaners included Niall Quinn in their number, and he's got no excuse. Unlike most of his peers in punditland, he's articulate and intelligent. But I suppose if you spend too much time around Ray Wilkins then this is what happens.

The Kompany sending-off also received copious coverage, most, if not all, seeing it as an entirely fair tackle. Replays showed that it was clean, albeit a much more forceful challenge than the one which had Nani leaping for cover in the FA Cup derby last year. So what happens? The FA overturn the decision. Great news, but yet another illustration of the power wielded by Ferguson. His comments after the Cup game were designed transparently to persuade the FA to uphold Vinny's ban, purely for United's benefit, and it worked. This time, he keeps his nose out of it, and the ban is rescinded. How many points a year is this guy's influence worth to them? They'll certainly miss him when he goes. If he ever does.

Back to Black

9 FEBRUARY 2013, PREMIER LEAGUE: SOUTHAMPTON 3 CITY 1

The new year continued to go well. A routine win over Fulham, with Silva excelling and for the first time scoring two goals in a game, set us up for a fourth round cup-tie at Stoke. Staying true to my word about never visiting Neanderthal Central again, I ended up as the lone TV addict in an Australian

Bar in Paris, watching City completely dominate the game and secure a narrow but thoroughly deserved win with a late Zabaleta goal. Everything was falling nicely into place. In the space of three weeks, we'd laid two long-standing away bogeys and were looking more solid, focussed and convincing than at any previous stage in the season. Just five points adrift and another thrilling run-in very much in prospect.

Next-up, QPR away, on a cold, wet, blustery night. Still bottom of the table although, under Redknapp, they'd become much more difficult to beat. But at least Mark Hughes' typically arrogant promise that Rangers would never again be at risk of relegation whilst he remained in charge had been fulfilled. He'd been sacked before it could happen.

On a tight pitch with a hostile crowd urging them on, this was always going to be tricky. From the start it was obvious that we were in for another night of bus parking, as Rangers showed next to no attacking intent. Zaba headed against the bar, Julio Cesar produced a couple of brilliant saves, but for all our possession and dominance we couldn't find a way through. The disappointment on the pitch was tangible, the players' body language at the end exuding sheer frustration. A great chance to pile the pressure on United had been lost, even if no one could criticise the performance or effort.

Five days later, we were at home to Liverpool. United had scraped two wins since our draw at QPR, leaving us ten points behind with today's game in hand. Victory was imperative. One man who wouldn't be helping us to achieve it was Mario Balotelli, who'd returned to Italy after a protracted transfer saga. He'd done next to nothing this season, a massive disappointment after his heroics at Euro 2012, but I'd still really miss him. There's something about him which makes me think we'll end up regretting it. With no sign of a replacement, a quota of just three strikers gave little margin for loss of form, injury or suspension. In contrast, Liverpool's signing of Daniel Sturridge had given them a real lift, and we were all bracing ourselves for another demonstration of the immutable law of the ex.

The game was enthralling and disconcerting in equal measure. City were second best for the most part, but took the lead when Dzeko finished off a slick, incisive attack. When Agger clattered through the back of the striker a few minutes later, the howls of derision at the officials for failing to penalise what looked an obvious foul intensified as Liverpool refused to put the ball out of play to allow Dzeko to be treated. When we did get the ball back, Garcia was distracted by the urgent desire to put it into touch, and clumsily ceded possession. Sturridge let fly with an unstoppable twenty-five-yarder, leaving Hart helpless and creating an incendiary atmosphere in the stands.

Dzeko promptly ceased his writhing, springing to his feet to give the linesman a mouthful. Good way to earn sympathy, Edin. No one imagined he'd been seriously hurt – how often are they? – but he *might* have been. How many times have we felt obliged to kick the ball into touch so that an obviously play-acting, time wasting, rhythm-destroying opponent can get treatment for an imaginary injury? We had a justifiable grievance, but the sooner we all get back to just playing to the whistle, the better.

The second half saw the visitors dominate completely, rewarded when Gerrard buried a trademark screamer into the corner. An air of resignation, not just for the day, but the whole season, engulfed the stands. The mood changed dramatically when Aguero chased a long ball beyond the corner of the area. Reina had taken it upon himself to come hurtling out of goal to shepherd Sergio further wide, into a position where he couldn't do any damage. Aguero glided past the keeper then, on the turn, clipped the ball towards goal from the most oblique angle, close to the corner flag. I was right behind the line of it. 'This could be going in.' 'It *is* going in!' One of the most astonishing goals I've ever witnessed and, from nowhere, we were level. But despite at last looking more threatening, we couldn't force a winner and two more dropped points saw the gap increase to nine.

It should have been a black day, yet somehow it didn't seem so bad. Sometimes you feel so privileged to witness an individual moment of brilliance that it transcends the outcome of the game and its consequences. This was one such occasion. Jamie Carragher's face as the ball hit the netting was an absolute picture. This may ultimately prove to be the day when the title slips from our grasp, yet I'll still look back on it with an element of warmth.

Mancini tries to remain positive, saying that nine points behind with thirteen games left is far from insurmountable. We're clinging to the hope that the Champions League will distract United from their domestic goal. Furthermore, the coming weekend looks promising, with them having to face an in-form Everton just three days ahead of their date in the Bernabeu. Before that, we'll have played at Southampton, hardly the most forbidding task.

We drive to St Mary's on a horrible, grey, drizzly afternoon. Not once does it cross my mind that we might not win the game. It's a last chance of what we hope will be a series of twelve or thirteen last chances. We need to finish the weekend closer to United than we are now; I really think we will.

Inside the ground it's a rocking atmosphere, Saints and Blues side by side behind the goal, and there's a tangible mood of optimism amongst us. We've had our little blip, now it's full steam ahead to claw those bastards back.

It's a fairly even start, as Southampton press hard and high, full of energy. We get a free kick on the halfway line, but Silva plays it with undue haste to Yaya, who's closed down immediately. Why the rush? Yaya quickly ships it off to Barry, who's also closely attended. Puncheon nicks the ball off him and a counter-attack is on. From behind the goal, we can see Rodriguez peeling off, making an unattended central run. If Puncheon sees him, we're in trouble. He does. We are. Joe's valiant sprawl keeps the ball out, but it rebounds kindly for Puncheon to roll into the empty net. It's a terrible start, and so utterly avoidable. A shocker from Barry, but he should never have been put in that position in the first place.

Saints and their fans are even more up for it now, and we need to stand firm and ease our way into the game. But they're swarming all over us, and after a couple of escapes we're breached again. Clichy allows Lambert way too much space and the striker easily cuts inside to fire a shot at Hart's near post. It's waist high and Joe's right behind it. He blocks the shot but the ball squirms from his grasp, bounces beneath his legs, and is prodded home by Davis. *Jesus!* Just like the first goal, it's a combination of sloppy general play with a shocking individual blunder. We're two down, and no one can believe it. This is the City of a long time ago. What the hell are *they* doing here?

We need three in seventy minutes. Play becomes more even, though it's still Southampton who look more dangerous. They get a corner which Dzeko clears, and he and Silva combine to release Zaba, busting a gut down the right into oceans of space. He plays a low cross into the marauding Dzeko, who spoons the ball into the empty net. It's a glorious counter-attacking goal, totally out of keeping with everything else we've produced so far, and we're right back in the game. You can almost hear the Saints' fans. 'Oh well, it was nice while it lasted'.

Now, we dominate possession, but have only a couple of unaccepted half-chances to show as half-time approaches. Saints mount one last attack, and as Rodriguez cuts into the area he's pursued by a leggy Yaya, far from fresh after the African Cup of Nations, setting himself to make a sliding tackle, 'For fuck's sake, don't foul him!' He does, and Martin Atkinson is just a few yards away. He looks closely at the incident before waving his arms to indicate nothing doing. I breathe a huge sigh of relief. Southampton fans go ballistic. Almost instantly it's half-time, and Atkinson leaves the field to cacophonous jeers. Quite right too. We've been let off big time. If we turn this round, we really will be turning into United ...

Just a few minutes into the second half, Southampton break down the left. The cutback from a dangerous position only finds Barry, under no pressure, with an easy clearance. He puts the ball out of play with considerable aplomb – slotting it past Hart into the corner of his own net. It may well be the only goal he's ever scored with his right foot. He can't have scored a more important one with either. Any lingering hopes of retaining the title have gone.

A few half chances come and go, but we – and the team – know the game's up. 'We never win at home and we never win away ...' makes an ironic and unwelcome return to our repertoire as time runs down on our title defence. Last year's events had instilled a hitherto unseen self-belief, but even that isn't strong enough to retain any hope that we can recover from this. A title so memorably, so thrillingly, so deservedly won has been limply tossed away.

As we sit on the bus back to the park and ride, the mood is wholly one of dejection and recrimination. Today has been a disaster, but its roots lie in the summer's failure to enhance the squad in order to build on everything we achieved last year. Everyone else is stronger, but we, the Champions, are weaker. We, the Champions, the club with more money to spend than anyone else, who've spent £54m to build the squad, but not recruited one single player to make us a stronger team here and now, not one player who'd have got into the side at its best last season. A golden, possibly unique, opportunity to establish a period of dominance, to stamp on those bastards' throats while they're down, has been feebly squandered. *Building A Dynasty 1.01.* Strengthen while you're on top.

Mancini is furious at the performance and, in particular, at the nature of the goals given away. He cites two of them as being totally unacceptable, the sort of goals he's never seen conceded before. Which of the three he regards as not being that bad isn't exactly clear.

The weekend's misery is completed the following afternoon when Everton, their shape disrupted when Distin injures himself in the warm-up, revert to type, rolling over and letting Ferguson tickle their tummies. We'll always be grateful for what they did last year, but that was just a one-off. We need to start thinking hard about next summer's recruitment programme to make sure our title triumph doesn't turn out to be the same.

Same as it ever was

16 MARCH 2013, PREMIER LEAGUE: EVERTON 2 CITY 0

After the capitulation at St Mary's, a few of the usual suspects were getting excited at the prospect of us going into decline and even missing out on a Champions League spot. Instead, we bounced back in some style, with an ultimately comfortable win over Chelsea and a narrow victory at Villa, bookended by two highly professional displays in the Cup. Leeds and Barnsley were both seen off with the minimum of fuss – as of course they should have been – taking us to the semi-final and another trip to Wembley. The draw pitted us against the winner of the United/Chelsea replay, and we all expected United. And most of us feared the worst.

They'd been blathering on for weeks about winning the treble, but had come a cropper in the battle of The Greatest Teams Ever To Have Met In Any Head-To-Head Sporting Occasion, as the media liked to refer to it. Looking well set to beat Real Madrid, 1-0 up after the 1-1 draw at the Bernabeu, they saw Nani sent off for a high challenge which would scarcely have been deemed a foul in Govan but which our continental cousins, with rather more regard for player safety, tend to interpret as recklessly dangerous. Ferguson belied his age by storming from his seat at breakneck speed to spew outrage at the fourth official: 'Just tell that jerk to let him back on the pitch at once. Now! Do you hear me? Thankfully, he doesn't have quite the same level of influence in Europe. United lost their shape and discipline totally, allowing Madrid to score the two they needed to win the tie. Out they went, to scenes of unbridled joy all across the country.

Their response at the end of the game was simply magnificent. Firstly Ferdinand marched up to the referee, shaped those unfeasibly undulating lips into a hideously hostile gurn, and applauded exaggeratedly and sarcastically in the official's face. Then, we waited, and waited, and waited for the words of wisdom from Ferguson himself. Alas, his complexion was deemed far too ruddy to pull off the ashen-faced look so essential to an occasion as solemn and tragic as this one, and Mike Phelan was assigned to the task.

Phelan was sensational. He stepped up to the plate to deliver his greatest ever performance. He talked as if in a library, hushed tones and economical use of words, each one carefully chosen to achieve maximum impact. Why isn't Sir Alex doing it? He and his players are too distraught to speak, he reveals, painting a dressing room scene of desolation and despair. This is such a terrible, cruel and unjust thing to happen to this magnificent football club. The tone and sentiment befitted a man emerging from the burning embers of his house to tell reporters about how his wife and children burned to death in their beds.

Phelan's interview showed exactly how Manchester United regard themselves. On some superior plane from everyone else, even a team that's won three times as many European Cups as they have. Their status is such that they should never, ever be the victims of a debatable refereeing decision, for it is these decisions, and these decisions alone which can act to deny this righteous club the spoils they've worked so hard to achieve and so richly deserve. 'How could they do this to us? *To us? Don't they know who we are?*'

Strangely, there was no talk about how United, with just thirty minutes to play, had simply fallen to pieces after the sending off, failing to respond to the introduction of Modric and conceding two quick goals. Even then, with ten men, they created plenty of chances to score and could still have won. However, to listen to this drivel, the red card instantly condemned them to defeat, and they might as well have come off the pitch there and then for all the chance they had of holding onto their lead. If you want to know why so many of us find this institution so utterly detestable, just watch the footage of Phelan on YouTube. It's truly beautiful.

Back in the mundane world of the Premier League, Mancini insists that he hasn't given up on the title, even though the twelve point gap remains. But whilst there might be a glimmer of hope that United will suffer a reaction to the Real defeat, history suggests that they tend to bounce back pretty strongly from bad results, and for them to lose four games in the last ten would take an awful lot of honest refereeing. We'd also have to win all our remaining games, starting at Goodison, not exactly a happy hunting ground.

Still, we'd laid the Arsenal and Stoke bogeys to rest, so why not Everton? Well, primarily because we played like drains. Smarting from their shock cup defeat to Wigan, and relishing as always the visit of moneybags City, Everton were in our faces from the start. Yet again we had no answer. Yet again they looked so much hungrier. Yet again they took the lead, this time through a screamer from Leon Osman, having already had a legitimate goal chalked off. And, yet again, we never looked like getting back into it, at least until Steven Pienaar saw red with some thirty minutes to go.

Could we do a Real Madrid? Could we come back to win, and reduce David Moyes to an ashen-faced gibbering wreck? Could we buggery. Tevez had a great chance, and we were denied an obvious penalty when Fellaini handled two yards inside the area, but the well-placed referee chose to give a free kick outside the box. If this had happened last year I'd have been apoplectic, and full of conspiracy theories. Instead, I just shook my head and wondered why I get so worked up about a game in which so many results are determined by decisions so obviously, so inexplicably, so unforgivably wrong. This one probably denied us a draw, although you could hardly have said we'd have deserved it, even if Everton's added-time, breakaway second gave the scoreline a misrepresentative gloss.

When United ground out another narrow win, at home to Reading, the gap became a monstrous fifteen points. Even those very few optimists who thought we had a shout at twelve points down had to face the facts. We were out for the count. Nothing to do but lick our wounds, make sure we get second, get some momentum to take into next season and most of all win that bloody Cup again!

You've got brown cows, we've got black and white ones …

14 APRIL 2013, FA CUP SEMI-FINAL: CHELSEA 1 CITY 2

The Old Trafford derby is looming large. Their players are all over the press again, saying how sweet it'd be to beat us and wrap up the title, then kick us out of the Cup the following weekend. At least 'Nanigate' means that the worst-case scenario – the treble – is off the agenda, but a grisly conclusion to the season is still very much in prospect, with months of hideous gloating to follow.

Easter brings some relief. Our comfortable win over a pitiful Newcastle is followed by Cup defeat for United at Stamford Bridge. Chelsea would be formidable semi-final opponents, and their loathsome, chavvy fans a complete pain in the neck, but it was still far preferable to the alternative. Before that, though, an appointment at Verminland.

This would be a much bigger game for them than it was for us. They so openly want to put us in our place, to start the celebrations for title number twenty while we're incarcerated in their hell-hole, and really rub our noses in it. For us, great as a win would be, we've got plenty of slack as far as Champions League qualification is concerned, and the main priority has to be the Cup.

I'm back in the Australian bar in Paris for this one, delighted to find a scum-free zone where I can watch in isolation. I convince myself that I'm not that bothered about the outcome; after all, there's nothing we can do to stop them winning the title and our ambitions and status are now such that local bragging rights don't matter as much as they used to.

We start well, composed on the ball, assured at the back and create a few decent openings without managing to break through. We look a much better side than them, which is heartening and depressing in equal measure. If we *are* much better, then why the hell are we so far behind them in the table? Giggsy's age – and voracious extra-curricular exploits – at last seem to be catching up with him, and he's grouchy from the off, committing countless niggly fouls, disputing every decision against him yet somehow dodging a card. Not to be outdone, Rooney flies in with an out of control two-footed lunge on Milner, infinitely more dangerous than anything in Kompany's repertoire, but his red card offence doesn't even incur a ticking off. It's Mike Dean's first Old Trafford appearance since he received Ferguson's forceful half-time lecture on the way things are done here, and he's clearly digested it well. Half-time, 0-0.

Soon after the restart, a smart move ends with the excellent Milner firing in a 20-yarder, which takes a slight deflection on its route past de Gea. My impulsive celebration is wholly disproportionate for a game that doesn't really matter. My mood is transformed. I'm agog, on the edge of my barstool, kicking every ball, as animated as Psycho in his earliest managerial incarnation. Of course it bloody matters. It's *them*!

United look to respond, and we concede a soft free kick which van Persie whips across, flat and at pace. Joe doesn't get anywhere near it and Jones can turn it into the empty net at the far post. He clumsily fails to connect properly, shouldering the ball across the face of the goal, but is spared what would have been one of the great derby howlers as the ball deflects off Vinny's back and into the net. The camera flashes of thousands of Japanese tourists capture the players' moment of celebration, and the rest of the inmates get very excited. This is where they push on and win.

Except that they don't. Our response is calm, controlled and impressive. We reassert ourselves instantly, Yaya dominant, Silva constantly probing, Milner a trojan, Tevez a thorn up front. Soon he's joined by Aguero, still recovering from yet another injury and eager to make his mark. A typically probing move ends with him in possession 25 yards out. A dip of the shoulder and he's in full stride, brushing past Ferdinand and Jones as he storms into the area at full speed. The ball seems to be stuck under his feet, but, with next to no backlift, he generates a shot of stunning power which is into the roof of de Gea's net at his near post before he can even flex a muscle. It's a fabulous strike, one of the great derby goals, and I'm making a right exhibition of myself.

We hold on in relative comfort for a tremendous win, which if nothing else will shut the bastards up for a few days. The message is crystal clear: we've screwed up this season, but we'll be straight back at you next year, so don't get carried away with yourselves. The only concern comes right at the end, as

David Silva limps off with a tight hamstring. If he's missing at the weekend, our win may have come at a heavy price.

There's praise aplenty for our display, and in particular for Aguero's magnificent, thrilling winner. There's also recognition that the injuries suffered by Sergio throughout the year have been really damaging to our chances. But, more than anything, the result and performance are used as a stick to beat us with. If we'd played like this all season, we'd still have been right in the hunt. So why hadn't we? Complacency, lack of commitment, poor team spirit, divisive management, underestimating how hard it is to retain a title, any bollocks they can think of, really. After such a tremendous win, the media response is to turn it round and praise United to the skies for being so far ahead of us when we've obviously got the stronger squad. Last year, maybe; this year, no way. But never let the facts get in the way of a good story.

The press can say what they like, but one thing a win at Old Trafford gives you in spades is a confidence boost. The Cup semi-final's next, and it's our biggest game of the season. Mike and Daz come down to stay on the Saturday, and we overindulge in predictable fashion. City at Wembley is still very, very special. You have to celebrate these things.

We arrive in London nice and early, meet up with Jersey Blue Mark, take in a few looseners and head for the stadium. Everyone reckons the game is too close to call. With Silva not recovered, we'll struggle to match Chelsea's creative trio of Mata, Hazard and Oscar. On the other hand, they've played a lot more games than us, most recently a trip to Russia, even if most of today's starting line-up didn't make it onto the field. We've got to be fresher.

It's a lovely day, a full house and a fabulous atmosphere. Not quite as intense as the United semi a couple of years ago, but what could be? We start superbly, totally dominant, moving the ball around beautifully and constantly threatening. Aguero's smart close-range flick is kept out by Cech, and a bewildering exchange of slick first-time passes ends with Tevez forcing another fine save. The movement of our front two is magnificent, reminiscent of this time last year, and Nasri is making up for Silva's absence by really imposing himself on the game.

We have a minor scare when Costel Pantilimon – a surprise retention, but consistent with Mancini's approach over the last two years – flaps at a cross, and Hazard's mishit volley bounces up and over the keeper. Vinny has immediately read the danger, and is back on the line to clear with comfort. We're still on top, if not so markedly, when at last we take a deserved lead. Great play from Yaya, our Wembley specialist, and Aguero sets up Nasri, who rides a lucky deflection to slot comfortably past Cech.

Chelsea struggle to respond, and in added time we miss a great chance to double our lead when terrific play from Milner sees him storm down the left with space and time to set up Sergio for a second. Instead he totally miscues his cross, but even then the ball breaks for the marauding Kompany, whose horribly mishit shot slices wide.

Squandering such a glorious chance casts a dampener over the half-time interval, but within ninety seconds of the restart it's all forgotten. Barry's measured cross is superbly anticipated by Aguero, pirouetting to get into position then leaping to send a precise looping header across Cech and in off the post. It's a wonderful goal, and such an accomplished header that it's hard to believe it's Sergio's first for the club.

We create another couple of half-chances, and it looks as though the afternoon might be more comfortable than anyone expected. Gradually though, there's a slight, but discernible, sense that we're taking our foot off the gas, showing a touch of nonchalance, knocking the ball around for the sake of it rather than looking to kill them off.

Chelsea have no choice other than to throw caution to the wind, and Benitez brings Torres off the bench. The striker makes an immediate impact without even touching the ball, distracting Kompany into misjudging a long punt forward. It allows Ba to swivel and hook a trademark acrobatic volley past Pantilimon, who seems to start his dive only once the ball hits the net.

There's certainly no nonchalance now, and Chelsea rip into us, totally revitalised. Costel makes a great save as Mata tries to take the ball around him, then does even better to deny Ba from point-blank range after slipshod, brainless play from Clichy allows Oscar to set him up. The momentum is all with them, and we're witnessing an object lesson in just how precarious a two-goal lead can be if you start to think you've done enough.

We dig in hard, and it starts to look as though we've weathered the storm, restricting Chelsea to long-range efforts and using the ball more effectively again. We're defending from the front, Aguero in particular showing prodigious strength and skill to hold off Chelsea defenders. A tussle with Luiz provokes consternation from both their bench and players, but Foy takes no action. I'm trying hard not to count the minutes, as Chelsea launch a tirade of long balls hoping to get Ba in behind Kompany and Nastasic once again. When they do it, it's a smart, well thought out tactic playing to their strengths; when Wimbledon, Watford *et al* did it, it was mindless long-ball hoofing. But West London sophisticates could never be reduced to anything so crass …

We're getting close to seeing it out and, with Yaya once again covering the Wembley turf with one stride to everyone else's two, even looking as though we might nick a third. There's one nervy moment as we move towards added time, when another hoof downfield – sorry, beautifully weighted sixty-yard pass – sees Torres and Kompany get in a tangle, provoking vigorous penalty appeals, but Foy mercifully waves play on. Shortly afterwards he puts us out of our misery and, for the second time in three years, we've come out on the right side of a thrilling, nerve-shredding semi-final. The celebrations are long and loud – and that's just inside the stadium.

We start in a local Wembley hotel, where we have a quick chat with Paul Lake as he returns from the bar with a few cans for his friends and family. It doesn't seem right that Lakey should have to queue for drinks, let alone pay for them, but he seems as happy as any of us. The days when your star players were also born and bred fans seem a long time ago. Absolute top man.

Back in central London, we end up in the lucky Strada. One win from one previous visit might not seem statistically significant, but it was the semi-final against the scum, *the* pivotal result in our renaissance. So now Strada boasts two wins from two, although maybe visiting it after the game's been won ought not to count towards the stats. We're shown through to the deserted back room, it being immediately evident that we might be a tad too raucous for the regular diners. A few minutes later, a young couple out for a romantic evening meal are shown to a nearby table. We close our eyes and shake our heads. 'Don't bring 'em in here …'

We can't stop ourselves spontaneously bursting into song, with the familiar favourites all getting an airing. 'You signed Phil Jones, we signed Kun Aguero, Kun Aguero …' is prominent amongst them. After a brief pause whilst we get to grips with our starters, Daz suddenly turns to Jersey Mark and launches aggressively into 'You've got brown cows, we've got black and white ones, black and white ones …' A startled Mark looks at Daz as though he's demented, a pretty fair appraisal really, and the rest of us are convulsed with laughter at this unexpected display of bovine expertise. I'm still singing it weeks later.

Our return back home coincides with the start of the TV highlights, which we savour over a couple more drinks. How Sergio avoided a red card for his two-footed stamp on Sideshow Bob is beyond comprehension, other than for the identity of the referee. Completely out of character for Sergio, but a retrospective three-match ban looks certain.

There's much angst from Benitez about the rejected penalty claim. Replays galore, from all angles, make it look like a classic 'six of one …', but stills show Vinny virtually pulling Torres' shirt over his head. Lucky to get away with it, then, but even a competent ref would have struggled to see anything in real time.

All are agreed that it was a magnificent game which we just about deserved to win, and that the final should be a lot more comfortable. As long as we don't underestimate our opponents, Wigan. But the days when we did that kind of thing are surely a long, long time ago …

What a Waste

11 MAY 2013, FA CUP FINAL: CITY 0 WIGAN 1

Our first game after returning from Wembley is a 'Cup Final Rehearsal', and allows any remote possibility of complacency in the final to be removed as Wigan dominate us for long spells. However, they fail to take their chances and succumb to an outstanding late goal from Tevez. Terrific goals from Aguero – beneficiary of the FA's ludicrous ruling that you can't be punished retrospectively if the referee saw the incident – and Yaya see off West Ham. We then look entirely comfortable at White Hart Lane after Tevez and Milner fashion a marvellous early goal for Nasri, but pay for missed chances when we concede three in seven minutes late on. There's now an unmistakeable sense that we're just waiting for the Cup Final.

In contrast, Wigan are fighting their usual desperate battle against the drop, and a disastrous defeat to Swansea just four days before the final looks set to condemn them to the Championship. While they were suffering this gut-wrenching setback, we were sealing our Champions League place by beating West Brom, and Mancini rested seven or eight of the players who'll start in the final. Things couldn't be playing into our hands any more nicely. We'll be the hottest favourites for many a year.

Concerned that we might be about to dominate the headlines again, United choose Cup Final week to announce Ferguson's retirement. It's out of the blue, hugely welcome but good reason to avoid buying any papers or watching TV for a while. A man who has bullied and manipulated his way to an array of ill-gotten prizes will be fawned over for days by a naïve and gullible nation. Feted for his list of trophies with the manner of their achievement being completely glossed over. Still, once the sick-making tributes are over, we'll finally be rid of this tyrant. It can only be good news.

It soon emerges that David Moyes will be replacing him. I can't be doing with the miserable moaning Minnie, so it'll be no effort to ratchet up my contemptometer to a level appropriate to his new role. Cut from much the same cloth as Ferguson, the only thing that concerns me is his extraordinary record against City, and particularly Mancini. But, at long, long last, they'll be subject to the uncertainty and potential upheaval that comes with a change in manager.

And maybe they won't be the only ones. Some people are still trying to convince us that Mancini himself won't be here next year, and we wake on Cup Final morning to yet more stories about him being on the verge of the sack, with Manuel Pellegrini nailed on to replace him. *Yawn.* Same old, same old. We, and Mancini, have had to put up with this for months now, as the press seem hell-bent on destabilising us at the most damaging times. I scarcely bat an eyelid. I hope Roberto reacts in similar fashion. Today, nothing can be allowed to distract us.

The desire to boost TV advertising revenues sees kick-off set at the not exactly traditional time of 5.15 p.m., much to the inconvenience of those fans needing to get back to the north-west that evening. It does, however, allow much more time for big match preparation, and we install ourselves in a West End pub just after midday, hooking up with Jersey Blues and the Delph Massive. Forecasts of two, three, and four-nil abound, though not from me; I'm naturally pessimistic and convinced that Wigan will make it really tough for us. Even so, I fully expect us to be too strong for them in the end.

We get to Wembley nice and early, and Lindsey and I have been invited to a champagne reception before the match. It's all very civilised, and we're soon joined by Dave, a guy who tells us he lives just down the road. He's worked on the buses for forty-odd years, recently suffered some serious illnesses, and his firm have treated him to Club Wembley seats for the final. He's brought his son along, and they're clearly hell-bent on going for the Champagne Speed Drinking World Record. The waiter is at our table every couple of minutes and Lindsey and I just cruise along in their slip-stream. They're lovely people, real salt of the earth types, but eventually we have to extricate ourselves and get to our seats before our vision becomes impaired. Dave and his lad don't look like they're going anywhere anytime soon.

Inside, it's the usual boisterous, celebratory atmosphere, with City fans noticeably the more prevalent. The only surprise in our team news is that Hart comes in for Pantilimon. It looks like an about turn on Mancini's previous policy, but stories that Costel's been talking about a transfer at the end of the season might have something to do with it. Not much point giving him big match experience if he'll be playing those matches for someone else. Sometimes, most times, it's better to say nowt ...

The game starts and we're bright enough, Aguero winning an early free kick which Tevez drills into the wall. The rebound falls nicely to Yaya, but his shot doesn't curve quite far enough away from Joel, who parries it to safety. The early possession is all ours, but we have a big scare when a smart Wigan break gives McManaman a real chance. He cuts inside and looks to bend one into the far corner; there's a sharp intake of breath as we watch the ball pass just beyond the post.

It's a warning that we don't heed, and from then on the game is even. Wigan are playing some nice stuff and showing defensive organisation beyond the level which most of us expected. We create the half's clearest opening, when a rare incisive move between Nasri and Silva sets up Tevez, just eight yards out. With the goal at his mercy, he doesn't strike the ball cleanly enough and his shot is deflected away by Joel's foot. It's a golden chance squandered, and our play is so ponderous that we don't look as though we'll be creating too many more.

Wigan don't test Hart directly, but their sharp counter-attacks look threatening, with both Zabaleta and Clichy looking uncomfortable against McManaman in particular. We stretch Joel a couple more times before the interval, but half-time comes with the scoresheet blank, and Wigan have very much held their own. They'll certainly be much the happier, and Mancini surely has to hammer home the need for more urgency when we resume.

We get it for the first few minutes, and when Tevez breaks free on the right, Sergio gets to the near post first, but superb defending from Boyce blocks his shot. That's as good as it gets. Yaya can't impose himself on the game at all, even when Rodwell replaces Tevez in order to free him to press forward. Silva is unable to find any spark, and his feeble defending doesn't even add nuisance value. We're lethargic, leggy and just not at the races. Maybe playing a series of 'don't really matter that much' games since the semi-final hasn't helped, but for players of this calibre that's hardly an excuse. Wigan have had no choice other than to be at maximum intensity week in, week out; rather than tiring them out, it's made sure they're battle hardened and right in the zone.

Wigan stifle our attacks with increasing comfort, the only space we can find being wide for Clichy, whose delivery is consistently poor. Not as bad as his defending though, as McManaman is running him ragged, passing him with ease to get in cross after cross. Zabaleta's not much better, saving his weakest performance of an outstanding season for the game that matters most. He gets a yellow card for a cynical foul as McManaman breaks away, then, when the same player pounces after a woefully misplaced pass from Barry, Zaba's mistimed slide scythes him down and brings an inevitable second yellow. Eight minutes left, a man down and up against a side that really believes they can do it. We've ceased to be an attacking threat, and I'm already wondering whether we'll be strong enough to get to penalties. It looks like the best hope.

As we reach ninety minutes, McManaman again skins Clichy; they appeal for a penalty, but a corner is all that's given. As Maloney shapes to take it, the board goes up for three minutes of added time. *Let's get through this and regroup.* We don't even get through three seconds. Watson strolls unattended to the near post, gets in front of Rodwell, and his glancing header flashes over Hart and into the net.

It's the first Wigan attempt to get through to Joe, but the stats don't tell the whole story. They've created plenty of threatening situations, had a number of potentially goal-bound shots blocked and it's hard to argue that they don't deserve it. Mancini throws on Dzeko as we strive desperately for salvation, but a few robust clearances are all that's needed to see time out on a stunning upset.

I'm absolutely gutted. How could we have performed so badly? We've so many big game players, so much big game experience, and our key men have all been rested to make sure they're in prime condition for the big day. It makes no sense. Had we underestimated Wigan, even though they'd outplayed us just three weeks ago? Had the 'Mancini to be sacked' stories got anything to do with it? But when you're playing for a place in history, surely you can put this sort of stuff to the back of your mind?

Despite the desolation, there's still a part of me that's pleased for Wigan. It's a great story, they play good football, and Martinez cuts such a consistently admirable and likeable figure that you can't begrudge him some success. Much the best part of the afternoon's proceedings is to see the gracious response of our management, players and particularly fans. We're totally shell-shocked, but most of us stay around for long enough to applaud the Wigan players as they make their way to receive the cup. It's one thing to be gracious if you're the underdogs, knowing in your heart that you'll probably lose and enjoying what might be your one and only Wembley final. It's quite another to do it when you've been overwhelming favourites, have seen your team play like drains, suffered the crushing disappointment of losing to a last-minute goal and know that all that lies ahead for the next few days is mockery and humiliation. No need to speculate on how United fans would have reacted in the same situation. We haven't got carried away with ourselves just yet – or maybe we're just nicer people altogether.

As we trudge out of the stadium, the heavens weep. Even God's a Blue. Time for a couple of beers in a local hotel where most of us are trying to put a brave face on it. 'We're shit, and we know we are', 'We never win at home and we never win away …' Then, we head back into town for a curry. What should have been a party risks turning into a wake, but we have an enjoyable enough evening, chatting about everything but the day's game. The last thing you want is people going over the match again and again. But even as the drinks flow and the laughter returns, no one can disguise the dark cloud hanging over us. It's going to be a long few days …

POSTSCRIPT

Back to the Future?

There are folks out there – and certainly plenty of commentators – who're describing the Cup Final defeat as one of our darkest days. Get real. Bitterly disappointing, yes. Worse than any of our almost countless relegations, no. Had it been our one and only chance of silverware for the foreseeable future, then maybe. We've had two fantastic years, and you can't win every time. But it won't half make the summer break drag.

Last year, I wanted the close season to last forever. This time, even with a couple of league games remaining, I almost wish we could fast forward to the start of the next campaign. We'll have learned from our mistakes, strengthened the squad, and be champing at the bit to get that title back. Ferguson's exit can only help – his influence over officialdom and the authorities has been immense, and it'll take years for Moyes to craft such an advantage.

I wake up on Sunday to yet more news reports saying that Mancini is on his way out, with Pellegrini all set to replace him. *Jesus, will they give it a rest?* We wouldn't sack him over just one result, would we? All through the day the rumours grow stronger, even though none of the parties directly involved are quoted. However, the intensity of the stories suggests that, this time, there's something in it. Well, I suppose if you print 'Mancini to be sacked' every day for three years, you've got to be right eventually.

Things are a bit quieter on the Monday, but late that evening, the truth emerges. Precisely one year to the day after providing us with the greatest moment in our history, Roberto Mancini has been fired. His three-and-a-half-year tenure is long term by today's standards, but given that the first two and a half produced constant improvement and almost unprecedented success, we're really looking at a dismissal for just one disappointing season, a dismissal which looks as though it would have happened even if we'd won the Cup.

The decision seems brutally harsh. Have we learnt nothing? Just one year of disappointment, and even then, in two competitions, we did better than every team but one. Nobody, but nobody, wins stuff every single year. A week later, Arsenal players would celebrate their fourth place finish as if they'd won the Champions League. For us, second place is a sackable offence. Who the hell do we think we are? Real Madrid? Chelsea? God forbid ...

However, it soon becomes apparent that this is about more than results. The owners have a clear vision of how the club will evolve 'holistically' and Mancini has evidently struggled with some of his broader brief. Also his confrontational style, his open criticism of players and on occasion the hierarchy, has made him a few enemies. So Ferguson has had cordial relationships with all and sundry over the past twenty-seven years, has he?

No one can deny that we've gone backwards this year, so much more negative tactically than for much of our title season. Our style of play is predictable, and too many teams have found it easy to combat. Mancini has bleated relentlessly about how he was denied access to his prime transfer targets in the summer, but surely he had some say in who we eventually recruited? With the exception of Nastasic, and even allowing for injuries, the signings have been disastrous. But worst of all by far were our Champions League displays. Another 'group of death', sure, but some of the performances were embarrassing. City fans may not yet have taken this competition to their hearts, but in terms of the worldwide profile so crucial to our owners it's the one that really matters.

So, plenty of evidence for the prosecution, but it's still been just *one* underachieving season. Surely everyone's allowed to have one below par year? The weight of evidence suggests a decision made as much on personal as professional grounds. Never good.

However, the season must go on. Pellegrini, if it is to be he, still has unfinished business at Malaga, and Kiddo takes the reins for the utterly meaningless trip to Reading. On the way there, via another park and ride, a Blue is giving the gentle folk of Berkshire the heads up on what's happening in the world of real big time football. 'I'll tell you what, we don't want that Pellegrino, he's done nowt.' I just roll my eyes. If you're going to diss a bloke you clearly know next to nothing about, at least get his fucking name right.

We show a bit more life than we did at Wembley, easing to a win amidst repeated and predictable shows of support and appreciation for Mancini. The final game is at home to Norwich, and it's impossible not to draw a contrast with this time last year. Then, the atmosphere was tingling with expectation; now it's as flat as could be, nothing resting on the game itself, and the whole ground still suffering from a

Cup Final hangover. Comedy defending and a general can't be arsedness allows the visitors to go home with the points, for what they're worth, and City's lap of appreciation to the fans plays to an array of empty blue seats.

So the season ends in a way that few would have imagined a year ago. You'd have got pretty long odds on us ending up with no trophies and no manager. But that's football, and that's City. The New City is only four years old, and I really don't think we should worry too much. There's an awful lot more growing up to do, and when the league and cup runners-up double is such a bitter disappointment it emphasises where we already stand in football's new order.

What's urgently needed is evidence that we've learned from this year's mistakes. It takes a few weeks for Pellegrini to be appointed, but even in this time we've made a couple of major signings, Fernandinho and Jesus Navas. And there are obviously more in the pipeline. And almost all of our existing main men have signed contract extensions. Some serious statements of intent there. Whatever we may think about the Mancini sacking, let's trust the owners, we know they're here for the long term, they've shown they have a real vision – and they know exactly what's really happened behind the scenes. And we don't. So thanks for everything Roberto, but we gotta move on.

A new man at the helm, a clear sign of lessons having been learned, a Baconface-free Premier League; next season can hardly come quickly enough. The New Manchester City isn't going anywhere just yet. So bring it on!

Lightning Source UK Ltd.
Milton Keynes UK
UKOW03f0437180714

235315UK00003B/9/P